The Contemporary Television Series

Edited by Michael Hammond and Lucy Mazdon

Edinburgh University Press

© in this edition Edinburgh University Press, 2005
© in the individual contributions is retained by the authors

Transferred to digital print 2013

Edinburgh University Press Ltd
22 George Square, Edinburgh

Typeset in 11/13 Ehrhardt
by Servis Filmsetting Ltd, Manchester, and
Printed and bound by CPI Group (UK) Ltd, Croydon, CR0 4YY

A CIP record for this book is available from the British Library

ISBN 0 7486 1900 3 (hardback)
ISBN 0 7486 1901 1 (paperback)

Front cover illustrations:
Buffy the Vampire Slayer
20th Century Fox Television / The Kobal Collection / Wolf, Jerry
Hill Street Blues
Mtm Enterprises / The Kobal Collection
Six Feet Under
Hbo / The Kobal Collection / Watson, Larry
The Sopranos
Hbo / The Kobal Collection / Wetcher, Barry
Twin Peaks
Lynch / Frost/ Spelling / The Kobal Collection

Contents

Acknowledgements

We embarked on this project with the hope that we would be able to bring together scholars who would approach the series/serial form in diverse ways. That hope was realised and we have been fortunate to work with this group of dedicated scholars and so first and foremost we would like to express our gratitude to our contributors for their patience and diligence throughout. Many thanks also to Sarah Edwards at Edinburgh University Press for all her support. As usual our partners and families have been equally generous in their encouragement and we would like to offer our thanks to them. Michael Hammond would like to dedicate this book to Sarah Hammond his 'telly buddy'.

Contributors

Sarah Cardwell is Lecturer in Film and Television Studies at the University of Kent, where she teaches courses on film and television aesthetics, and literary adaptation. She has published numerous articles about film, television and adaptation. She is the author of *Adaptation Revisited: Television and the Classic Novel* (Manchester University Press, 2002), and *Andrew Davies* (Manchester University Press, 2005), and is co-editor of 'The Television Series', a book series on notable television practitioners (Manchester University Press). She is currently working on two books: one about filmic temporality and the other on 'television aesthetics'.

J. Elizabeth Clark is a member of the faculty of LaGuardia Community College. She is active in the ePortfolio and First Year Academy projects at the college and currently serves as the Co-Director of Composition for the Department of English. Outside of LaGuardia, Dr Clark is a published poet and serves as managing editor of *Radical Teacher* magazine. Her work appears in publications such as *The Journal of Medical Humanities*, *Women's Studies Quarterly*, and *A & U: America's AIDS Magazine*.

Jane Feuer is Professor of English and Film Studies at the University of Pittsburgh. She is the author of *Seeing through the Eighties: Television and Reaganism* (BFI, 1995) as well as numerous articles on television.

Eric Freedman is an Associate Professor in the Department of Communication at Florida Atlantic University. He has contributed essays on public access cable television to *The Television Studies Reader* (Routledge, 2004), *The Television Studies Book* (Arnold, 1998), and the journal *Television and New Media* (Sage, 2000). His forthcoming book examines the assumptions that underpin the exhibition of personal images, occasional photographs and amateur video in public domains, an excerpt of which is included in *Hop on Pop: The Politics and Pleasures of Popular Culture* (Duke University Press, 2002). An independent video artist and former public access producer, his experimental video work has been shown at such venues as the Long Beach Museum of Art, the American Film Institute and Ars Electronica in Linz, Austria.

Michael Hammond lectures in Film at the University of Southampton. He has written extensively on the transnational reception of American cinema in Britain from 1910 to 1919, British cinema in the silent period and on contemporary Hollywood war films. He is author of *The Big Show: British Film Culture in the Great War*, published by Exeter Press, 2005.

Matt Hills is the author of *Fan Cultures* (Routledge, 2002) and has recently written on media fandom for edited collections such as *Teen TV*, *The TV Studies Reader*, *Studying TV: An Introduction*, *Movie Blockbusters*, and *The Blade Runner Experience*. He has also contributed fan studies to journals such as *American Behavioral Scientist*, *European Journal of Cultural Studies*, *Mediactive*, *Social Semiotics* and *The Velvet Light Trap*. Matt is a Lecturer in Media and Cultural Studies in the Cardiff School of Journalism, Media and Cultural Studies, Cardiff University.

Jason Jacobs is Senior Lecturer at Griffith University, where he teaches film and television studies. He is the author of *The Intimate Screen* (Clarendon Press, 2000) and *Body Trauma TV* (BFI, 2003).

Catherine Johnson is Lecturer in Television History and Theory at the Department of Media Arts, Royal Holloway, University of London. She has published on factual entertainment, early British television and contemporary US television, and is the author of *Telefantasy* (BFI, 2005). She is also co-editor (with Rob Turnock) of an edited collection on the history of ITV entitled, *ITV Cultures: Independent Television over Fifty Years* (Open University Press, 2005).

Janet McCabe is a Research Associate (TV Drama) at Manchester Metropolitan University. She has written several essays on American TV drama on British television, narrative form and gender, as well as with Kim Akass on female narratives and narration in American TV drama. She is author of *Feminist Film Studies: Writing the Woman into Cinema* (Wallflower Press, 2004), and has co-edited (with Akass) and contributed to *Reading Sex and the City* (I. B. Tauris, 2003) and *Reading* Six Feet Under*: TV To Die For* (I. B. Tauris, forthcoming 2005). She is currently researching a book on female narrative in contemporary American TV drama. She is a member of the editorial board for *Critical Studies in Television*.

Lucy Mazdon is Senior Lecturer in Film and Television Studies at the University of Southampton. She is the author of numerous articles on film and television. She is the author of *Encore Hollywood: Remaking French Cinema* (BFI, 2000) and the editor of *France on Film: Reflections on French Cinema* (Wallflower Press, 2001). She has also edited a special edition of *French Cultural Studies* on French television (2002) and a special edition of *The Journal of Romance Studies* on the cinematic remake (Spring 2004).

Angela Ndalianis is Associate Professor in Cinema and Entertainment Studies at the University of Melbourne. Her recent book *Neo-Baroque and Contemporary Entertainment* (MIT Press, 2004) explores the parallels between current entertainment culture and baroque culture of the seventeenth century. She has also published articles in a number of journals and has contributed to the anthologies *On a Silver Platter: CD-Roms and the Promises of a New Technology* (New York University Press, 1999), *MetaMorphing: Visual Transformation and the Culture of Quick Change* (Minnesota University Press, 2000), *Hop on Pop: The Politics and Pleasures of Popular Cultures* (Duke University Press, 2002), and *Rethinking Media Change* (MIT Press, 2003). She is currently writing a book about the history and cultural significance of theme parks.

Roberta Pearson is Professor of Film and Television Studies and Director of the Institute of Film and Television Studies at the University of Nottingham. She is the co-editor of *Cult Television* (University of Minnesota Press, 2004) and is co-authoring a book titled *Small Screen, Big Universe: Star Trek as Television*.

Greg M. Smith is Associate Professor of Communication and Graduate Director of the Moving Image Studies program at Georgia State University. His books include *Film Structure and the Emotion System* (Cambridge University Press, 2003), *Passionate Views: Film, Cognition, and Emotion* (Johns Hopkins University Press, 1999), and *On a Silver Platter: CD-Roms and the Promises of a New Technology* (New York University Press, 1999). He is working on his next book project, *Beautiful TV: The Art and Argument of Ally McBeal*.

Linda Ruth Williams is Senior Lecturer in Film Studies at the University of Southampton. She is the author of four books, including most recently *The Erotic Thriller in Contemporary Cinema* (Edinburgh University Press, 2005) and is co-editor, with Michael Hammond, of *Contemporary American Cinema* (forthcoming). She is a regular contributor to *Sight and Sound* magazine, as well as to TV and radio programmes on film issues.

Preface

Lucy Mazdon

This collection of essays began, like so many others, over a cup of coffee and a series of conversations during which Michael and I discovered that we shared the same enjoyment of the American dramas which were becoming an increasingly prominent part of the British television schedules. As we discussed our respective viewings of *ER*, *The Sopranos*, *Buffy* and so on, we came to the realisation that these shows were rather more than simply great entertainment. First and foremost we were *talking* about them and indeed they seemed to invite, if not demand, the very type of conversation we were having. These were programmes with highly complex narrative structures, back stories of which we may or may not have been aware and which enabled an exchange of information which would then impact upon subsequent viewings. These were programmes which, in many cases, attracted large audiences, spawned fanzines and websites and which garnered extensive column inches in the quality press. These were programmes which clearly played a vital role in the increasingly competitive and volatile television landscapes of both the United States and Britain and which were successfully exported worldwide. They were part of a process of transnational traffic and exchange which raised new questions about the national identity of contemporary television and its audiences, a process rather interestingly developed by our own Anglo-American conversations.

It seemed then very apparent that these television dramas which were providing us with so much pleasure as viewers were also fascinating cultural artefacts which perhaps invited a rather more sustained analysis than that provided by our hastily snatched discussions. Our solution was of course this collection and an invitation to a number of leading scholars to turn their attention to the prime-time quality series and serials. Our initial working title for the book was *Previously On*, a deliberate nod to the marker used by programme-makers to bring audiences up to speed on earlier events in a developing series or serial. For a number of reasons, we decided to drop this title in favour of the rather more prosaic *The Contemporary Television Serial*. In some ways this was perhaps a loss and yet to have kept that original title would we discovered, have been somewhat misleading. For in these dramas, events were not necessarily 'previously on' as the narratives frequently avoided the weekly, linear narrative progression of the more traditional drama serial in favour of complex story arcs, flashbacks and flashforwards and various forms of extra-textual spin-off. Indeed, as we began to read the chapters written for the collection, it became increasingly apparent that this complexity and the tendency to eschew linearity meant that the very definitions with which we had begun were perhaps no longer tenable. Were we looking at series or at serials? Was it still possible to posit a clear distinction between the two or, as I argue in the introduction to the first section of this book, 'Histories', was it now necessary to think in terms of a series/serial hybrid?

The chapters which follow provide a fascinating and cogent response to this question and to the quality drama series/serial in general. From a range of very different perspectives the authors give a lucid and very timely account of a number of ground-breaking television programmes. The essays are grouped into three sections: 'Histories', 'The Series/Serial Form' and 'Receptions'. Whilst we feel this is a useful subdivision which accounts for the rather different approaches employed in the chapters, it will quickly become clear to the reader that there is a certain degree of slippage between the three sections. An account of the history of the form does not of course efface either text or audience and similarly analysis of reception does not ignore the text. Indeed, we would like to encourage readers to keep this slippage very much to the forefront of their mind as they read the following chapters, for it does seem to lie at the very heart of both the programmes in question and the analyses here. *ER*, *The Sopranos*, *Six Feet Under*, *The X Files* et al. are, as we shall discover, very much a product of the particular industrial and historical conjuncture from which they emerge. Moreover, as our coffee-break conversations revealed, their meanings and impact were, and remain, heavily dependent on audience responses and the various inter- and extra-texts which supplement them. In this sense, whilst as Michael argues in his introduction to the texts section, these particular instances of seriality may have their roots in earlier written and cinematic examples of the form, they are also highly televisual. In other words, the very ways in which they combine and re-combine industry, text and audience mirrors the television experience in general. The shows we watch emerge from specific industries, they draw upon different textual forms and they invite and are subjected to various modes of reception. As these series/serials reveal only too well, in order to understand television and the ways in which we make sense of it, we must always be aware of the complex yet vital relationship between industry, text and viewer.

Clearly what follows is in no way intended as an exhaustive account of this prolific and extremely complex televisual form. However, we believe that this book does provide a broad overview of the contemporary television series/serial and its place in both British and American television schedules via a number of very different but equally stimulating approaches. It is our hope that this will in no way undermine the pleasures of these shows for fans like ourselves. On the contrary, we would be delighted if this book could provide further fodder for coffee-break conversations about this exciting, innovative and frequently addictive programming.

Part I: Histories

Introduction: Histories

Lucy Mazdon

For a number of years I have taught an introductory course on Television Studies to groups of undergraduate students here at the University of Southampton. An important element of the unit is time spent watching television, notepad and pen in hand, and I am always somewhat amused to discover my students' surprise at the revelation that I too indulge in a fair amount of television viewing. There seems to be an assumption among many that television is unlikely to hold much appeal for the academics who teach them and they often seem delighted, even relieved, to hear that we too can be found, remote control in hand, enjoying the pleasures of the small screen.

Of course these assumptions speak volumes about student–teacher relationships and perceptions of academic identity. However, they also tell us something about perceptions of television and the act of television viewing. The very fact that a good number of my students seem to believe that television might be 'below' the average university lecturer not only perpetuates the rather fanciful and outdated notion of the intellectual in an ivory tower, it also positions television and its audiences as less valuable than other cultural pursuits. I shall say more about this notion of quality in a moment; however, suffice it to say at this stage that in some way my students are right. For many of the programmes that have had me and a good number of my colleagues glued to the sofa in recent years have been productions clearly identified as 'quality' television, popular with audiences maybe, but in some way marked as more worthwhile, more significant and more enduring than much of the flow of contemporary television.

The programmes in question are the many prime-time series/serials which have been aired on British and American television, and indeed in many cases globally, in recent years (I will explain my rather clumsy use of the dual terminology, series/serials in a moment). There has been a proliferation of series/serials such as *ER*, *Six Feet Under*, *Twenty Four* and *The*

X Files, shows which, whilst distinctive in many ways, share the label of quality which sets them apart. A significant number of these shows, indeed I would argue the majority, originate in the United States and are then sold and screened in countries across the globe. Others, however, are conceived and produced in Britain. Whilst it would be problematic to draw up a definitive corpus of the contemporary quality series/serial – quality is after all necessarily subjective and open to change – there does seem to be a body of recent televisual work which shares the series/serial form, significant audience impact and a degree of cultural prestige. These are the shows which will be given detailed coverage in both popular magazines and the quality press. These are the shows which will be issued on DVD and video, suggesting that they merit re-viewing and should not disappear in the ebb and flow of everyday broadcasting.

It is striking that series/serials such as those mentioned above and a whole host of others, many of which will be analysed in more detail in this book, should have emerged during the last ten years or so, a period throughout which many commentators have identified the gradual dumbing down of television. Critics in Britain and the United States have decried the battle for ratings, the proliferation of reality television and the demise of serious television journalism and documentary and have blamed this on an increasingly market-driven television industry. It is in this very context that these much-praised series/serials have emerged. Indeed, as I shall go on to suggest and as Roberta Pearson, Catherine Johnson and Janet McCabe reveal in great detail later in this book, the emergence of these shows at this specific juncture is in many ways a direct result of the same industrial and material developments suggesting that accounts of television history which posit a move from innovation and quality towards repetition and dumbing down may need to be reconsidered. Moreover, it is striking that so many of these 'quality' series/serials emanate from the United States. Critics have often tended to condemn much American television, claiming it lacks the quality and integrity of British production. The arrival of early US television imports on British television in the 1950s coincided with the birth of ITV and the fledgling battle for audiences and this association between US production and a new commercialism have perhaps contributed to these hierarchies of cultural value. Nevertheless it is the United States that has led the way in the production of the contemporary 'quality' series/serials, again suggesting a need to revisit these very hierarchies.

All of this – the quality of these programmes, their critical and commercial success and the questions they raise about the status of television, national industries and audiences – makes the contemporary prime-time television series/serial ripe for serious analysis. Whilst many of the shows which can clearly be identified as 'quality series/serials' have received mention in overviews of television history and accounts of television genre, there has to date been very little in the way of sustained analysis of these prominent elements of the contemporary television landscape. Of course this is partly symptomatic of a historical failure in the academic world to take television drama seriously. Whilst television as a social phenomenon merited attention, the dramas we were busy watching were considered by many to lack the impact and longevity of their cinematic counterparts and for many years they were largely ignored. This situation has improved over the years as academic writing on television pays growing attention to the programmes on screen.[1] Nevertheless the absence of a detailed study of the contemporary television series/serial can perhaps be linked to this early silence.

When the 'quality' series/serial is mentioned in academic accounts of television history it tends to be traced back to the debut of *Hill Street Blues* in 1981. This American crime drama series was produced by MTM, an independent company which had acquired a reputation as a 'quality' production house throughout the 1970s. As Lez Cooke remarks in *The Television Genre Book*, the series marked a landmark in the history of American television (and, as the show was sold internationally, in televisions across the globe) as it broke all the rules of series drama (Creeber 2001: 23). Although the show combined 'traditional' televisual genre conventions, notably those of the soap opera and the cop show, it also utilised a large ensemble cast, plural and open-ended narratives, *vérité* style camera work and *mise en scène* and a notably liberal attitude towards social issues and the role of the police. Written and produced by Steve Bochco, who went on to create a number of other innovative and influential series/ serials (including *LA Law*, 1986–94, and *NYPD Blue*, 1993– present), *Hill Street Blues* set out to revivify television drama and indeed to establish it as a medium in its own right. Nevertheless MTM were very aware that despite its artistic innovation the show would also need to appeal to a broader viewing public, hence its very clear referencing of popular and well-established *televisual* forms alongside a rather more elite nod to cinema and documentary. As Jane Feuer points out in *The Television History Book* (London: BFI, 2003), *Hill Street Blues* was instrumental in redefining quality television drama and establishing it as its own genre (in Hilmes 2003: 98–102). Other shows followed, including the previously mentioned *LA Law*, *Moonlighting* (ABC, 1985–9), and *thirtysomething* (ABC, 1987–91, discussed by Feuer in this book) and gradually 'quality drama became a uniquely televisual form, its technological and narrative links to the medium more significant than its affinity to cinema or theatre' (in Hilmes 2003: 99).[2]

Feuer's account of the establishment of quality drama as a distinct televisual form clearly underlines the primacy of *Hill Street Blues* in this trajectory: this show indubitably paved the way for the development of the quality series/serial and many of the shows discussed in this book owe a great debt to Bochco's production. However, she also reminds us of the need to position the quality series/serial in the much broader history of television drama in general (an argument she reiterates and extends in her reviewing of *thirtysomething* in this book). If *Hill Street Blues* helped to establish quality television drama as a 'uniquely televisual form' it did this by turning towards (and perhaps more interestingly away from) its *televisual* predecessors. In other words, whilst the series/serials discussed in this book may well have been influenced by *Hill Street Blues*, they and their predecessors were also influenced by other forms of television drama.

As I have already suggested, the academic silence to which much television programming, including drama, was long subjected was perhaps instrumental in conveying the impression that this work was somehow not worthy of serious analysis. Unlike its cinematic counterparts, the audiovisual output of the small screen was considered too transitory, too light, too *small* for the type of critical attention which the cinematic movie had finally been accorded. Recent histories of British and American television reveal this to be a very unfair account of much television production and a growing interest in the televisual archive is beginning to provide us with a much clearer sense of the realities and indeed the cultural value of many of the programmes transmitted and viewed over the years. Drama provided the pioneers of early television with a means of successfully exploring the possibilities of the new medium. Although early transmissions often consisted of short extracts from popular West End theatrical productions, gradually the process of adaptation specifically for television was established and the BBC began to show more extended dramas based upon novels, plays or indeed original material (Hilmes 2003: 70). These early dramas were of course restricted by the constraints of live production; nevertheless improving technologies coupled with an ever expanding television audience and the concomitant need to increase output meant there were continuing efforts to produce innovative and exciting television drama. The decision on the part of the BBC to hire two staff writers, Nigel Kneale and Philip Mackie, dedicated to the creation of original material, speaks volumes about the place of fiction in contemporary schedules. The fact that Kneale went on to write the three *Quatermass* serials (*The Quatermass Experiment*, 1953, *Quatermass II*, 1955, and *Quatermass and the*

Pit, 1959), arguably some of the most popular and well-remembered productions of the period, suggests that the corporation's strategy was emi-
nently sensible. Television drama did then lie at the very heart of early
schedules. As John Caughie points out:

> [I]t is worth recording that the single play in the 1930s, and, later, in the 40s
> and 50s, seems to have offered some of the special attractions that films have
> for Christmas viewing now. The productions included *Hay Fever*, *Richard of
> Bordeaux*, *The Moon in the Yellow River*, *Charley's Aunt*, and *The Knight of
> the Burning Pestle*. In the immediate post-war period, drama usually occupied
> eight to ten hours of a very slightly expanded schedule. (Caughie 1991: 25)

Interestingly, Caughie goes on to discuss the prominent place accorded to
drama in the *evening* schedules, revealing that, 'on any evening when a full-
length drama was shown, it dominated the evening schedule, relegating
any other programming to supporting shorts' (Caughie 1991: 26). As
Caughie concludes, 'the single play was not simply a part of the flow of programming, but constituted a kind of anchor-point within the evening (and
perhaps within the week), which structured viewing in a different way, and
invited a different form of attention' (Caughie 1991: 26).

Clearly this was a time of innovation and experimentation and many
programme makers and schedulers were unclear as to quite what television
drama was or what it should be for. However, despite, or indeed perhaps
because of this confusion, drama consistently played a vital role in both
pushing the boundaries of television as a medium and in establishing the
identities of individual channels in an increasingly competitive audiovisual
landscape. ITV's decision to schedule the live *Armchair Theatre* series after
the highly popular *Sunday Night at the London Palladium* at the end of the
1950s heralded the advent of ground-breaking television drama also able
to attract vast audiences. The BBC gradually responded to this new competition with populist, realist dramas such as *Z Cars* (1962–78), challenging single dramas in the *The Wednesday Play* series and innovative sit-coms
such as *Steptoe and Son* (1962–74), *Dads' Army* (1968–77) and *Till Death
us do Part* (1966–74). In the United States drama also played a key role in
establishing television as a popular and influential cultural medium. Whilst
the variety shows and comedy serials which had proved so popular on radio
were prominent in early schedules, live anthology drama in programmes
such as *Studio One*, the *Hallmark Hall of Fame* and the *Kraft Television
Theatre* were important sites for innovation.

It is not my intention here to give an overview of the development of
television drama in Britain and the United States, however, as I think these
few examples demonstrate, it is clear that drama, despite the academic and

critical silence to which it was long subjected, played and continues to play a vital role in establishing television as a medium and an aesthetic form in its own right and in attracting audiences to the ever increasing programmes on offer. With this in mind, then, I think it becomes even more apparent that any account of the dramas discussed in this book must at the very least be aware of their position in the much broader trajectory of television drama – a simple tracing back to *Hill Street Blues* is clearly inadequate. Moreover it is imperative that we consider the place of these programmes in the development of the series and serial forms more generally. As Johnson and Pearson reveal in their essays in this book, the contemporary prime-time series/serial is very much a response to changes in the television industries and similarly the development of the series and serial formats has frequently been mobilised as a response to both aesthetic *and* material imperatives. The popularity and prominence of many of the shows discussed here, coupled with the tendency to trace them back to Bochco's 1980s police drama, can suggest that the series and the serial are quite recent phenomena. However, even the most cursory glance at television programming history reveals this to be far from true. Whilst the one-off drama, largely due to technical constraints, dominated very early television fiction, the serial and series forms had begun to take on an important role by the beginning of the 1950s (witness the aforementioned *Quatermass* films). In a process that prefigures the decision-making surrounding later successes such as *Buffy* and *Six Feet Under*, series and serials were perceived to save money (sets and costumes could be reused), to create an identity for the channel and to create some degree of certainty in terms of audience figures (increasingly important with the advent of new television channels in both Britain and the USA from the mid-1950s onwards).

The contemporary quality drama series/serial must then be positioned in the extended trajectory of British and American television histories. Moreover, it is vital to acknowledge the *differences* between these two television industries and the forms, genres and styles which they engendered. As Sarah Cardwell's later analysis of a number of British series/serials reveals, the impact of the American import has in no way precluded the existence of a domestic version and whilst there must surely be some dialogue between the two, there is equally a marked relationship between the different 'national' forms and the traditions and discourses of their specific context. *Cold Feet* is in no way a simple reworking of *thirtysomething*, although it may at times echo a number of its tropes and concerns.

This acknowledgement of the connection between programme and 'national' context reminds us that it is also imperative to consider the relationship between the contemporary series/serial and its specific historical context. I do not intend to rehearse these arguments here as the chapters which follow provide a far better account of the impact of industrial and cultural developments on this drama format than I could hope to include in a general introduction such as this. Suffice to say, however, that since the 1980s, a period during which we have seen the flourishing of the quality series/serial, television in both Britain and the United States has undergone some of the most profound changes of its history. That such a significant number of ground-breaking and popular dramas should have emerged during these turbulent and often difficult years is striking in itself and underlines the need to examine closely the relationship between text and social, political and above all industrial context. This brings me back to the explanation I promised at the outset of this introduction. Throughout I have used, somewhat reluctantly, the dual terminology series/serial. Whilst this decision may be far from felicitous from a stylistic point of view, it seems unavoidable as the traditional distinctions between series (a set of television programmes having the same characters and/or settings but with different stories) and serial (a television narrative presented in a number of separate instalments which may or may not reach a conclusion) form are broken down by contemporary programming. Whilst in 1982 John Ellis felt able to give a relatively confident account of the singularities of the two forms in his seminal work *Visible Fictions* (although even at this early stage he did point out some blurring of the boundaries; Ellis 1982: 145–59), today it has become increasingly difficult to categorise them straightforwardly. The contemporary series/serial, as we shall discuss further in Part Two of this collection, is a hybrid form which combines elements of both the series and the serial and in the very act of re-combining tells us much about the disparate, plural, fragmented landscape of contemporary British and American television and its audiences.

Notes

1. See Glen Creeber (ed.), *The Television Genre Book*, London: BFI, 2001, for a useful introduction to these analyses.
2. See also Robert J. Thompson, *Television's Second Golden Age: From 'Hill Street Blues' to 'ER'*, New York: Syracuse University Press, 1996.

Bibliography

Caughie, John (1991), 'Before the Golden Age: Early Television Drama', in John Corner (ed.), *Popular Television in Britain Studies in Cultural History*, London: BFI.

Creeber, Glen (ed.) (2001), *The Television Genre Book*, London: BFI.
Ellis, John (1982), *Visible Fictions*, London: Routledge.
Hilmes, Michele (ed.) (2003), *The Television History Book*, London: BFI.
Thompson, Robert J. (1996), *Television's Second Golden Age: From 'Hill Street Blues' to 'ER'*, New York: Syracuse University Press.

CHAPTER 1

The Writer/Producer in American Television

Roberta Pearson

The television producer 'prefers to turn the publicity spotlight away from himself so that it may shine fully on the program or the series he produces. He welcomes a secondary role and would embrace even anonymity if that would help his program achieve a higher Nielsen rating', said Frank La Tourette in his foreword to Muriel Cantor's 1971 book, *The Hollywood TV Producer: His Work and His Audience* (Cantor 1971: vii). In a 2001 interview with *The Los Angeles Times*, United Paramount Network President Dean Valentine shone the publicity spotlight on Joss Whedon, the creator and executive producer of the netlet's recently acquired *Buffy the Vampire Slayer*.

> Joss and the show are so respected in the writer and agent circles, a lot more quality writers are coming to the network. Frankly, we haven't always been in a situation where people are begging to work with us. Now we are. And it helps the perception of our network with our target audience of younger viewers. (Braxton 2001: 2)

By 2001, producer and programme had become inseparable; writers, agents and UPN's target demographic of younger viewers were said to be attracted not just by Buffy but by Joss Whedon's high-profile public (might we even say star?) image. The thirty years between the publication of Cantor's book and UPN's acquisition of *Buffy the Vampire Slayer* saw fundamental changes in the American television industry. Cantor's book was published during the height of three network dominance, a period that Michele Hilmes has dubbed the classic network system. When UPN acquired *Buffy*, the number of networks had doubled from three to six, all of which struggled for ratings in a multi-channel, fragmented audience environment. The transformation of the industry resulted in the television writer-producer, or hyphenate in *Variety*-speak, playing a much more prominent role in the industry than previously.

According to Hilmes, the classic network system (c. 1960 to 1980) was an oligopoly in which the three American networks, CBS (Columbia Broadcasting System), NBC (National Broadcasting Company) and ABC (American Broadcasting Company), secured control of production, distribution and exhibition through a 'tight vertical integration, similar to that of the movie studios before 1947' (Hilmes 2002: 194). The networks rapidly expanded their market penetration, purchasing stations in the largest metropolitan areas at the same time that the network affiliates, independently owned stations with contractual agreements to broadcast network programming in return for a percentage of advertising revenues, devoted an ever larger percentage of airtime to the network feed (Hilmes 2002: 194). The networks owned or had an interest in 91 per cent of the prime-time programmes produced for them by the big studios or independent producers (Hilmes 2002: 228). 'Despite the fact that a variety of players produced these programmes, the networks' oligopolistic control of distribution and exhibition mandated that producers conform to a narrow range of accepted practice' (Hilmes 2002: 229). The industrial organisation of the classic network system, asserts Hilmes, militated against artistry and originality, 'With a system that attracted a national audience and a market so neatly divided between the nets, few openings existed for creative, innovative productions that challenged the bland, formulaic network patterns' (Hilmes 2002: 230).

Muriel Cantor's book offers the best available account of the role of the producer in the classic network system. Most producers began 'their careers as free-lance script writers, contract writers, or story editors' and many considered themselves hyphenates (Cantor 1971: 92), continuing to be involved in writing 'since the function of associate producer and producer are closely tied to story writing, script selection, and idea formation . . .' (Cantor 1971: 101). But the producer's remit encompassed many other responsibilities, since he was 'both executive and creative authority', hiring the cast and directors, co-ordinating between the network and the producing studio and having the right to the final edit of the programme (Cantor 1971: 7). The producer also hired the writers and often worked 'with them, directing the tone and content of the script' (Cantor 1971: 8). This job description implies a great deal of creative freedom for producers, but it was the powerful networks that ultimately determined what went out over their airwaves. Said Cantor, 'Even when a man owns, creates, and produces his own show, the network retains the right to *final* approval of scripts, casts and other creative and administrative matters' (Cantor 1971: 9, emphasis in original). Network liaison men often sat in on the story conferences for new shows and producers of all shows, new and old, had to submit all scripts, and in some cases story ideas or presentations, to network censors (Cantor 1971: 122). Some producers sought ingenious ways to outfox the censors, but others internalised the networks' standards, selecting their stories and writing their scripts within these constraints (Cantor 1971: 31). Such practices ensured conformance to the bland, formulaic network patterns to which Hilmes refers. As Cantor put it, 'It is well known that networks are reluctant to try new ideas and would rather remake series with themes that have been successful, particularly in the recent past. When a show is considered "different," creative, or controversial, the networks take more interest in its production' (Cantor 1971: 127).

The reluctance to innovate stemmed from network executives' believing that the mass audience would immediately reject any show departing from the lowest-common denominator norm. Paul Klein, vice-president of programming at NBC in 1977–9, articulated this belief in his theory of 'least objectionable programming'. Klein thought that viewers would switch to another channel if they found a programme objectionable and that to succeed a show merely had to be 'least objectionable among a segment of the audience'. 'Thought, that's tune-out, education, tune-out. Melodrama's good . . . a little tear here and there, a little morality tale, that's good. Positive. That's least objectionable' (in Morgenstern 1979: 16–17). According to Cantor's interviews, most producers shared Klein's assessment of the viewers, seeing them as 'a mass audience, rather than a segmented one . . .' (Cantor 1971: 169) and having a 'low opinion of their audience's intelligence, urbanity, and discrimination' (Cantor 1971: 172). Said one producer, 'We try not to do anything controversial. Nor do we try to reach people of high intellect. Because of this we are a success . . . The formulas work for television and will continue to work' (Cantor 1971: 173). But some of the hyphenates believed that the networks' conservatism was 'losing a valuable group of viewers' who might watch 'higher-level television shows' (Cantor 1971: 173). Said one of these producers, 'I know the audience is smarter, more intelligent than they [the networks] think it is. One of the reasons so many shows fail is that the networks and others underestimate the IQ of the audience. How many of the same kinds of shows can be on the air? There should be shows with more character and originality that tap the more intelligent audience' (Cantor 1971: 174).

Shows with character and originality continued to be rare during the classic network system, but government regulation/deregulation and the rapid growth of satellite and cable weakened the power of the networks and led them to rethink their programming strategies. In 1982 the Department of Justice forced the National Association of Broadcasters to abandon the

Television Code that had previously provided guidance to the networks standards and practices departments. This, together with rapidly changing social mores, rendered network censors effectively irrelevant. The Federal Communications Commission's Financial Interest and Syndication Rules (Fin Syn) created opportunities for more independent producers to originate network programming by directing that networks could have a financial interest in only fifteen hours of programming per week and could buy a programme for only one or two runs (Hilmes 2002: 235). The FCC's Prime Time Access Rule, mandating that the network feed to affiliates begin at 8 p.m. rather than 7 p.m., created a need for independently produced programmes to fill this slot. The FCC's must carry rules, requiring cable operators to carry all local stations, made access to these stations much easier than had been the case when they broadcast on the weak-signal UHF spectrum (Hilmes 2002: 232). The resulting increase in viewers for the local stations created yet another market for producers. No longer reliant on the networks as their only distributors, producers could now risk making innovative programming such as *Star Trek: The Next Generation*, which in 1987 became the first hour-long drama to run off-network.

During the same period that regulation/deregulation threatened the three network hegemony, cable and satellite penetration grew exponentially and network viewership plunged. In the late 1970s the three networks combined to take over 90 per cent of the prime-time audience. By the end of 1989, the network audience had fallen to 67 per cent (Thompson 1996: 36–7) and by 2002 to less than 40 per cent, with cable picking up the other 60 per cent of the audience (Hilmes 2003: 65). As the networks' share of the audience diminished so did their expectations for an individual show's performance in the all-important Neilsen ratings. During the classic network system, programmes were cancelled if they failed to attract roughly a third of the viewers watching television during their time slot, but the advent of cable considerably lowered the cut-off point for cancellation (Thompson 1996: 39). *St Elsewhere*, the critically acclaimed hospital drama, ran on NBC from 1982 to 1988 with annual shares of from 19 to 22 per cent and a seasonal ranking never higher than forty-ninth out of one hundred shows (Thompson 1996: 40).[1] By the twenty-first century, shows succeeded, that is, warranted profitable advertising rates, with ever lower audience numbers. In its seventh season (2002–3), Joss Whedon's very successful *Buffy* often ranked below 100th place and achieved a highest rating of five, representing approximately 5 per cent of all households (as opposed to a share, which measures the percentage of households watching television during one time period).

The increasing fragmentation of the audience among the networks and their competition meant that a programme's demographic profile counted for more than sheer numbers, with advertisers seeking the 'right' viewers, those with disposable income and inclined to spend it. The trend away from the mass audience and towards the demographically desirable audience segment began in the 1960s, when executives at both NBC and CBS took an interest in the demographic breakdowns of the Neilsen and Arbitron ratings. This interest did not translate into programming policy, however, since attracting a desirable audience segment was still a secondary consideration compared to winning the numbers game (Alvey 2004). Shows which attracted the 'right' viewers but had low ratings still got cancelled, most notoriously the original *Star Trek*, even though having 'lots of young adult buyers' among its viewers partially accounted for its surviving past its first year (Alvey 2004: 51). But in the 1966 season, CBS, worried that its ageing, rural audience would not appeal to advertisers, began a reconfiguration of its schedule which culminated in the early 1970s (Alvey 2004: 54). The network cancelled several long-standing hits in favour of such groundbreaking programmes as *All in the Family* (1971–9), *The Mary Tyler Moore Show* (1970–7) and *M*A*S*H* (1972–83), all 'designed to appeal to urban, educated, upwardly mobile eighteen- to forty-nine-year-olds' (Jacobs 2003: 89). CBS's new line-up did not, however, signal the networks' total abandonment of the concept of the mass audience, for, as Jason Jacobs says, 'throughout the 1970s and into the 1980s, the "big three" broadcast networks alternated between long-held strategies for mass-ratings success and newer ideas for attracting more demographically specific audience segments' (Jacobs 2003: 93). But by the end of the twentieth century demographic thinking had become the norm among industry executives, guiding not only the acquisition of individual programmes but entire network schedules. The big three networks worked harder at establishing their brand identity among particular segments of the audience, while the three new networks established themselves by appealing to specific groups of viewers – Fox at first to African-Americans, WB (Warner Bros.) to twelve to 34-year-olds, particularly females, and UPN (United Paramount Network) to African-American and young male viewers (Perren 2003: 111).

In their tailor-made appeal to upmarket viewers, *All in the Family*, *The Mary Tyler Moore Show* and *M*A*S*H* were harbingers of the post-three network era. They also pointed to the future in the association between quality demographics and high-profile hyphenates that Joss Whedon and his *Buffy* now embody. Writer-producer Larry Gelbart, with experience in American television dating to the early 1950s, wrote the pilot for *M*A*S*H*, became the show's creative consultant in its first year, its co-producer in the second and left in the fourth, fearing that he was getting stale. Norman Lear, together with Bud York in one half of the Tandem Productions that originated *All in the Family*, had a television career that, like Gelbart's, went back to the early 1950s. Unlike Gelbart, however, Lear went on to further television success in the 1970s and his name is associated with several of the key, socially conscious comedies of the decade: *Maude*, *The Jeffersons* and *Mary Hartman, Mary Hartman*. Lear was a very hands-on hyphenate, present at the story conferences for all his series, even when six were airing simultaneously. Together with his then–wife Mary Tyler Moore, Grant Tinker formed MTM Enterprises in 1970 to produce *The Mary Tyler Moore Show*. The most influential and important producer associated with the three trail-blazing CBS comedies, Tinker was not himself a writer, although he and MTM nurtured an extraordinary stable of writers, many of whom themselves became prominent hyphenates. As Robert Thompson says in his book on American quality television, 'without MTM Enterprises . . . there would likely have been no second Golden Age of television. Formed around the *Mary Tyler Moore Show*, MTM went on to define the standard of quality in the television industry' (Thompson 1996: 46).

   Hill Street Blues, the pioneering cop show created by one of MTM's most imaginative and productive writers, Stephen Bochco, did much to define that standard of quality, as did Bochco to define the role of the Hollywood hyphenate in the post-classic network system. *Hill Street Blues*, which began airing on NBC in January 1981, epitomised the coming era in two ways:

1. Its producer's relationship with the network. In 1980, NBC was the third place network. The need to overtake CBS and ABC led network executives to commission a dangerously innovative show, to concede to Stephen Bochco's 'demands concerning production autonomy and freedom from network censorship' and to resist panicking at the initially disastrously low ratings (Marc and Thompson 1992: 221). Robert Thompson claims that *Hill Street* 'changed the way network execs thought about prime-time tv', initiating the new standard practices of giving creative freedom to a producer and waiting for his new show to find its audience (Thompson 1996: 73).
2. Its combination of low ratings and the 'right' viewers: the seeking of the 'quality audience' strategy CBS had initiated with its 1970s comedies began to become the industry norm with *Hill Street*. Although *Hill Street*'s rating were far lower than those of *All in the Family*, *The Mary Tyler Moore Show* and *M*A*S*H* had ever been, the show compensated

for its low over-all ratings by performing well among affluent eighteen to forty-nine-year-olds (Thompson 1996: 67) and among '"POMs" (an industry acronym for "professionals, operatives, and managers")' (Marc and Thompson 1992: 223). *Hill Street* would certainly have been almost immediately cancelled when CBS, NBC and ABC routinely split the audience three ways, but by the early 1980s 'the networks were freed to seek "class audiences" that lent themselves to target advertising' (Marc and Thompson 1992: 223).

Hill Street and Bochco's success helped to inaugurate a decade (1985–95) that Michele Hilmes believes 'may rank as one of the most creative periods in traditional broadcasting', with '"producer/auteurs" able to exercise a greater degree of creative control over their programs than they had before' (Hilmes 2002: 309). The networks granted this creative control because in the post-classic network system era the names of important hyphenates, the hyphenate brand as it were, proved more attractive to demographically desirable audiences than did the network brand, the new technologies of the remote control and the video recorder together with the proliferation of new networks and satellite channels inevitably diluting loyalty to the big three. As Hilmes says of Bochco,

> As one of television's premier auteurs in a fragmented business that provided few forms of continuity, his name had begun to mean more in terms of genre, quality, style, and audience than did the name of the network his shows appeared on. The stamp of an author – even when actual authorship was somewhat removed by the production practices of television – gave a program a degree of authenticity and legitimacy absent from television's earlier decades. (Hilmes 2002: 312)

Bochco, who went on to produce several more critical and commercial hits (*LA Law*, 1986–94; *NYPD Blue*, 1993–present; *Murder One*, 1995–7), became the most powerful and well-known of all the Hollywood hyphenates, with only David E. Kelley (*Picket Fences*, 1992–6; *Ally McBeal*, 1997–2002; *The Practice*, 1997–2004) rivalling him in terms of productivity and success. Other high-flying hyphenates include the so-far one-hit wonders Aaron Sorkin (*The West Wing*, 1999–present) and David Chase (*The Sopranos*, 1999–present) and the so-far two-hit wonders Chris Carter (*The X-Files*, 1993–2002; *Millennium*, 1996–9) and Joss Whedon (*Buffy the Vampire Slayer*, 1997–2003; *Angel*, 1999–2004). As did their classic network system counterparts, the new hyphenate-auteurs have control over the day-to-day running of the show, as Joss Whedon's description of his job makes clear:

A [film] director doesn't have to create anything, but he is responsible for everything. Same thing goes for an executive producer on TV. I don't have to write a line of the script – although there's not a script for my shows that I don't have a line in, or a scene, or a pitch, or something. I don't sew the damn costumes, I don't say the words – but I'm responsible for everything in every frame of every show. That's my job, whether or not I'm directing the episode.[2]

Unlike their classic network counterparts, however, the hyphenate-auteurs have relative freedom from the demands of studios and networks, their creative latitude deriving from the transformations of the American television industry and its audience(s) described above. The remainder of this chapter uses Whedon as a case study to explore the role of the 21st-century hyphenate-auteur. As *The New York Times* said in a lengthy profile, 'Television creators like David E. Kelley and Aaron Sorkin may be better known, but to many critics, Whedon is the more original artist, one who has been unfairly denied prizes and high ratings' (Nussbaum 2002: 56). In some ways, Whedon also better exemplifies the role of the hyphenate in the post-classic network system. Kelley, Sorkin and Bochco produce for the big three networks while the strong association among Whedon, *Buffy*, *Angel*, and the newcomer netlets WB and UPN (both launched by their parent studios in 1995) has helped to shape the latters' brand identity. *The Hollywood Reporter* said in a retrospective article at the end of *Buffy*'s seven-season run that the show 'became a pop-culture juggernaut that helped establish one fledgling network and gave a much-needed boost to another' (Hockensmith 2003). Whedon also enjoys that peculiarly intense relationship with his audience characteristic of cult, or, as the industry terms them, genre shows, but which also characterises producers' changed conceptions of their audiences.

Whedon began his career as a staff-writer with hit sit-com *Roseanne* (1988–97) and went on to work as a script doctor on feature films, receiving an Oscar nomination for co-writing the *Toy Story* (1995) script. It was his bitter experience with the *Buffy the Vampire Slayer* feature film (1992) that motivated his return to television. As he told *The New York Times*, he 'lost control of his screenplay' and saw 'his vision of "populist feminism" turned into a schlocky comedy.' He recalls sitting in the theatre, crying. '"I really thought I'd never work again," he recalls of the experience. "It was that devastating"'(Nussbaum 2002: 56). Three years after the critical and commercial failure of the *Buffy* feature, Gail Berman, whose Sandollar Television had inherited the property, thought it could be made into a television series. Says Whedon, 'They called me up out of contractual obligation: "Call the writer, have him pass." And I was like, "Well, that sounds cool"' (Robinson 2001). It sounded cool partly because Whedon thought that a television hyphenate would have more control over his material than would a film scriptwriter. Produced by 20th Century Fox Television, *Buffy* debuted on WB in 1997 and, according to *The Hollywood Reporter*, 'quickly became one of the WB's biggest draws, boosting ad revenues and shaping the network's image' (Hockensmith 2003). The newspaper quoted Stacey Lynn Koerner, executive vice-president and director of global research integration for media-buying giant Initiative Media North America. '*Buffy* was intrinsically linked to the WB. I think every viewer knew, "Buffy-WB. WB-Buffy"' (Hockensmith 2003). *Buffy* was ideally suited to the WB network brand as a teen- and young-adult magnet (Littleton 2003), quickly winning over young, female viewers (Hockensmith 2003).

The expiration of Fox's licensing agreement with WB at the end of *Buffy*'s fifth season in 2000 led to a bitter, highly public wrangle over the series' future, with media coverage that highlighted the creator's disappointment with the network attesting to the importance of the hyphenate in the television industry. A Cox News Service article headlined '"Buffy"' creator a bit cross with The WB' asserted that the programme had 'helped put The WB on the map'. According to the article, Whedon was particularly distressed at comments made by Jamie Kellner, WB's founder, which 'essentially downplayed the show's significant role in The WB's ascension' (Thompson 2001). A *Chicago Tribune* article headlined 'Why Can't "Buffy" Creator Get Any Respect?' made similar claims for *Buffy*'s and Whedon's centrality to the WB brand, saying that the 'series gave the mini-network serious credibility when it premiered in 1997 after a string of lame WB comedies and weak dramas fizzled' and that 'Whedon himself is respected in Hollywood as a writer, producer and director who shepherds a smartly written, well-executed show . . .' (Johnson 2001: 1). The dispute was resolved when the other fledgling netlet, UPN, 'signed a two–year, 44-episode deal for a reported $2.3 million per episode the first year and $2.35 million the second' (Johnson 2001). UPN paid over the odds to acquire the programme as part of a rebranding strategy, needing *Buffy*'s 'strong female demographic' after WWF wrestling and *Star Trek: Voyager* had made it the home for young male viewers (Johnson 2001: 1). Said Whedon, 'UPN says it wants to change its image, that it wants to sit at the grownup table' (Perigard 2001: 39). UPN president of entertainment Dawn Ostroff phrased it somewhat differently, saying that, '"Buffy" was an established franchise with a built-in fan base that advertisers wanted to reach'. The new acquisition, according to Ostroff, enhanced UPN's overall performance. '"Buffy" helped increase UPN's Tuesday night ratings while also providing a promotional platform for other shows on the network' (Hockensmith 2003).

In keeping with the tradition initiated by Bochco's relationship with NBC at the inception of *Hill Street*, both *Buffy* networks gave Whedon a high degree of creative freedom in acknowledgement of the show's centrality to their programming strategy. In an interview with *The Onion* at the beginning of *Buffy*'s sixth season on air and first season on UPN, Whedon was asked whether the change of networks would have any effect on the show.

> I don't think it'll affect it one iota . . . UPN has never said, 'Skew it this way, do this thing,' and they never will, because I'm not going to do it. I've had an unprecedented amount of control over the show, even for television, considering the show is a cult show. From the very start, The WB left me alone. You know, they collaborated, they didn't disappear, but they really let me do what I wanted. They trusted me. And UPN is on board for letting me do the show the way that works. (Robinson 2001)

Whedon couldn't resist a crack about UPN's signature show and audience profile, 'I don't think anything will change. I mean, there'll be wrestling. But tasteful wrestling. Wrestling with a message behind it' (Robinson 2001). Instead of wrestling, Whedon offered his new network the all-singing, all-dancing tribute-to-Hollywood musicals episode, 'Once More with Feeling'. *The Los Angeles Times* saw this as a somewhat incongruous way for Whedon 'to settle in to his new television home, the testosterone-charged UPN, which has cage-matched its way into young men's hearts by featuring wrestlers who attack each other with metal chairs and talk trash between gulps of Bud'. But Dean Valentine, UPN president, had no reservations. 'I couldn't have been more psyched when I heard about this episode . . . Joss is one of the few people who could do this and get away with it, and "Buffy" is one of the few shows that could attempt this and have the audience go along with it' (Stanley 2001: 6). Valentine's comments attest to the degree of creative freedom granted today's successful hyphenate. But successful is the all important qualifier. Network executives may wait longer for a show to find an audience and may be happier with smaller audience shares, but a show must still contribute in some significant fashion to a network's bottom line. When it ceases to do so, the happy marriage between network and hyphenate can rapidly sour into a bad divorce. *Buffy* ran for a lengthy seven seasons, ending to a chorus of critical acclaim and fannish laments. Whedon's newer projects didn't fare as well. In the wake of WB's cancellation of *Buffy* spin-off, *Angel*, after its fifth season and the Fox network's cancellation of gritty space-opera *Firefly* after a mere thirteen episodes, Whedon sounded less sanguine about the producer/network relationship than he had at the height of *Buffy*'s success, 'I think that it is a particularly twitchy time, but I also think there will always be shows the networks don't get. My only hope is that one day, I'll understand what it is the networks want' (Sullivan).

Unfortunately, as Todd Gitlin famously argued in *Inside Prime Time*, his seminal study of the American television industry in the 1970s, the networks don't know what they want or, rather, know they want hit shows but don't know how to get them. In times of uncertainty a daring network executive may take a chance, commission a *Hill Street* or a *Buffy* and wait for it to find its audience. If the ratings go south, however, networks will seek to rein in even the most high-profile of hyphenates. The curtailment of creative freedom often entails pressures to make the failing programme conform more closely to standard formulas. Network (and studio) executives particularly dislike lengthy narrative arcs, storylines that continue over several episodes or even an entire season, fearing that the dense backstory dissuades new viewers. As *Angel*'s ratings fell during its fourth season, WB executives briefly considered cancellation. In response, Whedon proposed ending the season with the vampire and his friends taking over evil law firm Wolfram & Hart, a setting which would lend itself to more stand-alone episodes (Villanueva). Whedon also lost two characters (Angel's son Connor and love-interest Cordelia) and brought back fan favourite Spike, the evil/good vampire, who had perished saving the world in *Buffy*'s final episode (McCollum 2003: 1). Twentieth Century Fox Television and WB arranged a mutually agreeable deal for the production and airing of the fifth season, although studio executives insisted that Whedon cut costs. Said Whedon, 'The series was not the pot of gold everyone might think: at least, that's what the suits told me. It was painful dealing with those people. But we rescued Angel from the grave, again, at least for this series and maybe the next.'[3]

The shows' ratings did improve but, to Whedon's disappointment, the reprieve lasted only a year; during the fifth season WB executives gave the producer advance warning that it would not be renewed for a sixth. *Angel*'s cancellation illustrates the complexity of the post-classic network system environment, for it was not due to a fall-off in ratings. *Variety* commented, 'Move on the surface is a head-scratcher. Twentieth Century Fox TV-produced skein is the net's second highest-rated hour among viewers 18–34 . . . and fourth among 12–34. Its numbers have been solid this year, even against brutal competish on Wednesday night' (Adalian 2004: 3). Why then did WB axe the show? Network president Jordan Levin offered two explanations. (1) *Angel* failed to attract new viewers. 'The show had a loyal core following, but it didn't have a tremendous amount of new audience upside' (Adalian 2004: 3). Presumably the 'new audience upside', having come to WB to sample *Angel*, would ideally have remained to sample the network's other offerings. *Angel*, unlike *Buffy*, was failing to act as a promotional platform for the other shows on its network. (2) *Angel* didn't repeat well, that is, there was a big fall-off in the ratings between the initial broadcast of an episode and its re-broadcast later that same week. Levin said that 'he needed to double run one or more dramas in primetime next season', presumably in order to earn the maximum advertising revenue relative to the license fee paid to the originating studio. 'We have to have more at-bats, and we need to create timeslots where we can repeat shows . . .' (Adalian 2004: 3). It's no longer enough for a hyphenate to produce a show that performs well among a desirable audience segment. Now that show must benefit the network in other ways, serving as promotional platform and repeating well, or the network will resort to tightening the creative reins or even to cancellation.

The producer's relationship with the network has changed in the post-classic network system; networks offer hyphenates greater creative freedom but at the same time place increasing demands upon them. Producers' conception of and relationship with their audience has also changed. As we have seen, classic network system producers had a rather disdainful view of the mass audience. By contrast, WB president Levin, in an interview at the time of *Angel*'s cancellation, talked of an audience that wants most challenging programming, not least objectionable programming, 'It's a little bit more of a challenge to support a show that has such an impassioned audience . . . They want storytelling that is open-ended and serialized and has a deep and complex mythology. That makes it very tough to bring a new audience in' (Villanueva). *Angel*'s loyal and impassioned audience are, of course, the fans, at whom hyphenates aim their shows and advertisers their products. Fans have come to play an increasingly significant role in the post-classic network system, but it was a classic network system hyphenate, *Star Trek*'s Gene Roddenberry, who first realised the importance of the fans and has even been credited for 'creating Fandom as we know it' ('The Gods of Cult TV': 67). Roddenberry not only created fandom, he set a pattern for hyphenates' relationship with their audiences (a pattern, admittedly, particularly appropriate for the producers of genre shows). Henry Jenkins speaks of Roddenberry's active courting of science-fiction fans. Roddenberry screened the *Trek* pilot episodes at a World Science Fiction Convention before the series aired, continually provided programme-related materials and even gave prominent fans access to the set (Tulloch and Jenkins 1995: 10). Roddenberry's investment in the fans paid off when NBC threatened *Star Trek* with cancellation at the end of the second season. The official *Star Trek* (www.startrek.com)

website's 'real world timeline' commemorates this seminal moment in the history of *Star Trek* and of television fandom.

1968 – Letter-writing campaign
Long time sci-fi enthusiast and author Bjo Trimble, along with her husband John, launch a letter-writing campaign to help save Star Trek. The pair are prompted by fears that the NBC network was about to cancel the show.
The campaign generates so much mail that after the March 1, 1968 broadcast of 'The Omega Glory,' NBC makes an on air announcement that Star Trek would be renewed for the fall.

An NBC press release said that 'from early December to date, NBC has received 114,667 pieces of mail in support of Star Trek, and 52,151 in the month of February alone' (Van Hise 1997: 47). Without this fan-led campaign, there may have been no third season. Without the third season's generating enough episodes for the syndication that kept *Trek* alive and eventually led to its revival with *The Next Generation*, there would have been no popular culture phenomenon. Without the popular culture phenomenon, there would have been no vast and highly organised Trek fandom for subsequent television fandoms to emulate.

But the *Angel* fans did have the Trekkie/Trekker fandom example, and, as their predecessors had decades earlier, rallied to save their favourite television programme (although with no success). The *Winston-Salem Journal* reported that fans had set up websites and started petitions and letter-writing campaigns within hours of WB's cancellation announcement. Fans, according to the *Journal* article, also drew hope from 'posts on fan sites by such members of the Angel production team as Whedon and Marsters indicating that they want the show to come back and that they feel they have more stories to tell' (Clodfelter 2004: 4). The internet, part of the technological and social transformations that led to the end of the classic network system, gives today's hyphenates a more accurate perception of their audience (or at least a part of it) than possible before the 1980s. As Muriel Cantor's research showed, some classic network system hyphenates believed that 'the audience is smarter, more intelligent that they [the networks] think it is' (Cantor 1971: 174). Joss Whedon can directly assess his audience's intelligence (or at least that of the core audience of fans) via the internet. Said Whedon, 'We found out we have a fan base on the Internet. They came together as a family on the Internet, a huge goddamn deal. It's so important to everything the show has been and everything the show has done – I can't say enough about it.'[4] Whedon seems to draw inspiration from fans' passionate responses to his creation, as he told *The Onion*:

You don't want to let them down. The people who feel the most strongly about something will turn on you the most vociferously if they feel you've let them down. Sometimes you roll your eyes and you want to say, 'Back off,' but you don't get the big praise without getting the big criticism. Because people care. So. Much. And you always know that's lurking there. It does make a difference. If nobody was paying attention, I might very well say, 'You know what, guys? Let's churn 'em out, churn 'em out, make some money.' I like to think I wouldn't, but I don't know. I don't know me, I might be a dick. Once the critics, after the first season, really got the show, we all sort of looked at each other and said, 'Ohhh-kay . . .' We thought we were going to fly under the radar, and nobody was going to notice the show. And then we had this responsibility, and we got kind of nervous. You don't want to let them down. (Robinson 2001)

Not letting them down doesn't mean slavishly responding to fan feedback. In an interview given between *Buffy*'s WB fifth season and UPN sixth season, Whedon's fellow producer Marti Noxon spoke at some length about audience response, which she said 'affects us in varying degrees'. When fan reactions split, as they did over Buffy and Spike's affair, 'it makes me think we are doing something right, because that means it's a really compelling situation'. The producers 'will definitely respond'; however, if 'we start to hear consistently that "we really don't like this, it's a downer," or when we feel people aren't getting what we are trying to say . . .' The producers definitely responded to perceptions that:

the show got perhaps a little too dark and intense last year, especially for younger viewers. It went to a real sexual place with Buffy and Spike, and Buffy was really going through a dark night of the soul . . . I think that one of the things we had already been striving to do, and one thing UPN really wants us to do, is to see that it doesn't get as dark this season. (Mazor)

The producers would sometimes defer to the fans but they also had the confidence to challenge them. Said Noxon, 'I definitely think that Joss and I can really take things to a really scary place, and I can understand why people don't want to see that all the time' (Mazor). With *Buffy*, challenging the audience often took the form of the inevitable changes in characters and settings demanded by the series' basic premise of a group of high-school kids fighting evil. The kids had to grow up, had to leave high school and had to suffer all the attendant traumas of the life cycle. Respecting his audience's intelligence, however, Whedon often went further than the premise demanded, for instance, killing Buffy's mother or Willow's lover. Challenging the audience also meant not just giving them the unexpected in the form of character deaths or all-singing, all-dancing episodes, but resisting the expected. Speaking of Buffy and Angel's relationship, Whedon said, 'That's why we had Angel go bad when he and Buffy got together. Because, and I've gotten into so much trouble for this phrase, what people want is not what they need. In narrative, nobody wants to see fat, married Romeo and Juliet' (Miller). It's unlikely that a classic network system producer would ever have uttered the words 'what people want is not what they need'. Not giving the audience what it wanted would have been anathema in the age of 'least objectionable programming'. Whedon can make this heretical claim and hyphenates more generally can now dare to be different because of the transformations of the television industry that have fundamentally altered their relationships with the networks and with the audience.

Notes

1. See also Robert J. Thompson, 'St Elsewhere', *Encyclopaedia of Television*, http://www.museum.tv/archives/etv/S/htmlS/stelsewhere/stelsewhere.html, accessed April 2004.
2. 'Interview with Joss Whedon', http://filmforce.ign.com/articles/425/425492p1.html, accessed 12/02/2004.
3. 'Interview with Joss Whedon', http://www.timesonline.co.uk/article/0,,2101-954416,00.html, accessed 10/02/2004.
4. Interview with Joss Whedon, http://filmforce.ign.com/articles/425/425492p1.html, accessed April 2004.

Bibliography

Adalian, Josef (2004), 'WB Decides it's Time for "Angel" to Fly Away', *Daily Variety*, 16 February 2004, p. 3.

Alvey, Mark (2004), 'Too Many Kids and Old Ladies: Quality Demographics and 1960s US Television', *Screen* 45(1), Spring, pp. 40–62.

Braxton, Greg (2001), 'Buffy Breathes Life into UPN', *The Los Angeles Times*, 2 October 2001, p. 2.

Cantor, Muriel G. (1971), *The Hollywood TV Producer: His Work and His Audience*, New York: Basic Books.

Clodfelter, Tim (2004), 'Fans Mobilize to Try to Save Angel After its Sudden Cancellation', *Winston-Salem Journal*, 20 February 2004, p. 4.

Hilmes, Michele (2002), *Only Connect: A Cultural History of Broadcasting in the United States*, Belmont, CA.: Wadsworth.

Hilmes, Michele (ed.) (2003), *The Television History Book*, London: BFI.

Hockensmith, Steve (2003), 'Fangs for the Memories', *The Hollywood Reporter*, 16 May 2003, http://www.trshows.nu/article.php3?id_article=958.

Jacobs, Jason (2003), 'Experimental and Live Television in the US', in Hilmes (ed.), *Television History Book*, p. 89.

Johnson, Allan (2001), 'Why Can't "Buffy" Creator Get Any Respect?', *Chicago Tribune*, 30 September 2001, Arts and Entertainment, Zone C, p. 1.

Littleton, Cynthia (2003), 'New Boss Levin in Sync with WB's Target Demo', *The Hollywood Reporter*, 2 October 2003.

McCollum, Charlie (2003), '"Angel" Makes Adjustments to Ward off Network Ax', *San Jose Mercury News*, 29 September 2003, Arts and Entertainment, p. 1.

Marc, David and Thompson, Robert J. (1992), *Prime Time, Prime Movers*, Boston: Little, Brown, and Company.

Mazor, David, 'Marti Noxon on the future of Buffy, the Vampire Slayer', http://www.prevuemagazine.com/Articles/Flash/540, accessed 08/02/2004.

Miller, Laura, 'The Man behind the Slayer', http://www.salon.com/ent/tv/int/2003/05/20/whedon/index-np.html, accessed 10/02/2004.

Morgenstern, Steve (ed.) (1979), *Inside the TV Business*, New York: Sterling Publishing.

Nussbaum, Emily (2002), 'Must-See Metaphysics', *The New York Times*, 22 September 2002, Section 6, p. 56.

Perigard, Mark A. (2001), 'After WB Finale, "Buffy" Gets ready to Slay 'em at UPN', *The Boston Herald*, May 20 2001, Arts and Life, p. 39.

Perren, Alisa (2003), 'New US Networks in the 1990s' in Hilmes (ed.), *Television History Book*, p. 111.

Robinson, Tasha (2001), 'Interview with Joss Whedon', *The Onion*, 5 September 2001, http://www.theonionavclub.com/feature/index.php?issue=3731&f=1, accessed 12/02/2004.

Stanley, T. L. (2001), 'Buffy, the Rules Slayer', *The Los Angeles Times*, 20 May 2001, p. 6.

Sullivan, Michael Patrick, 'Interview with Joss Whedon', www.ugo.com/channels/filmtv/features/firefly/josswhedon.asp, accessed 8/02/2004.

Thompson, Kevin D. (2001), ' "Buffy" Creator a bit Cross with the WB', *Cox News Service*, 21 May 2001.

Thompson, Robert J. (1996), *Television's Second Golden Age: From 'Hill Street Blues' to 'ER'*, New York: Syracuse University Press.

Tulloch, John and Jenkins, Henry (1995), *Science Fiction Audiences: Watching 'Dr Who' and 'Star Trek'*, London: Routledge.

Van Hise, James (1997), *The Unauthorized History of Trek*, London: Voyager.

Villanueva, Annabelle 'A vampire's search for redemption finds creative legitimacy and network success with 100 groundbreaking episodes', http://www.hollywoodreporter.com / thr / television / feature_display.jsp?vnu_content_id=2080596, accessed 10/02/2004.

'The Gods of Cult TV', *Cult Times Special*, 15, p. 67.

http://www.museum.tv/archives/etv/E/htmlE/ethicsandte/ethicsandte.htm

http://home.insightbb.com/~wahoskem/buffy7.html, accessed 08/02/2004.

CHAPTER 2

The Lack of Influence of *thirtysomething*

Jane Feuer

When I made *thirtysomething* (1987–91) my main example in *Seeing through the Eighties*, it was not because it was my favorite show but rather because I thought it was typical of 'something'. What that something was seems much clearer to me in retrospect: it used what this book calls 'prime-time serial television' to explore the inner lives of a particular class fraction otherwise not 'realistically' represented on American TV: what Barbara Ehrenreich calls the professional–managerial class and what I called 'yuppies'. The term 'prime-time serial drama' is no longer specific enough to account for the range of programmes that have populated the US television screens over the years since *thirtysomething* went off the air in 1991. 'Prime-time serial drama' is the most authored form of US television and each authorial franchise has put its particular stamp on the stream of shows produced. Not only do the shows take on individual voices, but also the term itself is now too general to have much meaning. Nearly everything on US prime-time television, from *Will and Grace* to *Survivor*, is now 'serialised' in the sense of having at least some continuing story arcs. The distinction between 'serialised' and 'series' television that once defined the difference between daytime and prime-time television formats no longer really exists. In addition, the term 'prime-time serial drama' does not distinguish between programmes as disparate as, say, *Ally McBeal*, *Buffy the Vampire Slayer* and *The Sopranos*. In order to discuss the influence, or lack of influence, of *thirtysomething*, I will need to use more precise terminology. I will need to distinguish between two strands active in prime-time serial television in the 1980s, 1990s and beyond. I will refer to these as, first, 'prime-time melodrama', a tradition of 'trash' or 'camp' TV dating from *Dallas* and *Dynasty* in the 1980s; *Melrose Place* in the 1990s, and certain 'reality' shows (e.g. *The Bachelor*) today. The second and more directly relevant tradition I will label 'quality drama', a term that Robert Thompson and I have used to refer to a particular *genre* of dramas in the 1980s and

1990s that today is most manifest in some of the 'HBO' dramas such as *The Sopranos* and *Six Feet Under*. By the 1990s, Robert J. Thompson was able to argue that:

> quality [drama] has become a genre in itself, complete with its own set of formulaic characteristics. As is the case with any genre. . .we come to know what to expect. All of the innovative elements that have come to define 'quality TV', even in its unpredictability, have become more and more predictable. By 1992, you could recognize a 'quality show' long before you could tell if it was any good. Quality television came to refer to shows with a particular set of characteristics that we normally associate with 'good', 'artsy' and 'classy'. (Thompson 1996: 16)

I will be using 'quality drama' in this way as a generic term, not as a judgement of aesthetic value. But what I want to argue is that *thirtysomething*, although clearly belonging to the genre was not in its mainstream, nor did it have as much influence on subsequent quality dramas as did other authorial franchises. Of all the prime-time dramas that followed, *thirtysomething* most influenced two important but lesser-known products of its own production company, 'The Bedford Falls Company' fronted by Edward Zwick and Marshall Herskovitz: the short-run cult teen TV show *My So-called Life* (1994–5) and the three-season *Once and Again* (1999–2002).[1]

Before explaining where *thirtysomething* fits within 'quality drama', I need to say why it is *not* typical of 'prime-time melodrama'. Although the show belonged to the genre of melodrama broadly speaking in that it focused on the interior emotions of the bourgeois class within a familial context, *thirtysomething* was not 'melodramatic' in the sense I believe this term applies to US television drama of the 1980s and after. For US television, 'prime-time serial melodrama' carries a particular edge. The most typical 1990s prime-time melodrama had to have been *Melrose Place* (1992–9), a show airing immediately after *thirtysomething*'s demise but with a different tone, audience and mode of reception. By that I mean that following in the tradition of *Dallas*, *Dynasty* and their clones in the 1980s, prime-time melodrama had to share with some film melodramas a tendency towards camp or at least excess. It could be said that these prime-time melodramas were in fact constructed by their audiences, subcultural groups and fan cultures, whose camp readings of the shows became the primary readings of the show as they were incorporated into subsequent scripts by the producers.

Prime-time melodramas could not be characterised by 'quality acting' or subtle psychological plot construction but rather tended like daytime soap opera to pursue an acting style that remained a little bit over the top.

In terms of theories of acting, we might say that while *thirtysomething* incorporated the kind of naturalistic theatrical acting associated with Stanislavski, *Melrose Place* was more in the tradition of Kuleshov. According to legend, the Kuleshov experiment was supposed to prove that all cinematic acting was an effect of montage. To this end, the same reaction shot of an actor's face could be juxtaposed with other shots to create different meanings from the same image. For example, a shot of an actor with a neutral expression would appear to represent sadness when intercut with shots of a funeral, or happiness when intercut with shots of a wedding. The crucial point here in terms of acting styles is that the Kuleshov experiment can be used to argue that film acting is not really acting, simply an effect of montage. This argument can then be used to denigrate soap-opera acting, relying heavily as it does upon reaction shots, at the expense of the more nuanced 'true' acting we find in the theatre where a performance can be allowed to unfold or in art cinema where theatrical acting technique is valued.

On an episode of *Melrose Place* (Season 3, Episode 73 'And Justice for None'), Jo is on trial for the custody of her child. One by one, the inhabitants of Melrose Place come to the stand to testify in her behalf. But as they are questioned, close-ups of each remind us of every ridiculous scandal to which Jo was subjected in the first three seasons of the show. As we look at each face, we are reminded of the backstory surrounding that character's interaction with Jo. The audience feels pretty certain that Jo is not going to get custody, but the effect is camp rather than tragic as we relive some of the more ridiculous storylines. In effect, the fan/viewer is filling in the gaps between the close-up shots and the backstories to which they refer.

Ultimately a show like *Melrose Place* makes us wonder if we really know the difference between Kuleshov and Brecht, who wanted to use a non-expressive acting style to make the audience think about the ideas being presented rather than getting carried away by emotional identification with the characters. A now-defunct fan website entitled 'Billy Campbell Master Thespian' pretended to want to replicate Kuleshov but wound up providing a Brechtian critique of soap-opera acting.[2] The site offers to give us 'a look at the vast emotional range of *Melrose Place*'s master of subtlety, Billy Campbell'. A series of identical photos of Billy/Andrew Shue has the actor looking into the camera with an admirable blank affect with each shot accompanied by a caption describing the emotion Billy is supposed to be showing, 'happy, sad, angry, distraught, excited, afraid, nervous, worried, and drunk'. Thus bad melodramatic acting becomes an unintended consequence of the Kuleshov effect. But when the Kuleshov effect is thus 'camped', it may have other outcomes. The effect of montage may be seen to have little or no effect if the acting is 'bad' enough. The effect may thus be distancing in the Brechtian sense. Not much has been written about the consequences of 'bad' (i.e. non-realist but also non-Brechtian, or, shall we say, 'failed realist' acting). Yet an effect of realism attempted but not achieved is crucial to the impact of the prime-time 'trashy' melodramatic serial and to the fan culture that surrounds it. In fact such an acting style may well be the crucial distinguishing mark between the higher 'quality' drama (such as *thirtysomething*) and the trashy serial (such as *Melrose Place*). Although fan culture around *thirtysomething* could also take on a mocking tone, it did not imply that the actors on that show were incompetent or that they were unable to embody the characters. When a fan website claimed that, '*thirtysomething* follows the lives of seven thirtysomething yuppies . . . linked by blood, love, fate and really bad taste in relationship partners', they are not talking about effects of 'bad acting' but rather about more or less authorially intended scripted effects. Whether or not *Melrose Place* validated the Kuleshov experiment, it cannot be said that *thirtysomething* invalidated Stanislavski.

Robert J. Thompson includes *thirtysomething* in his book on 'quality drama' , and the show certainly fits the genre's basic defining characteristics: the ensemble cast, continuing storylines, literate writing, etc. As I explained in *Seeing through the Eighties*, *thirtysomething*, perhaps more than any other show of its decade, attempted to capture the 'quality' audience in terms of demographics. Moreover, *thirtysomething* more than any of its contemporaries was able to define the quality audience on its own terms and in very specific age and social class dimensions: the show was crucial in delineating what the term 'yuppie' came to mean for the 1980s.

Being 'authored' is perhaps the most important factor distinguishing quality drama from ordinary TV, and this is even more true in the 2000s than it was in the 1980s. It was the MTM and Steven Bochco 'franchises' that initiated 'quality drama' with *Hill Street Blues* in 1981 and that defined quality drama for the 1980s and 1990s. This lineage pays particular attention to the television medium. It 'recombines', to use Todd Gitlin's phrase, traditional television dramatic genres, the cop show (*Hill Street Blues*, *NYPD Blue Homicide*), the lawyer show (*LA Law*, *Ally McBeal*, *The Practice*), and the doctor show (*St Elsewhere*, *ER*, *City of Angels*) with structural elements taken from the daytime soap opera and mixes in the personal 'quirks' of the show's *auteur*. For example, TV hyphenate-auteur (see Roberta Pearson's chapter in this book) David E. Kelley specialises in legal dramas, but he also specialises in 'quirky' often sexually perverse legal cases and odd character types. Thus he has worked on more or less mainstream quality dramas such as *LA Law* and *The Practice* as well as 'quirky' dramas such as *Chicago Hope*, *Picket Fences*, *Ally McBeal* and *The Brotherhood of Poland New Hampshire* (2003).

This tradition continues into the next decade with *The West Wing*, which I believe is a prominent descendant of TV's quality drama tradition, with the workplace setting (The White House), the serialised narratives, the large ensemble cast and hyphenate-auteur Aaron Sorkin's distinctive voice. Although *thirtysomething* continually referenced TV history (most notably in the 'Mike van Dyke' episode I described in *Seeing through the Eighties*), and although it was serialised and authored, I do not believe that *thirtysomething* fits the mould of the genre. When the 'Mike van Dyke Show' episode references a sixties TV sit-com, it does so by inserting the *thirtysomething* characters into the diegesis of the earlier show, an 'artsy' technique that stresses *thirtysomething*'s difference from a fondly remembered television tradition, not its continuity with one. As I have written, authorship on this show took a different form than it did in the mainstream of the 'quality' tradition. *thirtysomething* laid claim to a literary and theatrical idea of authorship found more often in British television dramas. *thirtysomething* did not really have a foundation in a traditional television genre, even though it complied with the home/workplace alternation central to MTM. If anything, the show took its generic material from the daytime soap opera, but as I have just explained, relocated this material in a realist social context. Its material was not the professional lives of highly valued or dramatic occupational groups, but rather the examination of the inner lives of a particular class fraction (yuppies) and a particular generation (baby boomers). The writers of *thirtysomething* set out to distinguish the show from the main tradition of television drama. The writers wanted to link the show more to an art cinema tradition than to anything televisual. In this sense, *thirtysomething* seems to me more closely related to an HBO drama such as *Six Feet Under* than to any of the more central quality TV dramas of the eighties and nineties. In both shows, the inner lives of the characters are individuated and linked to dream diegeses. Their occupations, advertising and funeral homes, respectively, are opposite to the heroic tradition of professionalism in the mainstream of TV drama. Yet the *thirtysomething* characters were not, to use a term beloved of TV writers, 'quirky' in the sense of another quality drama tradition running from *Chicago Hope* to *Twin Peaks* to *Northern Exposure* to *Picket Fences* to *Six Feet Under*. They were meant to represent social types that the audience could accept as 'real', not quirky types that the audience could accept as 'eccentric'.

Although *My So-Called Life* achieved cult status as teen TV, and although it can certainly profit for us to categorise it as teen TV,[3] what links it to *thirtysomething* for my purposes here is the continuing saga of the parents of the teenager at the centre of the show's narrative. Written and produced by Winnie Holzman, who also wrote for *thirtysomething* and would go on to write and produce for *Once and Again*, *My So-Called Life* is characterised by a reliance on what in literature is called 'interior monologue'. Certainly *thirtysomething* was obsessed with the interior psychic states of its characters, but the later shows would go even further in using subjective techniques to convey interiority. *My So-Called Life* employed the teenage Angela's voice-over narration in every episode, giving us a well-written and nuanced view of her private thoughts and making hers the only narrating voice we heard. *Once and Again* went further in employing the device of black and white 'confessional' sequences for all its characters. In these sequences, which interrupted the main narrative, the characters appeared to be confessing their innermost fears to an unseen therapist. The effect of having the sequences shot in direct address was that the audience of the show then became that therapist for the characters.

Since *My So-Called Life* made Angela the narrator, one would think that the show followed the teen film tradition of excluding the point of view of adults or of seeing parents only from the (jaundiced) teenage perspective. In spite of the voice-over narration, *My So-Called Life* frequently gave the parents equal time. Using the kind of pointed parallelism that *thirtysomething* borrowed from soap opera, *My So-Called Life* could interweave the angst of teenage life with the kind of generational perspective of the parents found in *thirtysomething*. The show dealt with the parents' lives apart from Angela's. Frequently we are shown the parents' point of view independent of hers. Even though Angela controls the voice-over narration, the parents are given equally confessional moments in the diegesis. Subjectivity is more than just an effect of narrative voice.

This is demonstrated in the 'Father Figures' episode.[4] So reliant is this episode on parallelism that even its plot summary on the TV Tome website uses a parallel sentence structure, 'in multi-generational father-daughter conflict, Patty must take control of the printing business from her father, and Angela approaches Graham for the first time as a person rather than a superhero'. The episode opens with a flashback to Angela (the teenager played by Claire Danes) as a little girl, waiting for 'Daddy' to come home. There is a match cut on an image of Graham's (her father's) briefcase and the audio of young Angela's words, 'Daddy's home' to a present-day continuation of the same scene in which the welcome home is far less enthusiastic. A bit later, we see Angela's younger sister cuddling happily with Dad. The episode parallels Angela's discussion of her father (with her friends Ricky and Rayeanne) with the parents' discussion of an impending

Internal Revenue Service audit based on the 1992 return that Patty (Angela's mother) filed when she took over her own father's business due to his heart attack. Later the parent/child alternation is replaced by a father/daughter one in which each father/child set confronts the other. In each generation, it is mentioned or shown that the daughter 'pushes the father away' if he tries to kiss her without shaving. I am not going to offer an interpretation of this episode because the oedipal conflict and its resolution are conveyed well enough by the writers. But I want to emphasise the structure whereby a shot of Angela hugging her grandfather from her parents' point of view carries as much weight as Angela's voice-over musings. As in *thirtysomething*, Graham and Patty are baby boomers for whom adulthood is a constant struggle. So much of this theme is carried by dialogue and by realist acting that cinematic techniques such as voice-over and point-of-view shots only reinforce the meanings conveyed by the scripts and by the realist acting style.

All three Bedford Falls shows involve nuclear families with children whom we see at home and at work. Unlike other quality dramas that meet these criteria, the focus is resolutely inward. The workplace is not a generic site for breeding exciting plots (as are the hospital, the courtroom and police precinct) but rather a place for further narcissistic self-examination.[5] For *thirtysomething* a story arc that spanned all seasons of the show's run involved the dissolution of the Michael and Elliot Company and their having to go to work for the large corporate firm headed up by evil yuppie Miles Drentell. When *Once and Again* was under threat of cancellation in its first season, the writers re-introduced the Miles character into a new diegesis. On *Once and Again*, he was the architect male lead Rick's most important client, now undertaking an enormous building project in Chicago. As an archetypal villain, Miles jars with the realistic inward bent of both shows, but in combining New Age spirituality and old-fashioned capitalist greed, he epitomises the class and generational emphasis that defines the Zwick–Hershovitz productions.

Reviewers speculated that *Once and Again* updated the material of *thirtysomething* from that of eighties parents with small children to a portrayal of nineties fortysomethings with teenage children. In many respects, the newer show was less experimental: it did not indulge in all kinds of dream diegeses, it did not define the social context for its decade, it played safe by catering to the teen-TV audience. Yet its resolutely inward, psychic focus made it unusual for the mainstream of quality drama. There is even less plot than on *thirtysomething*. The pilot episode shows the lead romantic couple meeting and immediately falling in love. Yet by the end of the first season (episode 22), they are only just introducing their children to one another. What, then, has transpired in the first twenty-one episodes? In terms of plot, not much. Lily moves towards divorcing Jake, Lily gets a new job, her sister Judy gets involved with a married man, Rick's ex-wife Karen gets involved with a younger man. But in terms of psychodrama, a lot happens. Unfolding primarily in a series of one-on-one emotional and sexual encounters, the characters have crept forward emotionally. The two legally separated couples have moved towards emotional separation. And the audience has heard approximately ten black and white therapeutic confessions per episode.

It is the confessional inserts that allow the audience to know the inner thoughts of the characters. I have said that the audience takes the place of a therapist in hearing these confessions. It's important to explain why I don't think we take the point of view of a priest, another figure accustomed to hearing private confessions. I believe the context of these black and white outpourings to be resolutely secular. Although *Once and Again* does have a spiritual side (as when Grace tells Lily upon viewing her brain-dead grandfather that she now knows what a 'soul' is), all three shows find salvation in the language of psychotherapy and not in the language of Judeo-Christianity. Part of the 'realism' of these shows consists in their having very well-defined characters, for example, ones that are explicitly labelled Jewish rather than stereotyped as generic American Christians. But psychotherapy *is* the religion of the educated professional–managerial class portrayed in all three dramas and it is also the source for their language, a vocabulary always adequate to the expression of fleeting emotional states. Therapy on these shows is always talking therapy, and the black and white sequences emphasise that. Yet the confessional sequences do not just convey hidden, darker thoughts. Often they are reminiscences, even happy ones. The characters black and white faces are keylit and they appear joyous. Just after Lily's father dies, we see him for the first time in black and white, fully alive and talking about what he plans to do after he retires. 'What do I want from retirement? The same as anybody else . . . time – that's what anybody wants – time to do the really important things.' He laughs in slow motion as the black and white dissolves back to the colour of the hospital corridor where, of course, time has run out for him. We are left to interpret the sequence as ironic, but the confession itself was a happy one.

The Bedford Falls shows are not populated by inarticulate characters whose emotions need to be conveyed exclusively by subjective camera or voice-over narration. The characters often do say what they are really thinking, then they say it again in the confessions and through the camera. Nothing is left unsaid. When in the finale episode for the first season, Lily finds a note in the pocket of her late father's old sweater, the camera shows us what it says, 'get gifts 4 kids'. The audience can interpret this as meaning that she now has four kids, because the families are about to be united. This kind of symbolism is fairly obvious to the show's audience. But just in case we missed it, Lily has to offer this interpretation to Rick later in the episode. Although the show appears to share with art cinema reliance upon the understated and the subtextual, in fact it is overwritten. Everything must be said.

This is a very different use of the confessional from its status as a trope of reality television from MTV's *The Real World* to *Survivor* to *America's Next Top Model*. When used, as it always is, on reality shows, the confessional is not so much a way of conveying subjectivity as it is a way of letting the audience know what the characters are really thinking as opposed to what they actually say in the interactions with other characters. The game structure of most of these shows and their voyeuristic bent make the confessionals much more of a direct address to the audience than a look inside the characters' psyches. On reality TV we always know more about the characters than they do about themselves, but they always know more about their true motives than do the other character/contestants.

For *thirtysomething* and its two offspring, subjectivity is not a game, rather it's the whole show. These shows are literary in a way that distinguishes them from the more televisual tradition of quality drama. Writing, and words, is the most important channel and although it appears that the writers speak for the characters, in fact the characters also speak as writers, as educated, articulate self-knowing literary types. This distinguishes the three shows from the tradition of melodramatic excess that feeds into reality TV as well. Strong emotions are the foundation of all these shows, but for the Zwick–Hershkovitz trio, the emotions never appear to be in excess of what the highly subjective narratives would demand. Ironically, *Survivor* expresses much more emotional excess than does *Once and Again*, which, in keeping with its high cultural roots, always shows those emotions repressed and kept in check and yet expressed verbally. Even though the two later shows do not pay as much attention to a specific socio-economic milieu as did *thirtysomething*, they nevertheless express the psychic zeitgeist of that class as much as the original show did. All TV drama is confessional, and all quality TV deals with the psychology of its characters but *thirtysomething* did so in a way particular not just to an educated demographic but to one conversant with modern art and drama. If all quality drama appeals to an educated audience, then *thirtysomething* and its offspring could be said to appeal to that segment of the educated audience that majored in English literature and that feels comfortable with the subjectivity of art cinema. *Hill*

Street Blues in the eighties and *The West Wing* in the nineties rewarded those viewers who had large vocabularies but *thirtysomething* et al. in addition rewarded viewers who had been psychoanalysed. In this sense, it was too specialised to have had much impact on the quality tradition of the 1980s-90s. It was not until the arrival of HBO with its far more specialised pay-TV audience that such a sensibility could have free reign in shows like *The Sopranos* and *Six Feet Under*.

Notes

1. The first season of *Once and Again* is available on DVD as is the only season of *My So-called Life*. The latter show was brought to DVD at the insistence of the internet fan community surrounding this show.
2. http://www.plj.com/bigshow/billycampbell.html
3. Teen TV is already emerging as its own genre. Matt Hills has convincingly argued that *Dawson's Creek* could belong to a subgenre called 'quality teen TV'. As such it straddles the line between being a 'mainstream cult' in the manner of *Melrose Place* and being a quality drama in the tradition of *thirtysomething* (Hills 2004).
4. The fourth episode was aired on 15 September 1994, written by Winnie Holzman and with a cameo by the writer in the role of the high-school guidance counsellor.
5. Of course most quality dramas deal with the inner lives of the characters. This is what distinguished them from old-fashioned cop, doctor and lawyer shows. But the Bedford Falls shows have an added element of narcissistic self-absorption that *ER* and *The West Wing* lack.

Bibliography

Feuer, Jane (1995), *Seeing through the Eighties: Television and Reaganism*, London: BFI.

Hills, Matt (2004), '*Dawson's Creek*: "Quality Teen TV" and "Mainstream Cult"?' in Glyn Davis and Kay Dickinson (eds), *Teen TV: Genre, Consumption and Identity*, London: BFI, pp. 281–305.

Thompson, Robert J. (1996), *Television's Second Golden Age: From 'Hill Street Blues' to 'ER'*, New York: Syracuse University Press.

CHAPTER 3

Twin Peaks: David Lynch and the Serial-Thriller Soap

Linda Ruth Williams

Like nothing else on prime time, or on God's earth.[1]

There is a moment in episode 4 of *Twin Peaks*,[2] David Lynch and Mark Frost's surreal/erotic detective/soap, when ditzy police receptionist Lucy (Kimmy Robertson), who has been watching *Invitation to Love* – the fictional soap much loved by Twin Peaks' citizens – is asked 'what's going on?' by her cop-boss Harry S. Truman (Michael Ontkean). Lucy replies:

> Thanks to Jade Jared decided not to kill himself and he's changed his will leaving the Towers to Jade instead of Emerald. But Emerald found out about it, and now she's trying to seduce Chet to give her the new will so that she can destroy it. Montana is planning to kill Jared at midnight so the Towers will belong to Emerald and Montana. But I think she's going to double-cross him and he doesn't know it yet. Poor Chet!

Ever the straight guy, Harry simply responds, 'What's happening *here*?' – here in the real of the police station, to which the answer is simple, 'Agent Cooper is in the conference room with Dr Jacoby.' Lucy's non-sequiteur betrays a guileless inability to distinguish the TV real from her *real* 'real' (police station or TV station?), just as *Twin Peaks* itself ultimately refused to mark the difference, or express a preference, between the dark seriousness of its dominant storyline (the murder of homecoming queen Laura Palmer (Sheryl Lee)) and its bizarre comic-surreal subplots. The elaborations of Lucy's beloved soap–within–a–soap mirror those of this pioneering series itself, which ran the gauntlet from the sublime (supernatural-melodramatic thriller) to the ridiculous (peculiar knowing humour) in its incomplete two-season run series on US channel ABC from April 1990 to June 1991. The oft-repeated adjective 'quirky' has become almost a synonym for *Twin Peaks*, though the series is as genuinely grief- and horror-driven as it is humour-laced. Viewers didn't know whether to laugh or cry, but usually did both. Then there is the Red Room, traversed by the intuitive FBI Special Agent Dale Cooper (Kyle McLachlan) in his dreams as he searches for far more than the answer to Laura's murder – a strange backward-speaking realm of the unconscious/unknown, hemmed in by red curtains and populated by dwarfs, giants and dead people. Unquestionably, the seductively disturbing Red Room is a place where no prime-time TV serial has gone before – or since.

Yet *Twin Peaks*' tears and fears are predicated on its deployment of two of TV's most predictable formats, soap opera and the crime/investigative thriller. Both genres haunt the opening of the startling pilot episode, in which Laura's body is washed up by a river in a small Pacific Northwest town, Twin Peaks itself, prompting the series' governing arc-question (which dominates season one at least), 'Who Killed Laura Palmer?' This proved to be a question to whet the appetite of soap and murder-mystery audiences alike. Indeed, Lucy's two answers might emerge from two different series, the first breathlessly articulating the interpersonal psychosexual complexities of prime-time soap opera (asking more questions than it answers), the second a simple statement of fact in the investigative serial's hopeful pathway towards the resolution of crime. Part-*policier* (centring on the developing buddy-partnership between Agent Cooper and Sheriff Truman), part ensemble-soap (myriad eccentric characters weaving in and out of the increasingly complex storylines, from genre-standards – the rich widow, the feckless businessman – to oddball one-offs – the Log Lady, the Man from Another Place), *Twin Peaks* injected a unique mix of compelling cult viewing and narrative undecidability in the schedules' standard entertainment fare.

Often read as the perfect hybrid of Lynch's cinematic strangeness and Frost's respectable televisual pedigree (he was by the late 1980s a veteran writer of such TV landmarks as *The Six Million Dollar Man* and the pathbreaking cop-soap landmark *Hill Street Blues*), *Twin Peaks* poses a series of questions about genre, seriality and auteurism for television studies. Its fantastically playful generic mix-and-match format contributed greatly to its cult hit status, but also provoked some of its problems. Though the question of whether it is possible to create a cult artefact with any degree of deliberation is a matter of debate, *Twin Peaks* may be the nearest the visual arts have got to a successful pre-sold cult show. I am particularly interested in the series' twin obsessions with weeping and the unknown/unknowable – with these as indicators of genre, and agents in the confusions bound up with the series' format. As I will discuss further below, *Twin Peaks* first promised the resolutions of an episodic series, but unfolded as an irresolvable continuous serial: Laura's tragedy is approached in two ways – as an unknown to be solved (or not), and as an agonised experience to be lived through. For all its comic quirkiness, *Twin Peaks* moves on a current of tears, both the cast's and the audience's, shed for Laura and themselves and for small-town Americana. Tears are the body fluid of soap opera, and perhaps their plenitude here (underpinned by a deeper question about whether Lynch's much-fêted strategies of post-modern irony should be read instead as straight-down-the-line sentiment) resolves some of the series' surreal generic undecidability into patently real tear-jerking. But running alongside this – to paraphrase Sandy in Lynch's previous film *Blue Velvet*, who can't figure out if Jeffrey is a detective or a pervert – *Twin Peaks* also makes detective-perverts out of most of its cast, in their search for answers to their proliferating questions. Laura's death is the emotive heart of the show, but it is also its primary epistemological focus, the first mystery of withheld knowledge which it poses then promises to (and fails to) reveal. As Cooper and Truman pick their way through the townsfolk's secrets – affairs, blackmail, drugs, all cheek-by-jowl with upstanding citizenry and wholesome intentions – Laura's friends, family, and those who preyed upon her become investigators in and perpetrators of new stories, running parallel to, or overlapping, Laura's posthumous tale. There is a liberal sprinkling of high-school angst (featuring bright young newcomers such as Lara Flynn Boyle as Laura's best friend Donna Hayward, or Sherilyn Fenn as small-town sexpot Audrey Horne) to attract younger viewers, and a heavier dose of adult intrigue (featuring established performers such as Joan Chen as Josie Packard, or Grace Zabriskie as Sarah Palmer). The uneasy line between investigation and involvement is crossed and recrossed, as is that between humour and melodrama, both of which are traversed by almost everyone. The show also develops David Lynch's insistent dark eroticism, though clearly going no further in its spectacles than could any regular prime-time series. Critical discussion of sexuality in Lynch is often subsumed into wider analyses of pervasive neurosis or his noirish fascination with eros as thanatos. *Twin Peaks* is predicated upon a set of sleazy shenanigans – Laura's death is an incestuous sex crime, com-mitted by the supernatural entity BOB who has taken possession of her father, and her backstory of prostitution and pornography is as ripe with Lynchian nefarious sexuality as any of his movies, from *Eraserhead* to *Mulholland Drive*. But the sexuality of the series is also more manifest. As a number of reviewers noted at the time, here the director gleefully show-cases a parade of nubile starlets in tight sweaters.

This mix of tears and sex, investigation and secrets, may seem quintes-sentially Lynchian, and I find that already I have marked the series with a particular auteurist brand. At least one critic (Page 2001) defines *Twin*

Peaks as prime postmodern drama, placing it alongside titles as diverse as *The Prisoner* and *Ally McBeal* in its self-reflexive refusal of naturalism, its mixture of styles and playful deployment/critique of master narratives. But perhaps the dominant master narrative with which it has continued to struggle is auteurism itself. Unexpected as its mainstream-Dadaism may be, all seems to be finally rendered meaningful via the overarching presence of a reliably bizarre product, David Lynch himself, who's marketing catchphrase is Expect the Unexpected. Critical reception insists on Lynch's cinematic allegiances dragging the form from the living-room into the theatrical auditorium, reading *Twin Peaks* as primarily the intersection of Lynch's erotic/surreal aesthetic with the serial television format. But there are significant contradictions inherent in reading *Twin Peaks* as a televisual event *as well as* a career 'event', one stage in the ongoing cult trajectory of Lynch-o-mania and primarily interpretable in a tradition of films from *The Grandmother* to *Mulholland Drive* and beyond. One question of this chapter concerns whether *Twin Peaks* is important because of what it tells us about Lynch, or because of what it tells us about generically hybrid serial television – is it, as Frost put it, 'the next evolutionary step after *Dynasty*'? (Woods 2000: 94) And what of its myriad collaborators, not least co–producer/writer/director Frost himself, who kept the show going throughout much of season two when Lynch departed to shoot *Wild at Heart*? How insistent must the discourse of auteurism still be if it continues to pervade a form as collectively produced as a TV series?

Big Screen, Small Screen

The blue-ish face of Sheryl Lee, who played that iconic corpse wrapped in plastic like a rose, has become emblematic of *Twin Peaks*. Hovering in a liminal state between life and death, Laura conjoins its soap-heart to its thriller-heart (at least as imagined by Lynch), an undead presence in a newly-invigorated form. In 1990 *Esquire* magazine named Laura Palmer 'Woman of the Year'.[3] Though Laura is dead, she haunts the series: Lee comes back to perform Laura's brunette but identikit cousin Maddie in episode 3,[4] and to star as Laura in the spin-off prequel movie *Twin Peaks: Fire Walk With Me* (1992; hereafter *Fire Walk With Me*). Like her namesake from Otto Preminger's 1944 film *Laura* – an absent woman who's iconic image (a painting) troubles the men who investigate her (presumed) death – Laura Palmer's death provides those who outlive her the context in which to rewrite their conditions of existence. If all the inhabitants of Twin Peaks are affected by her death, the series also promised new opportunities for future inhabitants and makers of TV drama.

But it was another dead blonde who first brought Frost and Lynch together, not Laura Palmer but Marilyn Monroe. After the success of *Blue Velvet*, Lynch was given the opportunity to direct a biopic charting the last days of the star's life, with a screenplay by Frost based on Anthony Summers' book *Goddess*. 'I loved the idea of this woman in trouble' Lynch has said (Rodley 1997: 156), recalling not just the Laura of *Fire Walk With Me* (a golden girl harbouring secret horrors) but the brunette Dorothy Vallens of *Blue Velvet* (trapped in a sexual-familial prison). Though *Goddess* didn't progress far into development, Frost and Lynch then began work on a fantasy/screwball screenplay entitled *One Saliva Bubble*, which got as far as casting Steve Martin and Martin Short, but failed due to the collapse of De Laurentiis Entertainment, itself partly precipitated by problems surrounding Lynch's earlier film *Dune* (Woods 2000: 92–3; Hughes 2001: 247). Lynch had been involved in some other short TV projects prior to his involvement with Frost, notably hosting a BBC *Arena* documentary on surrealism in 1987 (*Ruth, Roses and Revolvers*), and directing the comedy-western short *The Cowboy and the Frenchman*, made in 1988 for French television. But the cinematic false-starts with Frost meant that by 1988 the writer's native medium offered a more certain basis for project development for what came to be know as Lynch–Frost Productions.[5]

Cinema and television have a long history of interdependence; Peter Krämer even argues that the tendency for moving pictures to be 'caught up in the televisual imagination' dates from the early days of cinema (1996: 39). But one specific cross-fertilisation trend reached a peak around the moment of *Twin Peaks*. Martin McLoone points out that 'filmmakers as diverse as Stephen [sic] Spielberg, Peter Hyams, John Badham and earlier than these Don Siegel, Robert Altman, Sam Peckinpah and William Friedkin, had all worked in television' (1996: 103). In the UK television has often been seen as our national film school, with directors from Ken Loach and Mike Leigh through to Danny Boyle and Roger Michell first directing TV dramas before making the crossover to movies. But the late 1980s saw the development of a trend wherein A-list Hollywood directors made forays back into television through clearly delineated 'quality' forms. Oliver Stone's *Wild Palms*, Steven Spielberg's *Amazing Stories* and *Band of Brothers* are notable examples; Jonathan Kaplan has a long association with *ER*, as one of its producers and directors. *Twin Peaks* was a watershed in this movement. Though as we have seen Mark Frost had a much more resolutely televisual pedigree than Lynch, *Twin Peaks* could be pre-sold on the basis of Lynch's reputation as an internationally renowned maverick, the auteur of America's perverse underbelly. A weekly surreal/supernatural mystery-soap with Lynch's name attached promised an unprecedented televisual spectacle, and this unique selling-point ensured that before it reached networks interest was already high, even though the Lynch-brand also brought with it certain risks for a populist medium. However, the late 1980s and early 1990s was an exciting time for US television, and networks were willing to take risks. *Twin Peaks* did not spring fully formed from the genius of Lynch's auteur sensibility; it was part of a wave of more daring TV commissions between 1989 and 1991, including *The Tracey Ullman Show* and *The Simpsons* (both Fox). *The Village Voice* heralded this with a special issue on 'Rad TV',[6] and innovative programming was reflected in the Emmy Awards of 1990 – *Twin Peaks* garnered fourteen nominations, provoking one TV executive to comment, 'It's a clear sign that people are looking for smart fresh programming' (ABC vice-president Ted Harbert, quoted in Caldwell 286).[7] We might say – in homage to Jeffrey Sconce's seminal essay on late 1990s 'smart films' – that *Twin Peaks* was the smartest moment in a unique wave of US 'smart TV' production. It was also hugely successful, at least in its first series. Rosenbaum reports that the pilot episode reached 'almost 20 million households, roughly twice the number watching any competing show' (1995: 26), whilst Woods quotes a viewing figure of 35 million in the US for key early episodes (2000: 111), and cites ambitious merchandising plans which testify to its mainstream success, notably *Twin Peaks* logo coffee and a planned in-house promotional deal with Bloomingdales.[8] Successful products which did make it to the marketplace and still do brisk business in collector's circles include Jennifer Lynch's best-selling novella *The Secret Diary of Laura Palmer* from 1990, *The Autobiography of FBI Special Agent Dale Cooper* from 1991 (co-authored by 'Dale Cooper' and Scott Frost), the 'Agent Cooper Tapes' (dictaphone reports to the unseen Diane, recorded by Kyle McLachlan), as well as Cherry Pie T-Shirts, a Twin Peaks Murder Mystery Board Game, playing cards and cigarette lighters, some authorised, some not.[9] Meanwhile, at the end of the shooting of the first season, Lynch went 'on hiatus' to direct *Wild at Heart*, leaving Frost largely at the helm and a range of diverse writers and directors in charge of season two. This was when *Twin Peaks*' fortunes began to shift dramatically, as it refused to resolve its central narrative conundrum and saw its broadcast slot shift across the schedules, to damaging effect. It is, as once critic has commentated, a story of a 'spectacular rise and equally spectacular fall' (Dolan 1995: 30).

Twin Peaks thus articulates a sensational moment in recent television history, both in terms of its textual content and its substantial cultural splash. Yet however audacious it may have been as a televisual event, it is also haunted by cinema, largely because ever since it has been framed as a Lynch auteur-work. This is reinforced by other significant cinematic resonances. Certainly the series showcased some new young actors with little previous screen experience: Harry Goaz (Deputy Brennan), Eric Da Re (Leo Johnson), Madchen Amick (Shelley Johnson) and Sheryl Lee herself, plus pre-fame roles for Heather Graham (Annie Blackburne) and a dragged-up David Duchovny (Denis/Denise Bryson). But there was also a significant framework of cinematic has-beens whose faces reminded audiences of past big-screen glories: Russ Tamblyn (Dr Jacoby), better remembered for his roles in *Seven Brides for Seven Brothers* or *Tom Thumb*; Richard Beymer (Benjamin Horne), better known for his roles in *West Side Story* or *The Longest Day*; Piper Laurie (Catherine Martell), better known for her roles in *The Hustler*, *Carrie* or *Children of a Lesser God*. Lynch also deployed a number of 'Lynch mob' stalwarts including Jack Nance (Pete Martell, also Henry in *Eraserhead*), Catherine Coulson (Margaret The Log Lady, also a crew-member on *Eraserhead*, and 'star' of *The Amputee*), Charlotte Stewart (Betty Briggs, and Henry's hapless girlfriend in *Eraserhead*), plus McLachalan himself (Agent Cooper, as well as the star of *Dune* and Jeffrey in *Blue Velvet*). This mix of the known and unknown is standard practice in TV casting, but here it reinforces a relationship to cinema as Lynch's primary medium, anchoring the series to his established canon. Very soon into its broadcast history *Twin Peaks* had generated its own peculiar fanbase, not least on the embryonic internet, and one of its foci was the cinematic referencing perceived as central to the show's intricate narratives and symbolism, as well as Lynch the master-narrator (I will return to this below). The series, of course, also spawned a movie. But it is in academic discussion that *Twin Peaks* is most coloured by David Lynch's persona. He has always been attractive to intellectuals – critics, scholars and viewers drawn to complex visual experiences, and fans who appreciate a 'difficulty' which lends itself to decoding and mythicisation. Indeed, one aspect of *Twin Peaks* which brings certain academic approaches and those of the fan together is its textual 'thickness' – there is just so much to say about, so much to find in, *Twin Peaks* as an endlessly interpretable text which, tantalisingly, may outstrip critical and fan efforts exhaustively to decipher it (it is, like Laura, 'full of secrets'). Lynch has fun with the boundless fruitlessness of this enthusiastic will-to-interpret in an outlandish elucidation scene in *Fire Walk With Me*, when Agents Desmond and Stanley (Chris Isaak and Kiefer Sutherland) extemporise an elaborate interpretation of the layers of a 'Blue Rose Case' as pantomimically performed by a bizarre woman named 'Lil' (Kimberly Ann Cole).

Particularly since the successes of *Lost Highway* and *Mulholland Drive* there has been an upsurge in academic and more popular publications about the director. Lynch's career has navigated some rollercoaster highs and dips; three (not two) peaks characterising his history up to the early twenty-first century: (1) the rise in studio interest after early indie films like *The Grandmother* and *Eraserhead* which resulted in commissions to make *The Elephant Man* and *Dune*; (2) the personal and financial disaster of *Dune*, followed by the critical success of *Blue Velvet* and *Wild at Heart*, upon which *Twin Peaks* built;[10] (3) the critical and financial disaster of *Fire Walk With Me*, followed by the building successes of *The Straight Story*, *Lost Highway* and *Mulholland Drive*. Reflecting this career-trajectory, a number of publications have emerged about the director since the mid-1990s, with significant film studies 'names' pinning their colours to his weird mast (Michel Chion's *David Lynch* in 1995; Slavoj Žižek's book on *Lost Highway* in 2000) alongside a range of career-overviews (Nochimson 1997; Woods 2000; Hughes 2001; Sheen and Davison 2004). It may be that by the turn of the century Lynch had simply made enough films to merit completist canonical treatment. His penchant for 'bouncing back' has itself become part of the story which is told about him, an uneven director who provides consistently interesting material. Thus qualities of weirdness, eccentricity and (paradoxically) the unexpected take on a dependable regularity in Lynch's hands, becoming the characteristic used to launch his products into the marketplace. This cinematic reputation has infused how Lynch's television work has been marketed and received. *Twin Peaks* is forever 'David Lynch's' *Twin Peaks*. TV is traditionally seen as a producer's medium, yet here Lynch's role as executive producer takes on a directorial aura in the public mind. Academic discussions draw a fairly undifferentiated picture of 'the David Lynch universe' across the media with which he has involved himself, reading *Twin Peaks* as one episode in a career-long 'series' or chain of related moments rendered coherent by an auteurial arc. Contributors to the excellent 1995 collection, *Full of Secrets: Critical Approaches to Twin Peaks* did, admittedly, try to broaden the interpretative scope beyond auteurism, reading it variously as displaying 'reptilian' sexual ethics (George 1995: 119), as canonising Laura as secular saint (Desmet 1995), and for its innovative use of music (Kalinak 1995). But this diversity does not seem to have dispelled the glamour of auteurist interpretation here and elsewhere. It might also be said that *Twin Peaks'* exhibition 'afterlife' is haunted by auteurism. Cable channels and DVD have become the series' own Red Room, the 'other place' where a TV series may end its days if it is lucky. 'Cable has taught television that programs never die', writes Caldwell, 'they just keep resurfacing in the niche afterlife' (1995: 299). Yet even in its posthumous life of reruns, *Twin Peaks* continues to be dogged, for Caldwell, by a persistent Lynchianism, assuming 'its place within the aesthetic pantheon of European cinema and independent feature films on cable's auteurist boutique, Bravo' (1995: 299). It is then particularly difficult to read *Twin Peaks* as 'pure television' (if such a thing existed), infused as it is by its prime selling point (Lynch's name). For his part, Lynch's commitment to the project seems to have been ambivalently televisual. He hated the interruption of commercials every twelve minutes, resisted the 1:33 ratio with which he had to work, and – as a director committed to deploying powerful sound formations – had difficulties producing the haunting aural qualities he wanted. But though he laments the fact that 'Some little fences are put up that are smaller than the fences you're used to' (Rodley 1997: 178), he was also surprised at the artistic freedom he was given.

Yet even Lynch's absence becomes auteurially significant in the analysis of *Twin Peaks*' failures. The fact that Lynch moved on to the production of *Wild at Heart* between season one and season two of *Twin Peaks* is often given as the cause of the series' demise, lacking the cohering vision of its primary helmsman. This is despite the plain fact that Lynch himself only directed six episodes in the thirty-part run, with the remaining twenty-four directed by names prominent in film and TV directing, before and since, each with their own developing styles and bodies of work. These include Tim Hunter (*Control*, *River's Edge*, and episodes 5, 17 and 29 of *Twin Peaks*), Lesli Linka Glatter (*The Proposition*, *Now and Then*, and episodes 6, 11, 14, and 24 of *Twin Peaks*), Uli Edel (*Last Exit to Brooklyn*, *Body of Evidence*, and episode 22 of *Twin Peaks*), Diane Keaton (*Unstrung Heroes*, *Hanging Up*, and episode 23 of *Twin Peaks*), James Foley (*The Chamber*, *Glengarry*, *Glen Ross*, and episode 25 of *Twin Peaks*), and Stephen Gyllenhaal (*Homegrown*, *A Dangerous Woman*, and episode 28 of *Twin Peaks*). Perceived now in the relative 'completion' of collectable DVD and video releases, the series requires further analysis outside of this singular auteurist frame, perhaps through a collective production perspective. TV analysis is traditionally producer-focused, but given that such interesting cinematic careers have been forged by these and other collaborators in so many distinct directions, it would be worth looking at their impact beyond the insistent critical view that each formulated his or her own betrayal of the Lynch vision. This may ironically also be where discussion of Lynch's legacy is best placed – his role as a magnet, attracting talent to an exceptional TV project, which gave a number of directors unprecedented freedom.

Arguments around the quality of control commanded by Lynch or Frost at various stages in the series' fortunes also display interesting prejudices about artistic vision. Rosenbaum reads Lynch's popularity as the negative index of his artistic integrity: the more popular *Twin Peaks* is, and the more involved in it Lynch gets, the more it 'dilutes' his artistry (1995: 23).

Nochimson argues that Lynch's 'hiatus' from the series enabled Frost to take it in a more classically rationalising direction, true to the writer's interest in refiguring Agent Cooper as a latter-day Sherlock Holmes. But this is all in the service of an argument which casts Lynch as the more visionary force, pushing the envelope of the carnivalesque through the show's unconscious traces, with Frost as a conventional thriller-intelligence, seeking to resolve all with a narrative of good versus evil, reason versus the irrational, with the former categories ultimately privileged. In a detailed discussion of the very last aired episode, in which Cooper returns to the Red Room and is himself possessed by BOB, Nochimson argues that Lynch, like an emissary from the Cavalry of the unconscious, rescues the series at the eleventh hour.[11] Originally scripted by Frost but revised and filmed by Lynch as a refutation of the 'trite invasion of the banal into *Twin Peaks*' (Nochimson 1997: 94) which had occurred during his absence, this final episode is then quintessentially 'Lynchian' (1997: 97).[12] For Nochimson, Frost would make *Twin Peaks* a resolvable whodunnit, whilst Lynch 'redeems our connection to the subconcious' (97). I want to turn now to other readings of the series, thinking about its innovative mixture of TV genres, about Lynch/Frost as dark sentimentalists and, finally, why Lynch took Laura (back) to the cinema.

Tears, Genres and Textualities

The film – or programme or anything – has a certain smell to it. And a certain buzz on the street. I don't know what it is, but I think it's bigger. It's something to do with fate. (Lynch quoted in Rodley 1997: 177)

If *Twin Peaks* was an exceptional television series, then they were an exceptional audience who possessed all the cultural competencies necessary to fully appreciate its greatness. (Jenkins 1995: 66)

There are gallons of tears shed in the first episode of *Twin Peaks*, some of them positively Sirkian tears, dripping with the ironies and tragedies of small-town Americana. Tears are, of course, generically highly significant, but *Twin Peaks*' tears make it more slippery, ever harder to place. Its characteristic hip humour emerges at first surreptitiously, through the gaps defined by the uneven mystery-tragedy story which is woven around Laura's body. Yet Lynch wants us to be affected: weeping is for him like 'a yawn: it transfers over', cementing 'identification, and it's unleashed' (Rodley 1997: 167). This is soap as body genre (to borrow Linda Williams' term), a form which trades in the contagion of emotion passed from screen response to audience affect.

Twin Peaks was from the start discussed as a kind of soap-nightmare, even if it was 'Rad TV'. But why flirt with soap opera, 'that most conservative of media institutions' (Rodley 1997: 155)? Woods reports that Lynch became hooked on soaps playing on the workplace TV whilst labouring as a printer in pre-*Eraserhead* days, and fantasised about 'a long-running saga focused on one central locale' (2000: 94). There is, indeed, something supremely soap-like about *Blue Velvet* itself, with Lumberton more *Peyton Place* than *Melrose Place*, referencing Douglas Sirk's middle American small towns in its revelations of nefarious secrets hidden beyond the picket fence. Indeed, *Peyton Place*, which ran (also on ABC) from 1964 to 1969, a spin-off of two films from 1957 and 1961,[13] has itself often been heralded as the first high-profile, star-led US soap series, which established 'a place for melodrama in the prime-time schedule' (McCarthy 2001: 49). Sirk's sly social critique melodramas have also been read as influencing the genre, under the auspices of wider analysis of so-called 'women's genres'. What Lynch and Frost did with this territory was already begun in Lynch's cinematic sagas of the dysfunctional-domestic. 'It was a TV show about free-floating guilt' said writer-producer Robert Engels; 'Something was captured there that people responded to emotionally' (Rodley 1997: 156). Guilt, of course, is a driving force for both crime and soap-scenarios, though in the first it is a mystery to be uncovered (who is *particularly* guilty?), whilst in the second it is a generously disseminated neurosis (which of us is *not* guilty?).

This also has implications for how we read its generic form: is *Twin Peaks* formally as innovative as some of its outlandish content? Marc Dolan reads the show as playing fast and loose with serial conventions as they had been established by the late 1980s, from the episodic and continuous serial forms up to the 1970s (individual stories are resolved in each episode, as in *Star Trek*, or else stories carry over in a continuous stream, as in soap opera), to the sequential series of the 1980s (*Cheers*, *Hill Street Blues*, which combines the satisfactions of narrative closure 'with the expectation elicited by the narrative 'hook' (Dolan 1995: 34)). *Twin Peaks* is remarkable for Dolan (even 'television at its best' (1995: 45)) because its different narrative and character demands make it a strange (or original) combination of the episodic and the continuous (1995: 35). This tension rests on its uneasy development of crime-story and character:

> Instead of choosing one consistent narrative mode for all aspects of its scripting, the creators of *Twin Peaks* chose two by letting a serialized detective story (the joint local and federal investigation into the death of Laura Palmer) serve as an expositional framework for the introduction of an off-centre soap opera (the ongoing plots of daily life in Twin Peaks, Washington). (1995: 35)

Dolan calls this a 'continuous-serial-within-an-episodic-serial pattern' (1995: 36), but most interesting for me is the implication that the first can be borne of the second – 'the branches of the various soap-opera plots were intended to "grow" out of the central detective-story plot' (1995: 36). Soap thus becomes the progeny of the investigative thriller. So how skilfully did *Twin Peaks* do both – providing answers as well as asking the unanswerable?

Henry Jenkins describes the series as combining 'the syntagmatic complexity of a mystery with the paradigmatic plenitude of the soap' (1995: 54), and Lynch himself betrays in interview a greater allegiance to the soapier elements than the detective trajectory. Whilst ABC were pushing for the mystery of Laura's killer to be solved up-front, Lynch and Frost saw a number of TV genres mingling in the series, ideally diminishing the need to solve the central mystery. Lynch articulates this in a way remarkably similar to Dolan's notion that the crime story 'births' the continuous (sentimental/character-driven) threads:

> The way we pitched this thing was as a murder mystery but that murder mystery was to eventually become the background story. Then there would be a middle ground of all the characters we stay with for the series. And the foreground would be the main characters that particular week: the ones we'd deal with in detail. We're not going to solve the murder for a long time.
> . . . They did not like that. And they forced us to, you know, get to Laura's killer. (Rodley 1997: 180)

Thus both Lynch and Frost favoured something that was more character-driven with renewable, developing plot-lines – something of a definition of soap opera, which is characterised by stories which 'are never finally resolved' and which 'project themselves into a non-existent future' (Geraghty 1990: 11). In conversation with Lynch Chris Rodley remarks 'I sort of assume that Twin Peaks is still there, it's just that no one is pointing the camera at it now' (1997: 181), which may characterise viewers feelings about other soap-locations, from Walford to Coronation Street between episodes. One critic has defined soap opera as a genre within which characters 'become as real as family, good friends, and neighbors, and the audience learns to track their every mood, share their thoughts, dream their dreams, and weep their disappointments' (Cassata 1985: 131). Postmodern qualities of the stylised surreal may in this series' case militate against deeply developing characterisations, but the ensemble focus, the posed-then-resolved sexual–emotional cliffhangers, and the attention given to telling personal peccadilloes, shows a clear direction for the series, albeit through parody or pastiche. Christine Geraghty cites one critic as defining soap through its 'openness, the rejection of endings anticipated or already known' (1990: 3). Though it only ran to two seasons, *Twin Peaks* is also characterised by a sense of ongoingness, not predicated on dramatic realism but on the twin compulsions of addictive storylines and compelling characters who seem to take up residence in one's psychic space. Lynch also deployed a classic cliffhanger strategy of filming two possible outcomes to a dramatic situation (who kills Maddie? Leland Palmer or Benjamin Horne?) to protect against leaks revealing the 'true' killer. Still, there is a sense that *Twin Peaks had* to self-destruct given that it was pitched across such unsettling and perhaps incompatible generic demands.

Yet European viewers were privy to the curious experience of at first seeing a version of *Twin Peaks* which *did* offer some kind of closure, unavailable to US audiences. I vividly recall watching what we then understood to be the 'pilot' episode in 1990, which featured much of the action from the opening two episodes, but concluded with the capture of Laura Palmer's killer, wild-man BOB as a manifestly corporal being. Before the series itself ever wove its regular weekly course towards finding Leland guilty of his daughter's murder, UK viewers of this chilling chunk of gripping television (which played out more like a completed mini-series than an ongoing saga) thought we already knew Who Killed Laura Palmer. The pilot programme which now appears on the DVD of the first series is not this European version, but rather a feature-length splicing of episodes. Consequently the European release is now referred to in the context of 'ancillary' *Peak* paraphernalia, to be categorised alongside Julee Cruise albums or guide books to Snoqualmie, Washington (the 'real' Twin Peaks). It is then testimony to the power of the series that when it started playing in its 'proper' form we all started watching again, only to discover that the 'real' series took a different narrative route, with BOB implicated as the demon who drives Leland to filicide. Thus even when answers are provided, we are still hooked, still asking for the questions to be asked again in weekly dollops of prime-time TV, and left in a kind of liminal space of satisfaction/dissatisfaction: what ended has become endless, what we knew we must now un-know. Or perhaps we sensed that, however complete the storyline of the European 'mini-series' version of *Twin Peaks*, there was still something unsettlingly incomplete about it, suggesting that finding out who killed Laura Palmer was not really what was at stake. As Lynch puts it, 'it had the feeling of an ending that may or may not relate to anything else' (Rodley 1997: 167), an episode, perhaps from Another Place, and certainly *for* another place.[14]

How, then, did other audiences approach the show? One fascinating avenue of enquiry has been into the *Twin Peaks* fanbase, particularly Henry Jenkins' 1995 supplementation of his seminal work on the active productivity of TV fans (*Textual Poachers*, 1992) in an analysis of internet fan activity around *Twin Peaks*. This study evidences the avid and ardent passions of many devotees – Jenkins cites an estimate of 'some twenty-five thousand readers' subscribing to alt-tv.twinpeaks in the early 1990s (1995: 53). 'Trekkie' had long been a popular name for enthusiastic fans of *Star Trek* (though the proponents of this particular televisual church prefer to call themselves Trekkers). 'Peakie' was adopted in some quarters as the fond term of nerdy-designation attached to *Twin Peaks* aficionados and aficionadas (another term is 'Peaks Freak'). But what kind of animal is the 'Peakie'? Though the show was a mainstream success at first, Peakies characterise themselves as offbeat kinds of fans. All cult fan groups colour themselves through their particular specialist knowledge, but the Peakie can take pride in the outlandishly esoteric nature of the original subject matter which fuels their obsession. Yet Jenkins also shows that auteurism has invaded even that most viewer/reader-oriented domain of the fan webgroup, with discussion circulating around Lynch as 'the master programmer', the perverse and unpredictable 'trickster', who may also provide the answers to the mystery, if only the Lynchian code could be cracked (Jenkins 1995: 61–3; see also Hills 2002: 132–3). Unlike early fans of shows such as *Star Trek*, *Dr Who* or *The Prisoner*, the Peakie might also be characterised by their access to the new exhibition technologies which *Twin Peaks* could capitalise on, broadcast as it was at the end of the decade in which the VCR became a common domestic appliance in US and UK living rooms. Video was also important for its role in augmenting the series' sense of 'collectibility'; for the fan, rerunning an episode after its original airing helped to negotiate the semiotic and symbolic labyrinth of the show's rich textuality. Jenkins quotes one net-fan as writing, 'Can you imagine *Twin Peaks* coming out before VCRs or without the net? It would have been Hell!' (54) – analytic hell, perhaps, in which it is not possible to review, revisit and above all relive the intense semiotics of the text. Video has thus made the pleasure of cult TV partly a process of 'going back over' through interpretative repetition, bringing past experience back into the present, even as the 'continuousness' of the series spins off into the future.

This rich hermeutic irresolution may also be key to *Twin Peaks*' cross-gender appeal. Jenkins offers some evidence of a gender divide between respondents on the web-forum, suggesting that male fans were obsessed with solving the mystery whilst female ones 'focused on the bonding between Harry Truman and Dale Cooper' (1995: 60). Female fans responded, in other words, as soap-viewers, whilst male fans responded as thriller-viewers. Both Christine Geraghty and Charlotte Brunsdon address the common model of soap as a genre for housewives, whilst Gripstrud quotes one writer as calling *Dynasty* 'the ultimate dollhouse fantasy for middle-aged women' (1995: 2). But it may be that *Twin Peaks* could be characterised as 'soap for boys' (and girls too), nearer to the kind of neo-soap which Geraghty also discusses as arguably threatening the traditional view of the genre as women's territory. Jeffrey Sconce reads smart cinema as Generation X-oriented texts, 'dark comed[ies] and disturbing drama[s] born of ironic distance; all that is not positive and "dumb"' (2002: 358). We may also read smart movies such as *Punch-Drunk Love* or *Eternal Sunshine of the Spotless Mind* as rom-coms for boys – films which enable men to enjoy romance and sentiment as long as they are cloaked in the paraphernalia of ironic cleverness. *Twin Peaks* had a multi-gendered audience, but one wonders how the large swathes of its viewership which were geeky and male weathered the floods of tears. Perhaps its Lynchian surrealism functioned to make its romantic emotionalism more palatable for guys, in a way which is similar to Michel Gondry's deployment of a crazy time-warp conceit as a vehicle for lost love in *Eternal Sunshine*, or Paul Thomas Anderson's psychotic complication as a vehicle for a happy-ever-after story in *Punch-Drunk Love*.

Perhaps none of these characterisations fully accounts for the phenomenon of the series as an international mainstream cult hit, as well as a niche-cult, prompting hundreds of articles and profiles, and viewing figures which run across a wide cross-section of audiences. *Twin Peaks* is something other, melodramatically inflected perhaps, but predicating its success on its 'talkability' and cross-generic appeal to a wide range of viewers. In this sense it was classic 'watercooler TV', first aired on a Thursday night, the perfect slot for fostering discussion the next day at the workplace. Geraghty cites the ability of soap opera's storylines to provoke audiences 'in such a way that they become the subject for public interest and interrogation' (1990: 4) as key to its ongoing dynamism as a form, which might constitute prime-time soap as the predominant 'watercooler' genre. However, the debates which *Twin Peaks* provoked were worlds away from most mainstream television. The questions 'Who Killed Laura Palmer?' and 'Who Shot JR?' may sound similar, but the answers could not be more different, to the point that Lynch considered *never* answering what began as the primary trajectory for the show. This 'unanswerableness' may account for some of *Twin Peaks*' fascination, and the series quickly complicated its terrain so dramatically that questions such as 'What does Margaret's log know?' and 'Who is the Man from Another Place?' made the original whodunnit conundrum, with its promise of a definitive answer, seem simplistic if not irrelevant (Cooper's somnambulistic visit to the Red Room at the end of episode two,[15] culminating in the waking announcement that he *does* know who killed Laura Palmer and it *can* wait until morning, is a classic example). This bizarre audacity required – at the very least – some public airing around what it all could possibly mean. The series' reliance on its Thursday slot to capitalise on its sheer 'talkability' is evidenced by the dramatic impact a slot change had on *Twin Peaks'* fortunes. Chasing ever higher ratings, ABC shifted the show to Saturday nights, a far less watercooler friendly slot: it's hard to remember something you saw on Saturday when you get into work the following Monday. Subsequently, *Twin Peaks* began to lose its 'buzz', and ratings dropped. Lynch then participated in an (eventually successful) campaign to get the Thursday slot reinstated (the last six episodes went out in the show's original slot), but not before its public fortunes had been terminally damaged. In itself this tells us something about who the series played to in this first run. Significant elements of *Twin Peaks'* textuality may draw it towards soap-inflected melodrama, but as watercooler TV it was squarely aligned with prime-time 'quality' television. As Lucy (and even Lynch) have shown us, soap is not just the domain of the housewife. Lucy watches 'Invitation to Love' at work, whilst Lynch watched seventies soap at his print-plant – daytime soaps, of course, which play *as you work*, meaningful in and through the context of the workplace. *Twin Peaks* was television which required a social context to establish itself as supremely 'discussable'.

The final chapter of the *Twin Peaks* story returns us to Lynch. *Fire Walk With Me* was conceived and received as a return to Lynchian form, redressing the series' cute quirkiness, dispatching the epistemological smugness of the FBI, and going straight to the heart of Laura's appalling predicament. Here Lynch reminds us, with deep sympathy for the central woman but in no uncertain terms, that Laura Palmer is an incest victim. Sheryl Lee deserved an Oscar for her performance, but the film was critically trashed. The movie's merits are dealt with in greater detail by writers such as Nochimson (1997: 173–97), but what is material here is how (or whether) it closed the *Twin Peaks* chapter. Certainly, it concludes Lynch's involvement with this Northwestern world, by making the whole terrain once more subject to his 'vision'. This is borne out by John Orr's analysis, positioning the film as the auteur's revenge on a TV show which had gone out of *his* control into the control of networks and collaborators. The movie thus gives Lynch the opportunity to make 'his final cut second time around' (Orr 1998: 152). It is, then, a wholesale dark revision of the TV series:

> Usual processes of film-to-video and film-to-TV are reversed and challenge our cultural expectations. The *Twin Peaks* familiar (i.e. the TV version)

deemed by fans to be surreal and excitingly unfamiliar, really is made unfamiliar . . . the television cannot cope with Lynch's frontal attack on Laura's tragic life. (1998: 151)

Famously Lynch opens *Fire Walk With Me* with an extreme close-up of a television tuned between channels, which is then smashed. TV is dead, long live cinema, the image seems to be saying. But if the exploding TV is an act of warfare against Lynch's former medium, it is also a moment of perverse self-destruction – Lynch continued to work in television, albeit sporadically, throughout the 1990s, and his name will, for good or ill, continue to be associated with *Twin Peaks* as courageous television. *Fire Walk With Me* was also one of the decade's most critically reviled movie (second only, perhaps, to *Showgirls* or *Waterworld*). Whatever its artistic merits, it proved too tainted by its proximity to the series, which became the filter through which it was read (and found wanting). Here Lynch cannot entirely erase his televisual legacy: the image of the dead Laura was, of course, where *Fire Walk With Me*'s living Laura was first born.[16] *Twin Peaks* on cable, video and DVD will always be *Fire Walk With Me*'s more populist context. The cinematic TV may explode, but long live television.

Notes

1. From the *Time* magazine review of the pilot episode of *Twin Peaks*, quoted in Woods 2000: 101.
2. Cited as episode 5 in the chapter breakdown section of Lavery (1995: 217). This discrepancy results from whether the pilot is counted as the first episode or not.
3. Discussed by Lavery 1995: 17. It is, of course, highly significant for feminist readings of the series that the 'Woman of the Year' for a magazine such as *Esquire* could be a dead one.
4. Cited as episode 4 in the chapter breakdown section of Lavery (1995: 216) – see note 2 above.
5. Lynch's interest in seriality is also manifest in the long-running cartoon-contribution he made to the *LA Reader*, 'The Angriest Dog in the World', which ran from 1982 for nine years. Here, an unchanging set of images of a dog, the same week after week, is augmented by a new caption, provided by Lynch, which changed every week. The visuals thus provide an arc of continuity, the words injecting a sequence of different moments of experience.
6. See *Village Voice*, 10 April 1990, 32–42, discussed by Caldwell (1995: 282 and 393n).
7. See Caldwell (1995: 286–7) for a discussion of this period. Despite these nominations, the series won none, though participants remained bullish: "'We

kind of like the idea that we didn't get any Emmys,' protested Ray Wise (Leland Palmer in the show) defiantly. 'We're not about winning awards'" (Woods 2000: 111).

8. Lynch also shot four commercials for Japanese television for a product called Georgia Coffee, 'set in Twin Peaks and featuring many of the regular characters' (Rodley 1997: 256).

9. Appropriate to its status as a cult show, the Twin Peaks collectables market is vast. As I write, a drinking-glass napkin used on the set of One Eyed Jack's is currently up for auction on e-bay, along with signed photos, posters and genuine merchandise produced in different forms for different international markets.

10. 'Peakies', the dedicated Twin Peaks fan, might note therefore that *Twin Peaks* came at the crest of the second peak in Lynch's career.

11. For Matt Hills, this concludes *Twin Peaks*' run with a 'grand Non-narrative', an open question concerning its hero's fate guaranteed to denote immortality on 'the martyred cult show' (2002: 137).

12. There is also some debate about whether the soap-within-a-soap 'Invitation to Love' should be regarded as pastiche, and what function Lynch 'originally intended' it to fulfil: 'Lynch conceived "Invitation to Love" not as an ironic device but as a fully developed parallel world charged with subconscious energies' (Ayers 2004: 96); 'As I understand Lynch's original thoughts about *Invitation to Love* (from him), it might have served a function similar to that of Glinda in *Wild at Heart* . . . Lynch thought that he and Frost were in agreement on this and was surprised to find that Frost had created a clichéd mockery of the soap-opera form' (Nochimson 1997: 75–6).

13. Russ Tamblyn, *Twin Peaks*' Dr Jacoby, was Oscar nominated for his role in the 1957 film *Peyton Place*.

14. British viewers also experienced the particular reception phenomenon which often characterises the release of a media product outside of the US, when there is a time-lag between US release and arrival on our shores. This time-lag enables media coverage to intensify, and can involve the leakage of key plot information via the internet. In the UK, *Twin Peaks* was heralded largely through the advanced publicity of newsprint and television documentaries. *Wild at Heart* won the Palme D'Or, functioning to showcase Lynch's name in Europe and further feeding in to the 'highly anticipated' label which came to be attached to *Twin Peaks*. Lynch's next movie was also 'highly anticipated' *because* of *Twin Peaks*, but the prequel *Fire Walk With Me* bombed, perhaps influenced by the TV *Twin Peaks*' mixed fortunes.

15. Cited as episode 3 in the chapter breakdown section of Lavery (1995: 215) – see note 2 above.

16. Laura also 'lives' in the bizarre fan practice which involves fans wrapping themselves in plastic and posing as corpses on the banks of the Columbia River at Snoqualmie (see Hills 2002: 201).

Bibliography

Ayers, Sheli (2004), '*Twin Peaks*, Weak Language and the Resurrection of Affect', in Sheen and Davison (eds), *The Cinema of David Lynch*, pp. 93–106.

Brunsdon, Charlotte (2000), *The Feminist, the Housewife, and the Soap Opera*, Oxford: Oxford University Press.

Caldwell, John Thornton (1995), *Televisuality: Style, Crisis, and Authority in American Television*, New Brunswick, NJ: Rutgers University Press.

Cassata, Mary (1985), 'The Soap Opera', in Brian G. Rose (ed.), *TV Genres: A Handbook and Reference Guide*, Westport, CT: Greenwood Press, pp. 131–43.

Chion, Michel (1995), *David Lynch*, London: BFI.

Desmet, Christy (1995), 'The Canonization of Laura Palmer', in Lavery (ed.), *Full of Secrets*, pp. 93–108.

Dolan, Marc (1995), 'The Peaks and Valleys of Serial Creativity: What Happened to/on *Twin Peaks*, in Lavery (ed.), *Full of Secrets*, pp. 30–50.

George, Diana Hume (1995), 'Lynching Women: A Feminist Reading of *Twin Peaks*', in Lavery (ed.), *Full of Secrets*, pp. 109–19.

Geraghty, Christine (1990), *Women and Soap Opera: A Study of Prime Time Soaps*, Cambridge: Polity Press.

Gripstrud, Jostein (1995), *The 'Dynasty' Years: Hollywood Television and Critical Media Studies*, London and New York: Routledge.

Hills, Matt (2002), *Fan Cultures*, London and New York: Routledge.

Hughes, David (2001), *The Complete Lynch*, London: Virgin Books.

Jenkins, Henry (1992), *Textual Poachers: Television Fans and Participatory Culture*, New York and London: Routledge .

— (1995), '"Do You Enjoy Making the Rest of Us Feel Stupid?": alt.tv.twinpeaks, the Trickster Author, and Viewer Mastery', in Lavery (ed.), *Full of Secrets*, pp. 51–69.

Kalinak, Kathryn (1995), '"Disturbing the Guests with This Racket": Music and *Twin Peaks*', in Lavery (ed.), *Full of Secrets*, pp. 82–92.

Krämer, Peter (1996), 'The Lure of the Big Picture: Film, Television and Hollywood', in John Hill and Martin McLoone (eds), *Big Picture, Small Screen: The Relations Between Film and Television*, Luton: University of Luton Press, pp. 9–46.

Lavery, David (ed.) (1995), *Full of Secrets: Critical Approaches to 'Twin Peaks'*, Detroit, MI: Wayne State University Press.

McCarthy, Anna (2001), 'Studying Soap Opera', in Glen Creeber (ed.), *The Television Genre Book*, London: BFI, pp. 47–9.

McLoone, Martin (1996), 'Boxed in?: The Aesthetics of Film and Television', in John Hill and Martin McLoone (eds), *Big Picture, Small Screen: The Relations between Film and Television*, Luton: University of Luton Press, pp. 76–106.

Nochimson, Martha P. (1997), *The Passion of David Lynch: Wild at Heart in Hollywood*, Austin, TX: University of Texas Press.

Orr, John (1998), *Contemporary Cinema*, Edinburgh: Edinburgh University Press.

Page, Adrian (2001), 'Post-modern Drama' and '*Twin Peaks*', in Glen Creeber (ed.), *The Television Genre Book*, London: BFI, pp. 43–6.

Rodley, Chris (ed.) (1997), *Lynch on Lynch*, London: Faber.

Rosenbaum, Jonathan (1995), 'Bad Ideas: The Art and Politics of *Twin Peaks*', in Lavery (ed.), *Full of Secrets*, pp. 22–9.

Sconce, Jeffrey (2002), 'Irony, Nihilism and the New American "Smart" Film', *Screen* 43(4), Winter, 349–69.

Sheen, Erica, and Davison, Annette (eds) (2004), *The Cinema of David Lynch: American Dreams, Nightmare Visions*, London and New York: Wallflower Press.

Woods, Paul A. (2000), *Weirdsville USA: The Obsessive Universe of David Lynch*, London: Plexus.

Žižek, Slavoj (2000), *The Art of the Ridiculous Sublime: On David Lynch's 'Lost Highway'*, Seattle: University of Washington Press.

CHAPTER 4

Quality/Cult Television: *The X-Files* and Television History

Catherine Johnson

The X-Files (Fox, 1993–2002) appeared on our screens at a crucial moment in the history of US television, as the industry gradually adjusted to the increased market fragmentation brought about by the expansion of new services (satellite, cable, pay-TV) and the deregulation of the communications sector. In this chapter I will argue that an understanding of *The X-Files'* place within the historical development of US television can enable us to tackle the diverse and conflicting academic analyses that circulate around the series. Such a historical perspective is particularly important in analysing *The X-Files*, because the series has frequently been constituted as a 'unique' programme in television broadcasting, in part because of its fan followings and cult status, and has been consequently situated outside of television history.[1]

More recently, *The X-Files* has been linked with the development of 'quality' television in the US. However, there has been little attempt to combine historical analysis of the series as quality television with a consideration of its cult status.[2] This chapter will bring these two aspects together to argue that the series can be understood as a new kind of quality television that emerges in the early 1990s – 'quality/cult' television. While academic analyses of the series tended to read the series as either subversive/progressive, or reactionary, this chapter will argue that the construction of a text able to sustain such divergent interpretations is actually a characteristic of quality/cult television.

The Origins of Quality Television

In the 1960s, the costs of advertising slots on US network television were calculated in relation to an estimation of the *total* number of viewers tuned to a particular programme at any one time. However, in the early 1970s, a consideration of the demographic *composition* of the television audience began to be considered as an additional factor. Economic profitability no longer resided purely in the total number of viewers, but also depended on the type of viewer watching.[3] These changes altered the kinds of programming that the networks favoured, leading to the production of what Feuer et al. (1984) term 'quality' television. Quality television in the early 1970s attempted to appeal to a specific audience demographic: urban, 18–49, liberal, professional and culturally educated. It drew on traditional criteria of aesthetic value, such as authorship, artistic freedom and creativity, formal and narrative experimentation, complex characters and sophisticated writing, to attract what was perceived as a discerning 'quality' audience that was ambivalent towards the aesthetic and cultural value of television as a medium. Such quality television was therefore concerned with promoting itself as different from 'regular' television, even though as Feuer points out, the quality series created by the production company MTM for the network CBS signalled 'quality' and 'regularity' simultaneously, inscribing a number of different positions within a single text:[4]

> The appeal of an MTM programme must be double-edged. It must appeal both to the 'quality' audience, a liberal, sophisticated group of upwardly mobile professionals; and it must capture a large segment of the mass audience as well. Thus MTM programmes must be readable at a number of levels, as is true of most US television fare. MTM shows may be interpreted as warm, human comedies or dramas; or they may be interpreted as self-aware 'quality' texts. In this sense also, the MTM style is both typical and atypical. Its politics are seldom overt, yet the very concept of 'quality' is itself ideological. In interpreting an MTM programme as a quality programme, the quality audience is permitted to enjoy a form of television which is seen as more literate, more stylistically complex, and more psychologically 'deep' than ordinary TV fare. The quality audience gets to separate itself from the mass audience and can watch TV without guilt, and without realising that the double-edged discourse they are getting is also ordinary TV. (Feuer et al. 1984: 56)

The 'quality' television produced by MTM therefore accommodated multiple readings to combine an appeal to the 'quality' demographic with a broader consensus appeal. These programmes signalled themselves as literate, complex and 'deep', while simultaneously offering the familiar pleasures of 'everyday' television, inscribing different reading positions within one text. As a consequence, the representation of a working single woman in her thirties in *The Mary Tyler Moore Show* can be interpreted as both 'reactionary' (replicating the ideological structures of the patriarchal family in Mary's worklife) and/or 'progressive' (exploring and valuing the experiences of single working women) (see Feuer et al. 1984: 56–9).

The valuing of programmes that are open to multiple readings in US television is both specific to this particular historical period, and a general characteristic of US television production. As Todd Gitlin argues, 'television entertainment takes its design from social and psychological fissures' (Gitlin 1994: 217). For the US networks, whose profitability is based on audience numbers, programmes with messages that are open to divergent interpretations are favoured, as these are most likely to attract the largest audience. As a consequence, 'in television success often comes from finding the main fault lines of value conflict in society, and bridging them' (Gitlin 1994: 218). However, Gitlin argues that while television may attempt to resolve these social and cultural conflicts, it is not always successful, particularly when the industry attempts to appeal to the desires of conflicting social groups (Gitlin 1994: 248). In attempting to attract the 'quality' audience while not alienating other network viewers, 'quality' television is precisely concerned with appealing to divergent desires. As a consequence, these programmes do not simply explore or expose contemporary social conflicts, but offer their viewers the possibility of divergent, even conflicting, interpretations within one text.

Quality Television in the 1980s and 1990s

John Thornton Caldwell argues that the 1970s MTM series, along with other 'quality' sit-coms produced by Tandem such as *All in the Family*, constructed their quality status in relation to content rather than to style (Caldwell 1995: 57). Furthermore, the production practices and budgets of serial television had led to the favouring of stylistic techniques based on efficiency, rather than on visual style. As Gitlin argues, 'instead of style there were techniques' (Gitlin 1994: 290). However, Caldwell argues that in the 1980s there was a significant shift in the definition of 'quality' television, a shift that encompassed an increasing emphasis on visual style as an indicator of quality. Caldwell sees this as partly a consequence of the rise of quality television, arguing that 'once the aura of artistry became a conscious part of the industry hype, a *critical expectation for stylistic accomplishment* followed' (Caldwell 1995: 61). Series such as *Hill Street Blues*, which is often cited as the initiator of the development of visually stylish quality television in the 1980s, led the way with a new form of quality television whose visual distinctiveness and stylistic flourishes were as much an indicator of its 'quality' status as the complexity and depth of its characters and scripts.[5] *Hill Street Blues* demonstrated the potential economic return for visually distinctive 'quality' television, garnering critical and financial success for NBC despite initial low ratings.[6] As Caldwell states, 'a shift in cultural capital has clearly occurred by the early and mid-1980s, one that made stylistics a more valuable kind of programming currency' (Caldwell 1995: 67).

The increasing emphasis on style (what Caldwell refers to as 'televisuality') is not just a formal development, but an industrial strategy in a saturated media market, that responds to the economic crisis in US network television production in the 1980s. With the deregulation of the telecommunications industry in the early 1980s, the three networks (ABC, NBC and CBS) faced increasing competition from cable, satellite and new network stations.[7] As a consequence the networks' ability to attract a large consensus audience was undermined and the networks began to target their programmes at differently defined (although not necessarily mutually exclusive) 'niche' markets. Celia Lury argues that with the shift to niche marketing, 'taste cultures' became as, if not more, important than socio-economic criteria in delineating and targeting market segments:

> The term [taste cultures] was introduced in market planning as a way of exploring the role of non-demographic factors in the organisation of the audience-as-market, and as part of the recognition of the often fleeting and overlapping nature of audiences within a market. It is used to group individuals according to acts of media choice seen to display similarity of content or style – in short, according to market notions of taste – rather than to demographic variations, and has begun to be used as a basis on which to plan new products. (Lury 1993: 46)

With the growing fragmentation of the US television market over the 1980s and 1990s, the television audience was increasingly conceived and addressed as a coalition of taste markets (rather than demographics). Within this increasingly fragmented marketplace, the display of a distinctive visual style was a means by which the networks differentiated their programmes from the competition and attracted specific audiences defined in terms of their tastes.

The X-Files as Quality/Cult TV

While Robert Thompson sees *The X-Files* as an extension of earlier network 'quality' television (Thompson 1997: 184–5), I want to argue that the series represented a new form of 'quality/cult' television that marked a shift in network programming in the 1990s. Unlike the earlier quality television discussed by Thompson, Feuer and Gitlin, *The X-Files* was not produced by one of the three established networks, but was part of the nascent Fox network's move into hour-long prime-time drama. The Fox

network had emerged in the wake of a series of corporate mergers following the deregulation of the broadcasting industry in the mid-1980s and
first became profitable in 1989. By the early 1990s Fox was keen to build
on its reputation for successful comedies (*The Simpsons*, 1989–present,
Married . . . with Children, 1987–97) and teenage dramas (*Beverly Hills,
90210*, 1990–2000) by moving into hour-long drama production that
would extend its demographic range into the 18–49 age group (Caldwell
1995: 11). *The X-Files*, scheduled alongside the western drama *The
Adventures of Brisco County, Jr.* (1993–4), made up Fox's first full evening
of hour-long drama series, competitively scheduled at 9 p.m. on Friday
evenings against ABC's successful comedy line-up. As a consequence of
Fox's position as a new network, the production strategies that it adopted
differed from those of the three established networks. While NBC, CBS
and ABC were trying to retain their audiences from the threat of the new
cable and satellite services, Fox was attempting to break into the network
market. Fox was therefore concerned with attracting viewers from the
existing networks *and* from their rival cable and satellite stations. This balancing act is central to understanding the particular way in which *The X-
Files* situated itself as 'quality/cult' television.

The *X-Files* depicts the investigations of two young FBI agents, Fox
Mulder (David Duchovny) and Dana Scully (Gillian Anderson) into 'X-
files', inexplicable cases of supernatural phenomena rejected by the bureau
mainstream.[8] The series combines stories of detection and investigation
with the iconography and narratives of the science fiction and horror
genres, as Mulder and Scully explore reports of alien abductions, polter-
geists, artificial intelligence, human mutations and demonic creatures, as
well as becoming embroiled in a government plot to conceal the existence
of paranormal phenomena from the general public. The series therefore
signals its distinctiveness in part through its generic hybridity, a strategy
that Thompson argues is particularly indicative of quality television
(Thompson 1997: 15). Furthermore, the series' sophisticated scripts,
complex multi-layered narratives, and visually expressive cinematography,
combined with its exploration of contemporary anxieties concerning late
capitalism, such as environmental issues, the role of medicine, the threat
of scientific experimentation and, most overtly, the duplicity of the US
government, is characteristic of quality television.

However, in addition to this appeal to the 'quality' audience, the series
was also produced to appeal to another market segment, the fan-
consumer.[9] As Reeves, Rodgers and Epstein (1996) point out, when *The X-
Files* was initially produced, there were two different kinds of cult
television on US television. The first, like *Star Trek*, were prime-time

network shows that failed to gain high ratings when initially released on the networks but subsequently attracted large fan followings. These network shows were not produced specifically for the fan audience, but went on to gain fan followings, often (as was the case with *Star Trek*) through repeat runs in syndication. The second kind of cult television, such as *Mystery Science Theater 3000* and *Beavis and Butthead* were series that were narrowly targeted at niche audiences on smaller cable channels with the precise aim of attracting small but loyal fan audiences (Reeves et al. 1996: 31). For these smaller non-network channels that could not expect to gain the large audience figures of the networks, the loyalty of the smaller fan audience was particularly valuable. Reeves, Rodgers and Epstein argue that the production of *The X-Files* marked a new form of cult television that can be attributed to the Fox network's nascent status in the early 1990s (Reeves et al. 1996: 31). *The X-Files* differed from earlier cult television in two ways. First, unlike earlier series that had been produced for the niche fan audience, this was a network series produced by a new network attempting to compete with NBC, ABC and CBS. Second, rather than being a network series produced for a consensus audience that was 'found' by fan audiences and subsequently gained the status of a cult, *The X-Files* was actively produced by Fox as a cult series designed to attract the fan-consumer taste market.

The fan audience is valuable to a network such as Fox, attempting to break into an increasingly competitive environment, because of the loyalty of fan viewers. As a consequence, as Matt Hills argues, in the 1990s 'fandom has begun to furnish a model of dedicated and loyal consumption which does, in point of fact, *appeal* to television producers and schedulers within a fragmented multi-channel environment' (Hills 1999: 5). In addition, fans are not only loyal consumers of television programmes, but also of the ancillary products that are produced around such programmes. The exploitation of the ancillary market was particularly valuable for Fox, a media conglomerate with holdings in a range of different companies. As Reeves, Rodgers and Epstein argue, Fox was able to exploit *The X-Files'* appeal to the fan market in order to promote their other media holdings and to offset the financial risks of investing in the series:

> In Britain, first run episodes of the series appear only on Sky One, part of Rupert Murdoch's satellite network. Fox also attempted to use *The X-Files* to promote Delphi, its online service; Delphi became the official home of *The X-Files*, and writers and producers were encouraged to frequent the discussion areas related to the show. By using the show's cult status to multiply its revenue streams, Fox has taken away some of the pressure on *The X-Files* to be a ratings hit. (Reeves et al. 1996: 31)

The X-Files therefore combined the production strategies of the existing networks with those of their rival cable channels in an attempt to infiltrate the network prime-time market and to minimise risk by attracting a specific, commercially valuable niche fan audience. In doing so it combined quality television's dual address to the 'everyday' and 'discerning' viewer, with an additional address to the fan-consumer.

The negotiation of this layered address to different taste markets is apparent in the series' use of genre. *The X-Files*' creator, Chris Carter, claims that the idea for *The X-Files* stemmed from a desire to redress the lack of horror in the prime-time network television schedules. Carter states that when working on the initial premise for *The X-Files* he sensed a void: 'You look at the TV schedule . . . and there's nothing scary on television' (quoted in Lowry 1995: 10). As Glen Morgan, former co-executive producer on the series, explains, 'Horror had been relegated to the slasher movies, and I think the networks felt that you couldn't do horror without lots of blood' (quoted in Coe 1995: 57). Here, the series' use of the horror genre is evoked in a rhetoric of distinctiveness. The implication is that *The X-Files* appealed to Fox because it offered something different from the other networks (horror), in a new way (without 'lots of blood'), allowing Fox to fill a void left open by its competitors. However, the precise nature of this difference is constructed in relation to the generic conventions of existing forms and the network's conception of acceptability. The attempt at horror functions as a viable aesthetic strategy as long as the series avoids the generic associations with 'lots of blood', which would be unattractive to a network broadcaster keen to maximise its audience and extend its demographic reach.[10]

This negotiation of difference and acceptability is apparent in the construction of the visual style of the series. *The X-Files* has a distinctive 'signature' style, a production strategy that Caldwell (1995) argues is increasingly important as a form of product differentiation within the saturated media environment of US television. Through the display of visual style, signature styles immediately signal the distinctiveness of a television programme, and for series with high production values are also important indicators of quality. Distinctive signature styles are also useful in the production of ancillary merchandising by creating a visual style that is immediately associated with the series and can be replicated across a range of different products. However, the creation of *The X-Files*' signature style needs to be understood in relation to Fox's strategy of balancing product differentiation and an appeal to the quality and cult audiences, with existing notions of acceptability in US network television.

The X-Files' Signature Style

Both John Bartley (Director of Photography on the series for its first three seasons) and Chris Carter describe the logic behind *The X-Files'* visual style in terms of lack. Bartley claims, 'You don't want to show the audience too much. You just want to feel that there's something there' (quoted in Probst 1995: 32), while Carter states, 'You're always more scared of what you don't see than what you do see' (quoted in Martinez 1995: 22). In an article in *American Cinematographer* (Probst 1995), Bartley discusses the techniques he used on the series to evoke a visual style that Carter describes as 'dark, moody, mysterious and sometimes claustrophobic' (quoted in Probst 1995: 28). Bartley explains how he consistently underexposed actors' faces to create a shrouded image, and used blue lights in the background to give the effect of a dark hue while still showing some detail and allowing background and foreground to be distinguished. While this is most pronounced in frightening and mysterious scenes, the series as a whole tends to avoid high key lighting. The exception to this is the use of strong bright lights. A visual motif is established over the series, which associates brightness with alien abduction, medical invasiveness and memory. These three elements are repeatedly connected in the series, in which recovered memory is the only means of recollecting the medical procedures performed on alien abductees during their abductions. However, these white lights, in their blinding intensity, are not a revealing source of brightness but are as obscuring as the shadowy darkness.

The series' characteristic use of darkness and bright lights to obscure rather than reveal places a visual emphasis on concealment. When the series does represent the fantastic it tends to be glimpsed in the shadows rather than clearly displayed. Both Bartley and Bill Roe, the Director of Photography who replaced him for the series' subsequent seasons, emphasise their reliance on practicals – lights that have a real and discernible source – in shooting the series.[11] This gives the visual style of the series a plausible basis and also makes the light sources very directional, enabling the general look to be dark, while allowing beams of light to illuminate necessary details. This effect is heightened through the use of smoke, which gives the image an underlying ambient glow while picking up beams of light as they cut through the murky darkness. This particular style of lighting is most pronounced in what can be described as a signature *X-Files* shot, in which Mulder and Scully enter darkened spaces shining bright flashlights.[12]

Bartley describes how they shot such a scene for the season two episode, 'Dod Kalm':

In 'Dod Kalm', which ends up in a frigate that is supposed to have been dormant for thirty years, the only lighting sources in the halls and cabins are the Xenon flashlights. [. . .] I use the pebble-bounce [off-screen reflectors] so the actors can shine the flash-lights into the reflector, which bounces the light back into their faces. (Bartley, quoted in Probst 1995: 30)

The extent of the darkness in these scenes is pronounced. At times the screen is almost entirely black. Yet the use of strong directional light, combined with close-ups, allows the pertinent (and rather gruesome) details to be glimpsed within the bright beams of the flashlight. The series' signature style can be characterised, therefore, not only by the extremes of darkness and brightness in the screen, but also by the use of strong contrast. This enables the series to employ a visual rhetoric whose emphasis on concealment (what is hidden or obscured by the dark shadows and bright flashes) simultaneously opens up spaces for the fantastic to be occasionally and fleetingly exposed. This visual 'lack' functions as an ideological strategy, whereby the series can *suggest* all manner of horrors, rather than representing them. This allows the series to explore such topics as necrophilia, childhood abduction and torture without compromising the network's notions of acceptability. Within the construction of the series' signature style, there is a negotiation between offering subjects not found on the networks while still functioning within the networks' existing notions of acceptability.

This signature style works in tandem with the series' narrative structure to create a basic formula that can be sustained over time. Drawing on the emphasis placed on continuing storylines in quality television over the 1980s, *The X-Files* combined one-off 'genre' episodes that centred on a single investigation, with ongoing and increasingly complex narratives. The consequent interweaving of character history and conspiracy narratives became a prevalent feature of the series. This dual narrative structure enabled the series to be accessible to the casual viewer, while simultaneously rewarding the loyal viewer with character and story development.

However, despite the use of a series structure that provided space for character and story development, *The X-Files* depends on the maintenance of a certain sameness. The series' basic premise is constructed around Mulder and Scully's search for *elusive* proof about the existence of paranormal phenomena. In order to give this quest value and meaning, the series must continually suggest that 'the truth is out there' (to borrow from the series' tag line), while never allowing it to be fully established. The series' signature style based around suggestion, in which the fantastic is glimpsed, rather than displayed, is central because the narrative logic of the series is constructed around continuation, which is possible only if ambiguity remains as to the reality of the fantastic.[13]

Progressive or Reactionary?

It is this basic ambiguity at the heart of the series' narrative and stylistic formula that has lead to the divergent interpretations of *The X-Files*. Just as Feuer argues that the MTM 'quality' sit-coms were open to 'progressive' and/or 'reactionary' readings, much of the academic debate surrounding *The X-Files* is concerned with its interpretation as either a subversive/progressive or reactionary text. For example, Douglas Kellner argues that the series attempts to subvert dominant ideologies to comment 'on some of the most frightening aspects of contemporary society, including government out of control, science and technology out of control' (Kellner 1999: 174). Adrienne L. McLean, borrowing from the theories of Marshall McLuhan, takes this a step further by arguing that the series has progressive potentiality. In her argument the divergent responses to *The X-Files* suggest that the series offers spaces for counter-hegemonic resistance to consensual ideology. At its most progressive, she argues, 'it helps us achieve what McLuhan calls a consciousness of the "revolutionary transformations caused by new media," thus giving us the means by which to "anticipate and control them" rather than being their slaves' (McLean 1998: 9).

However, the series' representation of the fantastic and its deliberate refusal of narrative resolution has lead other theorists to argue that far from being a progressive text, the series 'demonstrates the infantilism of the American psyche, where a loss of faith in a political vision has given way to the ingenuous belief in everything else' (O'Reilly 1996: 6). In this counter-argument the series' critique of traditional institutions of knowledge and power (such as science, technology and government), which Kellner sees as progressive, is interpreted as a reactionary attack on rationality, which is solidified by the series' foregrounding of the paranormal and mythological over the sceptical and logical.[14] As John Lyttle writes:

> Mulder and Scully don't want you to wake up, and be responsible for, say, CIA involvement in the illegal overthrow of Chile's President Allende, or even the budget deficit. They want you to wake up, and be responsible for, the Loch Ness monster, for liver-eating mutants who live for hundreds of years, for Bigfoot. Which is no responsibility at all. [. . .] *The X-Files* promotes the very powerlessness it pretends to challenge. (Lyttle 1996: 17)

Lyttle argues therefore that the series functions as an apolitical attack on capitalism that rejects the rationalism that has let down society in favour of an unformed insecurity against an unnamed and secret conspiracy around phenomena that can never be proved.

While these readings might on the surface seem opposed, for Keith M. Booker they reflect the ways in which the series 'presents a postmodern view of the world while simultaneously straining against and protesting certain characteristics of the postmodern age' (Booker 2002: 126). However, while Booker offers a complex reading of the series, he ultimately refutes the arguments for *The X-Files* 'subversiveness', arguing that 'those who see the series as subversive [. . .] are probably underestimating the ease with which the style and content of *The X-Files* can be absorbed by the commercial television context in which it exists' (Booker 2002: 148). For Booker *The X-Files* can never be truly subversive because of 'the thorough embeddedness of commercial television within the system of late consumer capitalism' (Booker 2002: 156). Yet Booker's rigid ideological model, which ultimately implies the rejection of all television because of its mode of production, does not adequately address either the context of production or the context of reception for television drama.

As I have argued, the ambiguity of *The X-Files* can be understood in relation to the industrial context within which the series was made, in particular its attempts to combine an appeal to the quality, fan and network audience markets. As Gitlin (1994) argues, by attempting to generate programmes with mass audience appeal, the networks are inevitably drawn towards social and cultural conflicts. While some television offers resolutions for these conflicts, the history of 'quality' television indicates that television drama is quite capable of generating programmes that build in multiple (and potentially opposed) readings. Indeed in the production of quality television, this strategy becomes particularly valued by networks which are attempting to appeal to a number of different taste markets and demographics. To suggest that the capitalist mode of production of US network television ultimately contains such contradictions is an oversimplification of the context of production. Furthermore it fails to address the reception of television programmes. Indeed Fox's specific attempt to appeal to the fan audience creates an emphasis in the production of *The X-Files* on complex, multi-layered and open storylines that are deliberately constructed to leave the space open for audience engagement and debate, which is clearly evidenced by the wide range of fan sites, chat rooms and academic debate generated by the series.[15]

However, this is not to suggest that we should privilege the progressive reading of the series over the reactionary reading. Rather it is to suggest that *The X-Files* invites both of these readings. For example, Booker argues that *The X-Files*' insistence that 'the truth is out there', combined with its inability to ever offer this truth to its audience, replicates the deferral of desire that characterises the ideology of late capitalism (Booker 2002: 148).

Yet while the series certainly defers any definitive 'truth' of the paranormal, in doing so it also offers this very deferral as a central problematic. As a consequence the deferral of desire becomes not just a characteristic of the series, but a central theme, explored through Mulder and Scully's struggles to keep the X-files open and through the increasing personal sacrifices they have to make in order to continue searching for the truth. In the later seasons Mulder and Scully defer their desire to be together shortly after their relationship is first consummated, as Mulder goes into hiding and Scully is left to bring their child up alone. This deferral of desire becomes increasingly difficult for Scully, who ultimately gives her child up for adoption. If, as Booker argues, the postponement of the fulfilment of desire is a characteristic of late capitalism, then *The X-Files* does not simply replicate this logic, it also represents the deferral of desire as a problem. By both replicating the deferral of desire in its overarching narrative and thematic structure, and problematising it through the experiences of the central characters, the series is able to be read as both critical of and conforming to the logic of late capitalism. Rather than trying to close down analysis of such series into these either/or dichotomies, it is important to examine how these dichotomies function as a specific characteristic of US television production. As I have argued, this openness to divergent interpretations is not a historical anomaly but a consequence of the series' historical position as 'quality/cult' television, and a prevalent feature of the contemporary US television series.

Notes

1. For example, Douglas Kellner claims that the 'aesthetically innovative and thematically challenging texts [of *The X-Files*] are rather unique in the history of mainstream television' (Kellner 1999: 164), while Jan Delasara describes *The X-Files* as 'a unique television experiment' (Delasara 2000: 27).
2. While *The X-Files* is mentioned in Jancovich and Lyons' edited collection on 'must-see' cult television (2003), there is no sustained analysis of the series' place within this new category of contemporary US television.
3. The reasons for this shift are complex, arising from competition from satellite- and cable-delivered pay-TV, changes in syndication, shifts in personnel at the networks and socio-cultural changes (such as the women's liberation movement, youth culture and civil rights). For more detail see Feuer et al.'s edited collection on MTM (1984), Gitlin's study of Hollywood television industry (1994), and Thompson's study of the 'quality television' debate (1997).
4. The independent production companies MTM and Tandem have been understood as central to the historical development of quality television, pro-

ducing sit-coms and dramas that appealed to the young, urban audiences that the networks aimed to attract in the 1970s. MTM produced *The Mary Tyler Moore Show* (CBS, 1970–7), a number of spin-off series such as *Lou Grant* (CBS, 1977–82) and *Rhoda* (CBS, 1974–8) and *Hill Street Blues* (NBC, 1980–7) among others. Tandem has a reputation for more socially 'relevant' sit-coms, such as *All in the Family* (1971–9) (based on the BBC's *Till Death Us Do Part*), *Maude* (1972–8), and *Sanford and Son* (1972–7) (based on the BBC's *Steptoe and Son*).

5. For discussion of *Hill Street Blues* as quality television see Thompson (1997), Gitlin (1994), Kerr (1984) and Jenkins (1984).

6. *Hill Street Blues* averaged in the low-20 share of the audience for most of its first season (Gitlin 1994: 302). However, the series went on to receive 21 nominations and eight awards in the 1981 Emmy ceremony. After this, the audience ratings increased, and by autumn 1982 it was the top-rated show in prime time for male viewers aged 18–34 (Gitlin 1994: 322–3).

7. ABC, CBS and NBC had dominated network broadcasting from the mid-1950s, regularly commanding 90 per cent of the total television audience in the 1960s and 1970s, a figure that slipped to 60 per cent by the 1990s (see Caldwell 1995: 11).

8. At the start of the eighth season David Duchovny left the series as a regular cast member and was replaced by John Doggett (Robert Patrick). Later in that season, Monica Reyes (Annabeth Gish) also joins as a regular cast member, and in season nine, Reyes and Doggett are assigned to *The X-Files* in the place of Mulder and Scully, although Scully continues as a regular cast member throughout the series.

9. This is not to imply that the fan and quality audiences are mutually exclusive, but that the network differentiated between them.

10. The need to function within the existing networks' notions of acceptability differentiates *The X-Files* from more recent examples of quality television produced by the subscription network HBO (such as *The Sopranos* and *Sex in the City*), which is able to experiment with programmes that offer more overt depictions of sex and violence because it is funded by subscription (see Rogers et al. 2002).

11. For Bartley, see Probst (1995), for Roe, see Holben (2000).

12. This shot is repeated each week in the series' opening title sequence.

13. The final two-part episode of *The X-Files* does offer some narrative resolution. As Mulder is placed on trial for murder, a number of characters from across the history of the series offer testimony that brings together and explains previously unresolved narrative strands. However, these testaments are dismissed by the court because of the lack of corroborating evidence, ultimately maintaining the series' premise in which the existence of the fantastic can be witnessed but never proved.

14. In his 1996 Dimbleby Lecture on BBC 1, Richard Dawkins took a similar line in criticising the series' attack on reason. As Thomas Sutcliffe wrote of the

lecture, 'week after week, he [Dawkins] pointed out, sceptical enquiry is vanquished in favour of moronic credulity' (Sutcliffe 1996: 36).

15. Matt Hills argues that cult texts tend to display the textual attributes of the 'perpetuated hermeneutic' (a central mystery that repeats familiar characteristics but is never fully resolved) and 'hyper-diegesis' (an internally logical, stable, yet 'unfinished' fictional world) (Hills 2002: 131). These attributes, which are in evidence in *The X-Files*' ambiguous representation of the fantastic and complex conspiracy narratives, leave 'a space for interpretation, speculation and fan affect which cannot be closed down by final "proof" or "fact"' (2002: 143). This 'space for interpretation' is apparent in both the extended debate and speculation generated by fans of the series, and the continuing academic debates about how the series should be understood.

Bibliography

Booker, M. Keith (2002), *Strange TV: Innovative Television Series from 'The Twilight Zone' to 'The X-Files'*, Westport, CT, and London: Greenwood Press.

Caldwell, John Thornton (1995), *Televisuality: Style, Crisis and Authority in American Television*, New Brunswick, NJ: Rutgers University Press.

Coe, Steve (1995), 'Networks Take a Walk on the Weird Side', *Broadcasting and Cable*, 125(43), 56–7.

Delasara, Jan (2000), *PopLit, PopCult and 'The X-Files': A Critical Exploration*, Jefferson, NC, and London: McFarland and Co.

Feuer, Jane (1984), 'The MTM Style', in Feuer, Kerr and Vahimagi (eds), *MTM: 'Quality Television'*, London: BFI, pp. 31–60.

Feuer, Jane, Kerr, Paul and Vahimagi, Tise (eds) (1984), *MTM: 'Quality Television'*, London: BFI.

Gitlin, Todd (1994), *Inside Prime Time*, revised edn, London: Routledge.

Hills, Matthew (1999), 'From *The Radio Times* to *Cult Times*: Market Segmentation in TV Consumption', paper presented at the 'Consuming Markets, Consuming Meanings' Conference, University of Plymouth, September 1999.

Hills, Matt (2002), *Fan Cultures*, London and New York: Routledge.

Holben, Jay, (2000), '*The X-Files*: Cinematographer: Bill Roe', *American Cinematographer*, 81(3), 88–91.

Jancovich, Mark and Lyons, James (eds) (2003), *Quality Popular Television: Cult TV, the Industry and Fans*, London: BFI.

Jenkins, Steve (1984), '*Hill Street Blues*', in Feuer, Kerr and Vahimagi (eds), *MTM: 'Quality Television'*, London: BFI, pp. 183–99.

Kellner, Douglas (1999), '*The X-Files* and the Aesthetics and Politics of Postmodern Pop', *The Journal of Aesthetics and Art Criticism*, 57(2), 161–75.

Kerr, Paul (1984), 'Drama at MTM: *Lou Grant* and *Hill Street Blues*', in Feuer, Kerr and Vahimagi (eds), *MTM: 'Quality Television'*, London: BFI, pp. 132–65.

Lowry, Brian (1995), *The Truth is Out There: The Official Guide to 'The X-Files'*, London: HarperCollins.

Lury, Celia (1993), *Cultural Rights: Technology, Legality and Personality*, London: Routledge.

Lyttle, John (1996), 'Do We Need *The X-Files?*: The TV Phenomenon About Strange Phenomena Has Taken International Hold of Paranoid Minds. It Could be a Conspiracy', *The Independent*, 6 May, pp. 8, 17.

McLean, Adrienne L. (1998), 'Media Effects: Marshall McLuhan, Television Culture, and *The X-Files*', *Film Quarterly*, 51(4), 2–11.

Martinez, José (1995), 'An Interview with Chris Carter and Howard Gordon', *Creative Screenwriting*, 2(3), 20–3.

O'Reilly, John (1996), 'Arts: A Jump-Cut Above the Rest', *The Independent*, 6 September, pp. 6–7.

Probst, Chris (1995), 'Darkness Descends on *The X-Files*', *American Cinematographer*, 76(6), 28–32.

Reeves, Jimmie L., Rodgers, Mark C., and Epstein, Michael (1996), 'Rewriting Popularity: The Cult Files', in David Lavery, Angela Hague and Marla Cartwright (eds), *'Deny All Knowledge': Reading 'The X-Files'*, Syracuse, NY: Syracuse University Press, pp. 22–35.

Rogers, Mark C., Epstein, Michael, and Reeves, Jimmie L. (2002), '*The Sopranos* as HBO Brand Equity: The Art of Commerce in the Age of Digital Reproduction', in Lavery, David (ed.), *This Thing of Ours: Investigating 'The Sopranos'*, London: Wallflower Press, pp. 42–57.

Sutcliffe, Thomas (1996), 'TV Review', *The Independent*, 13 November, p. 36.

Thompson, Robert J. (1997), *Television's Second Golden Age: From 'Hill Street Blues' to 'ER'*, Syracuse, NY: Syracuse University Press.

Part II: The Series/Serial Form

Introduction: The Series/Serial Form

Michael Hammond

At the time of writing this introduction I have, in the interests of research of course, been confronted with a dilemma; the satellite system to which I subscribe has channels that run episodes of the series/serials *Deadwood* (HBO/Roscoe Productions, David Milch, 2004), *The West Wing* (Warner Bros./John Wells Productions, Aaron Sorkin 1999–present) and *The Sopranos* (HBO/David Chase Prod./Brad Grey Prod, David Chase, 1999–present) , in such an order that I cannot watch all of them (due to a peculiarity in my system I can only record the programme I am watching). I can of course choose to catch the rebroadcast of both of these later in the week so in that sense my dilemma is a false one. In any case I can record both of those later broadcasts since they don't clash. However, given the limits of my system I am forced for that moment to make a choice between *Deadwood*, which begins at 10.00 p.m., and *The Sopranos*, which starts a half an hour later at 10.30 p.m. I decide to watch the first thirty minutes of *Deadwood* (episode 4) and then to switch over to *The Sopranos* (episode 65 'All Due Respect') primarily because I am more involved in *The Sopranos* and specifically whether Tony (James Gandolfini) will kill off Tony B. (played by Steve Buscemi) thus avoiding a blood feud with Johnny 'Sack' Sacramoni's (Vincent Curatola) gang across the river in New York. During the advertisement breaks in *The Sopranos* I switch back to *Deadwood* keeping myself abreast with the progress of that narrative in a more general sense. I will then record both later and watch *Deadwood* in its entirety.

For this evening I am engaged in what the advertising industry refers to as 'zapping', or at least a form of zapping since the actual definition for zapping refers to surfing channels in between commercial breaks.[1] In both cases I am involved in the negotiation with two texts simultaneously, or to be more precise I encounter them alternately. This common type of viewing presents problems for any form of textual analysis that looks for *immanent* meaning, that is meaning that solely resides in the text independent of any surrounding historical or cultural influences. More obviously the remote handset signifies viewer control over his or her own personally chosen text. My remote in fact is doubly significant since it has the facility of operating the video, so when I finally do come to watch *Deadwood* in its entirety I can 'zip' through the commercials, thereby exercising my ability to disrupt the 'flow' of the televisual text much to the dismay of advertisers.

It may seem a little strange to begin an introduction to the section on texts with an example of my viewing activity but it illustrates quite neatly two points. The first is that the text, even in my casual viewing, is limited to the drama's narrative and that I am actively engaged in erasing or 'zipping' through the interruptions of commercials. The commercials are not my main interest and therefore are not part of my experience of the narrative, or at least the narrative as I wish to experience it. Second is the fact that the hybrid shape of the series/serial format makes it possible for me to glean some general sense of the longer story arcs in *Deadwood* when I switch over from the five to seven minutes of commercials interspersed in *The Sopranos*. It is the last episode of *The Sopranos* in season five and I am involved in the specific resolution of a number of narrative problems that have been set up earlier. I am also paying close attention to the specific shorter storylines that are in this episode, particularly the relationship between Tony Soprano and Dr Melfi. In short these 'quality' dramas are characterised by both the serial format of the long story arc with open storylines and their combination with the shorter more contained plot-lines that come to an end within one episode. The use of this hybrid form affords the programme-makers a number of advantages in developing deeper characterisation through the longer story arcs while maintaining the advantages of shorter, episode-length stories. Shorter storylines allow both new viewers access and, as Greg Smith in this section points out, in the case of *Ally McBeal* they help to define and deepen the motivations and characterisations of the main players. So the viewer activity and the hybrid series/serial form make attention to the text essential to any understanding of how these contemporary television dramas are constructed and what might be their appeal both to audiences and therefore to the programme-producers.

At the end of the introduction to the Histories section we suggested that the terms series and serial were difficult to usefully distinguish. We could make the case that this is true not only in contemporary television dramas, but also sit-coms, think of Ross and Rachel's long-term off-and-on relationship in *Friends*. This seems to be a general trend in contemporary narrative television. Kristin Thompson has noted that 'the notion of firm and permanent closure to any given narrative has loosened across media. Series television, with its broad possibilities for spinning out narratives indefinitely, has been a major impetus in these tendencies' (Thompson 2003: 105). This hybridity is evident in the structure, characterisation and plot development of television dramas and this section offers some specific studies which take as their starting point a consideration of the way particular programmes are constructed.

Given the choice afforded by technologies for the consumer to 'zap' and 'zip', what is the role of the text in this viewer/consumer-centred relation that seems to characterise contemporary television? The question of the text in television studies is not new and traditionally considerable attention has been given to textual analysis in television studies from the early 1980s with the publication of George Brandt's *British Television Drama* (1981) or as far back as 1959 with Howard Thomas' *Armchair Theatre*. In both cases, as Charlotte Brunsdon has shown, these early approaches arose from 'traditional literary and dramatic criticism' and the type of television studied here is 'home theatre' (Brunsdon 1998: 97). As Brunsdon notes, the history of television studies is marked by the tensions between the study of the text in this tradition, a tradition which emphasises the 'cultural value' of a programme, and the simultaneous treatment of television by the social sciences as a sociological phenomenon. Added to this is the influence of cultural studies in the 1970s and 1980s that, in response to an evaluative model of textual analysis such as *Armchair Theatre*, had the effect of treating all of television as text rather than simply those identified as 'serious drama'. Here textual analysis provides a tool by which to analyse specific programmes regardless, and/or in spite of their perceived 'quality'. Nevertheless textual analysis of television has presented problems for the cultural studies tradition which was concerned that judgements of cultural value were inherent to most forms of textual analysis, and therefore to be avoided or to be qualified, often, as indeed we have, by surrounding the term quality in inverted commas. Christine Geraghty has noted:

> In this framework, television is placed at the popular end of the high/low binary that has underpinned much cultural studies work, and judgements are then made on the basis of ideological readings. Somewhat tautologically, programmes that aspire to a different kind of cultural value, such as the classic serial or some arts or history programmes, are criticized for precisely that. (Geraghty 2003: 27–8)

While all of these from differing perspectives have had their role in weakening the resistance to popular forms as legitimate objects of study in the academy as Geraghty points out this results at times in a refusal to make aesthetic judgements (Geraghty 2003: 28).

Because of these tensions it seems that any account of the value of textual analysis in television studies must start with a justification of the concentration on one specific textual example. Pitched against arguments that television texts are not indicative of the experience of the viewer, many text-based studies of television begin with a reference to Raymond Williams' concept of 'flow'. Kristin Thompson in her study on storytelling in film and television provides an instructive example when she points to the nuances of Williams' concept in setting out the parameters of her own study. Williams' experience of watching television in the United States resulted in his trying to determine ways of accounting for the constant interruption by commercials 'a single irresponsible flow of images and feelings . . . [and that] . . . In all developed broadcasting systems the characteristic organization, and therefore the characteristic experience is one of sequence or flow' (Williams in Thompson 2003: 6–7). Thompson points to an element in Williams' concept of flow which runs counter not only to contemporary viewing practices but to the broader history of mass entertainment forms at least from the nineteenth century. She points out that Williams suggested that the disruptive basis of the organisation of broadcast television was therefore an indication of the disrupted experience of the viewer. Further Williams' assumption overlooks the history of entertainment and print culture in the West which was characterised by variety formats (Thompson 2003: 7). Audiences have accommodated changes, interruptions and disjunctions in all manor of entertainment and mass-media forms. One need only take the reading of a newspaper, where choices made by the reader are not necessarily consistent, to recognise the long history at least of 'disruption' in encountering media texts. Indeed, journalistic practice is predicated quite often on the reader getting the gist of the article in the first few paragraphs on the assumption that the reader will jump from article to article before deciding, if at all, on which to devote the most concentration. Seen this way it may be more useful to recognise that organisation of programming does not necessarily reflect the viewer's experience and that there may be some advantage in considering the texts of specific programmes for reasons which are less to do with trying to establish any certainty about their cultural value and more to do with simply trying to understand how they are put together and why they constitute a significant shift in the format of television drama.

The series/serial then presents us with a need for paying attention to the text in a more focused form, if only to gain a better understanding of how this form works and then subsequently what may be the constituents of its appeal. However, for a moment it may help to reinforce the need for this type of analysis by turning to the industry. It stands to reason that technological developments which have increased the range of consumer/viewer choice have posed a problem for networks and producers who wish to sell advertising space and advertisers who wish to reach audiences with some degree of predictability. Recently the appearance of TiVo, a digital video recording system has given the viewer the possibility of even more control over the texts. The system has rewind and slow-motion facilities that can work on the programme being broadcast at that moment, it offers the ability to record up to 140 hours of programmes and a selection facility that enables the search and recording of particular programmes. This would allow the follower of a series/serial the opportunity to record all of the programmes of one season and then watch them, if they wished, back to back. This level of sophistication in programme selection will continue to develop in the coming years and it has not escaped the scrutinising attention of advertisers. Henry Jenkins has written recently:

> Right now, 43 percent of all households skip commercials. TiVo and other digital video recorder users skip between 60 and 70 percent of advertisements. These numbers are producing panic within the consumer economy. Many worry that the effectiveness of a spot during a top rated television show will be about the same or less than the clickthrough rate on the web. (Jenkins 2004)

Such a 'democratic' technology would seem to bring into high relief the way in which audiences choose to deal with 'flow' in Williams' sense by making their choices manifest through new technology. However, Jenkins asks that we consider these figures in another way: 'It isn't that 70 percent of TiVo users skip commercials altogether; people use TiVos to decide which commercials to watch. Marketers are trying to understand what kinds of commercials people choose to watch and why' (Jenkins 2004). Jenkins reminds us that the advertising industry works to incorporate these viewing practices in their own strategy. In this case advertisers respond by trying to target the programmes which generate the most return viewers.

> Industry researchers are discovering that the most valuable viewers may be loyals (or what we call fans). For most shows, less than 5 percent of all viewers regard the program to be a favorite. For some shows (and these include many cult and reality television programmes), the numbers may reach 40 or 50 percent of viewers. Loyals are significantly more apt to watch the entire show each week, seek out additional information, watch advertisements, recall brands, and talk about them with others. (Jenkins 2004)

Many of the cult shows that Jenkins refers to are series/serials, while many reality television programmes such as *Big Brother* or *I'm a Celebrity get Me out of Here* are serial in format. The relationship between establishing 'loyals' and the serial format has considerable historical roots. The serial format in cinema arose in the early teens, alongside the feature and was a design for ensuring loyal audiences. *The Adventures of Kathlyn* (Selig, 1914), a US serial with 'cliffhanger' endings, reached Britain in 1914 and was the first serial to be released in bi-weekly instalments. The effect on gaining returning audiences and ensuring a profitable programme was, in the words of one exhibitor, 'the greatest attraction I have had at this hall up until now'.[2] Another noted how profits had improved with each instalment, 'the takings of the last one (episode) no. 10 were over 30% more than those of no.1'.[3] As with the serialisation of novels in the nineteenth century, the form of the serial was central in gaining and retaining audiences and readers that the advertising industry now terms 'loyals'. This form was helpful in the early teens for cinema exhibitors particularly where competition with other local exhibitors was intense. Without making ahistorical claims for precise parallels it is probably not surprising that the serial format appears as a significant trend in the late twentieth century at a time when competition for audiences has increased, but more importantly where the televisual landscape is so populated with options that finding specific audiences with any degree of accuracy has become the primary motivation for advertisers and producers. It is clear that in the last decade much of the answer to that for the industry has been found in the series/serial format.

This section takes as its object the texts of the series/serial in a set of studies with different emphases on the role seriality plays in achieving the kind of character development and narrative complexity that not only differentiates it from other episodic series but also from the feature film, another competitor for audience attention and loyalty. Angela Ndalianis begins with a formal and diagrammatic study of the forms of seriality as they exist across programmes from *Dallas* to *Millennium* and *The X-Files*. Greg Smith works through the way seriality functions to create complexities of characterisation in the main characters in *Ally McBeal* to show the way that the attitude the narration has to these characters shifts across episodes. Jason Jacobs undertakes an analysis of the way that serialisation and the use of psychotherapy as a character motivating device in *The Sopranos* works to provide the kind of character complexity and thematic concerns which appeal to a knowing audience. Such complexity and specific cultural and inter-textual referencing (Carmella: 'Godfather 3, what happened!?') seems to be addressed to a media-savvy audience, who apparently respond to what Jane Feuer in the previous section has referred to as 'quality drama'. In both Smith's and Jacobs' chapters the attention to detail and form in these shows helps to establish a stronger sense of how the serial/series format helps to create empathetic attachment to characters and in the process begin to encourage 'loyals'.

Kristin Thompson's own concern in outlining the formal structures of contemporary television storytelling is productively limited to 'looking at storytelling techniques that may help constitute the specificity or at least the salient differences characterizing television' (Thompson 2003: 18). Careful to outline the parameters of her study Thompson differentiates her formal analysis which looks to find the normative principles in contemporary narrative television from the wider analyses of the text as 'flow' and also the analysis of content in the interests of establishing the political nature of the programme. From another paradigm the advertising industry concerns itself with texts with an eye, in Henry Jenkins' words, to 'reshape our emotional bonds with brands' (Jenkins 2004). Such a desire to wrap commodities in narratives, and the emotional affect of those stories does indicate among other things that the structure of the text has significance beyond the analytical laboratory of the academy. To this end, Eric Freedman looks at *Smallville* (Alfred Gough, Miles Miller, 2001–present) and *Buffy the Vampire Slayer* (Joss Whedon, 1996–2003) and the way in which the serial text, in structuring the two realms of fantasy/horror and teenage realities, seeks to connect with a teen market within the tradition of youth marketing organised around various depictions of the body, fantastic and real.

Most of the examples above relate to the US market, industry and viewers. One of the important means by which programme-makers outside the US differentiate their product from the ubiquitous US programming is by trying to address the specific experiences and concerns of the nation. Sarah Cardwell's study of the series/serials *This Life* (BBC2, 1996–7) and *Queer as Folk* (Channel 4, 1999–2000) explores the way these two programmes utilise specific textual elements and devices to address a 'twentysomething' audience, a demographic which marketers had termed a 'lost generation', and to differentiate their programmes from the general fare on British television screens.

Finally the value of textual analysis in exploring the way that series/serials function as storytelling forms and as marketing strategies lies in obviously divergent fields of interest, the academy, whether seeking to explore the normative principles or outlining audience address, and the advertising industry's intention of exploiting the intersection of affect and commodity. Yet both implicitly or explicitly recognise the viewer's ability to separate the text from 'flow', as I did in my zapping to *Deadwood* during the commercials in *The Sopranos*, and this affords more productive understanding of how these texts encourage the acquisition of 'loyals'. They also point towards the links to surrounding inter-texts from industry-generated official products to fan or 'loyal'-generated objects, or even, in the case of fan cultures and 'loyal communities', social relationships. This unpredictable outcome of finding loyal audiences is one that both the industry and the academy seek to understand and one that, however diverse the approach, they recognise lies at least partly in the structures of the programmes themselves.

Notes

1. Zapping is apparently the practice of surfing channels while commercials are on in the main programme. Zipping is a process of searching out a programme to watch or for something that catches the viewer's interest (Marshall 1998).
2. Letter from Charles Burgess, Manager of the Belgrave Cinema, Leicester (1914), in Folder 10, Selig Collection, Margaret Herrick Library, Academy of Motion Picture Arts and Sciences, Beverly Hills, California.
3. Letter from T. W. Goodison, The Empire Palace, Denaby (Rotherham) (1914), in Folder 10, Selig Collection.

Bibliography

Brunsdon, Charlotte (1998), 'What is the "Television" in Television Studies', in C. Geraghty and D. Lusted (eds), *The Television Studies Book*, London: Arnold, pp. 95–113.

Geraghty, Christine (2003), 'Aesthetics and Quality in Popular Television Drama', in *International Journal of Cultural Studies*, London: Sage Publications, pp 23–45.

Jenkins, Henry (2004), 'Affective Economics 101', in *Flow, A Critical Forum on Television and Media Culture*, http://idg.communication.utexas.edu/flow/?jot=view&id=411

Marshall, Caroline (1998), *Pocket Advertising: The Essentials of Advertising from A–Z*, London: Economist Books.

Selig Collection, Margaret Herrick Library, Academy of Motion Picture Arts and Sciences, Beverly Hills, California.

Thompson, Kristin (2003), *Storytelling in Film and Television*, Cambridge, MA: Harvard University Press.

Williams, Raymond (1974, reprint 1992), *Television, Technology and Cultural Form*, Middletown, CT: Wesleyan University Press.

CHAPTER 5

Television and the Neo-Baroque

Angela Ndalianis

Writing an article about television, the series and seriality, the temptation was too great: I simply had to begin by retelling the events that occurred in that infamous final episode of *The Colbys* (1985–7). *The Colbys'* narrative premise centred on the exploits, loves, hates and intrigues of the wealthy Colby family and other characters that entered their story space. Week after week, audiences watched as characters fell in love, fell out of love, fell into comas, were kidnapped, blackmailed, and murdered. A labyrinthine web of stories unravelled at a pace that left the daytime soap storylines miles behind in the drama stakes. Then, during the final season of 1987, the ABC network announced that the show was to be cancelled. In a strategy that is, to this day, unparalleled for its sheer audacity, the writers decided to let the series go out with a bang. One of the show's main characters, Fallon Carrington Colby, the wife of Jeff Colby, had spent many seasons suffering from amnesiac episodes. In the final episode, Fallon is driven by an inner urge to take to the Californian highway in her car, as if drawn by some mysterious energy. As her family search for her (a storyline that itself follows narrative paths too complex to go into), Fallon experiences 'technical difficulties' with her car, which eventually goes totally dead in the middle of the desert, miles from anywhere. Looking up at the sky, she sees fantastic lights that lure her out of her car. Then, in a scene that would do Steven Spielberg of *Close Encounters of the Third Kind* (1977) and Chris Carter of *The X-Files* (1994–2002) fame proud, an enormous space ship lands, its doors open, the silhouetted figure of a spindly alien emerges, and Fallon disappears into the ship, the willing recipient of the alien's embrace. And as the space ship takes off, and the mystery of Fallon's amnesia is resolved (clearly, she had been victim to numerous alien abductions), *The Colbys'* presence in television history comes to an end. This was sheer television magic!

But this wasn't the end. *The Colbys* had been a spin-off of the other popular ABC series *Dynasty* (1981–9), which had itself copied the successful CBS series *Dallas* (1978–91). Having migrated to *The Colbys* from *Dynasty*, the producers wanted this popular character back on the earlier series, and come back she did: yes, Fallon was found again, suffering yet another amnesiac episode that was conveniently denied the fantastical conclusion provided in *The Colbys*. It was replaced instead with a rational one – Fallon was, according to doctors, suffering from a case of severe neurotic episodes. However, while relishing the virtuoso finale of *The Colbys*, audiences also did not find it too difficult to accept this alternate explanation offered by *Dynasty*, which shared a narrative reality with its spin-off.[1]

If anything, the narrative scenarios of these shows reveal the extent to which television series since the 1950s have increasingly favoured an open narrative form that not only weaves into and between multiple story formations that traverse episode and series time, but that also cross over distinct television series into other spin-off shows. The series (which consists of a succession of self-contained narrative episodes that progress in a sequence) and the serial (which comprises a series of episodes whose narratives resist closure and continue into the next episode(s) within the sequence) have increasingly collapsed into one another, so much so that, in more recent times, it has become difficult to distinguish one form from another. Since *The Colbys* and *Dynasty*, the series format integral to television has become even more rampant, and writers and producers have become more sophisticated in juggling, dispensing of, and returning to story formations in strategic and ingenious ways that keep audiences actively engaged with the narrative universes presented.

From its inception in the 1940s, television learned a valuable formal lesson from the comic book industry: like comics, which had flourished since the creation of Superman and Batman in the late 1930s, television's fundamental logic relies heavily on the series format. By giving media consumers familiar characters and continuing storylines, it was more likely that these fictional universes could weave themselves within the everyday world of the viewer. This new medium asserted and ensured the success of what it had to offer, managing to rely especially on serial motivation that steadily expanded its market and warded off loss of audience to other media competitors. It became a successful strategy, one that the cinema experienced to its detriment during the 1950s and 1960s. However, while the series has always been integral to television, its formal properties become more extreme as it approaches the late twentieth and early twenty-first centuries, during which time it has succumbed to the serial format.

In an article written about the function of the serial in popular culture of the late nineteenth and early twentieth centuries Roger Hagedorn has argued that serials tend to dominate as a narrative form within a specific medium when the competition of other media becomes more prominent (Hagedorn 1988: 4–12). Operating on a cliffhanger logic, serial narratives strategically delay closure. Instead, the reader or viewer is woven into one or multiple narrative threads that remain unresolved within one independent episode, the result being that consumers are encouraged to return for more. Considering Hagedorn's assertion that series and, in particular, the serial tend to dominate during periods of intense media competition, it comes as no surprise that today's entertainment media are imbued with a serial structure the likes of which has not been witnessed before.

Many of the aesthetic and formal transformations currently confronting the television series are played out against and informed by cultural and socio-economic transformations. Since the 1980s, national markets have been integrated into an expansive system of economics that spans the globe through transnational corporations whose concern for capital extends across multiple countries and multiple media (Jameson and Miyoshi 1998: 55–7). The conglomeration of the entertainment industry has resulted in an industry that has multiple media interests. The outcome has been new convergences between diverse entertainment forms – comic books, computer games, theme-park attractions and television programmes. All these configurations have formal repercussions. Even when part of the same conglomerate, subsidiary companies must still vie for audience attention by offering their own media-specific experiences, and they attempt to ensure success and a faithful audience by relying on a serial logic. This market is intensely competitive and each medium struggles to draw attention to its presence. Television – like the other media it competes with – is a dynamic being that has had to redefine itself in the midst of intense competition. So, where do we begin in mapping out the nature of these transformations? One pattern is certain: the television series has become more excessively serial-like. The 'relationship between economics and aesthetics' evident in the formal properties of entertainment media: economics gives rise to new aesthetics and to new formal patterns – evident, in this instance, in the shape of serial narrative formations (Wyatt 1994: 160). Reflecting the multi-centred rationale of the economic infrastructure that supports it, narrative 'meaning' becomes increasingly reliant upon an audience that is capable of traversing multiple 'texts' in order to give coherence to an independent episode within a series. As Omar Calabrese explains, the result is a 'polycentric', open structure (Calabrese: 1992).

In *The Open Work* Umberto Eco states that the 'theory of the open work is none other than a poetics of serial thought' which is 'open and polyvalent' (Eco 1989: 218). The poetics of the open work is characteristic of our contemporary era, an era that Eco was to characterise as the 'neo-baroque'

(Eco 1992: viii–ix). It is the articulation of the neo-baroque aesthetics inherent within the television series as serial that concerns me in this essay. Whereas structural thought is concerned with discovering and tracing signs back to an original source, serial thought develops along alternate paths: it is intent on destabilising the singular, linear paths that are familiar to classical, Aristotelian narrative patterns – Eco's 'structural thought'. Instead, it is concerned with form itself, with what Deleuze has called the 'infinite work in process' (Deleuze 1993: 34). The formal logic of the neo-baroque narrative (Eco's 'serial thought') is to resist classical attention to linearity and closure. Writing in the 1960s, Eco was more concerned with the seriality typical of modernist traditions of writing and in the possibilities inherent in interpreting a work 'in a way that differs from the intentions of the author' (Eco 1992: ix). In Eco's foreword to Calabrese's *Neo-Baroque: A Sign of the Times* he states that, in the 1960s, openness was a phenomenon found in the avant-garde but extraneous to the messages circulating in mass media. However, 'Since the 1980s the distance between the avant-garde and mass media has closed. We are no longer dealing with works and interpreters but with processes, flows and interpretative drifts that concern not single works, but the totality of messages that circulate in the area of communication' (Eco 1992: ix). Clearly, this shift that Eco locates is one that is aligned with the phenomenon of postmodernism. In this essay, however, I follow the lead of Omar Calabrese, who embraces the neo-baroque and the postmodern as kindred spirits. Like Calabrese, I suggest that the neo-baroque (as the late twentieth–early 21st-century manifestation of its more famous seventeenth-century baroque counterpart) provides a more focused method with which to analyse the formal properties that are inherent to postmodernism. It is a specifically neo-baroque spatial logic that is embedded within the postmodern that remains the primary point of reference. The central characteristic of the neo-baroque that informs the analysis that follows is the lack of respect for the limits of the frame. Closed narrative forms associated with the classical are replaced by neo-baroque open structures that favour the movement of the serial – the 'infinite work in process'.

As I have argued elsewhere, the baroque is not merely a specific period situated within the seventeenth century (its traditional, temporal home), but a formal quality that crosses the boundaries of historical periodisation (Ndalianis 2004).[2] Formally reflecting the open and multifarious nature of the redefined entertainment industry, the protean forms in the television series reveal a fascinating metamorphosis from a closed, structural form to an open neo-baroque form that displays 'a loss of entirety, totality, and system in favour of instability, polydimensionality, and change' (Eco 1992:

xii). While cultural theorists such as Martin Jay and Christine Buci-Glucksman have also liberated the baroque from its historical confines, they have persisted in understanding the baroque as a form primarily associated with the visual – or, more precisely, the spectacular. However, the inherent 'madness of vision' that Buci-Glucksman associates with the baroque is equally manifest as a 'madness' of narrative formations. The seriality and polycentrism that began to emerge in television shows from the 1950s with increased fervour is typical of a shift towards a neo-baroque attitude concerning narrative space. Henri Focillon, for example, has stated that baroque forms

> pass into an undulating continuity where both beginning and end are carefully hidden . . . [The baroque reveals] 'the system of the series' – a system composed of discontinuous elements sharply outlined, strongly rhythmical and . . . [that] eventually becomes 'the system of the labyrinth', which, by means of mobile synthesis, stretches itself out in a realm of glittering movement. (Focillon 1992: 67)

Neo-baroque narratives draw the audience into potentially infinite or, at least, multiple directions that rhythmically recall what Focillon labels the 'system of the series', or the 'system of the labyrinth'. While the porosity of narrative form that is the result of seriality has been present throughout television's history, it was not until the 1950s and especially the 1960s that the serial became more prominent as a narrative system within popular culture. It is television, in particular, that had a fundamental role to play in familiarising audiences with serial form. While television turned to the series as a strategy that could maintain a constant audience, its lesson, in turn, came to dominate the entertainment industry on a grander scale. Evaluating the development of the series within the context of television, Calabrese outlines the evolving polycentrism of five neo-baroque narrative prototypes.[3] Significantly, as each prototype moves progressively from the 1950s towards the 1980s the polycentrism becomes far more evident in the form of story arcs and multiple storylines that unravel within and beyond single episodes and, eventually, across the series whole, revealing a shift in preference for the series as serial. The analysis that follows is greatly indebted to Calabrese's ideas, but, in addition to diagrammatically displaying each prototype, I will also move beyond the 1980s to consider the ways in which Calabrese's model has transformed over the last two decades. Specifically, whereas Calabrese understands the movement from prototypes 1 to 5 as a linear and evolving one (with points of overlap occurring when one prototype is being replaced by the other), it will be argued that, since the 1980s, all five prototypes have returned and co-exist. As will become clearer below, while dominant prototype patterns remain distinct, the tendency in contemporary television series has also been to blur the boundaries by sharing characteristics with other prototypes.

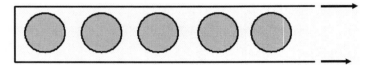

Figure 5.1 The First Prototype – distinct episodes with
common characters but no overall series narrative.

For Calabrese, the first prototype embodies the series as adopted by television in the late 1950s and 1960s. Including television shows such as *I Love Lucy* (1951–7), *The Honeymooners* (1955–6), *The Adventures of Rin Tin Tin* (1954–9), *Star Trek* (1966–9) and the earlier seasons of *Get Smart* (1965–70) within the first prototype, each episode repeats the same main characters and remains self-contained, sacrificing overall serial development for the sake of the closed, self-sustained narrative episode. In this sense, each episode within the series is influenced by and contains within it the classical (Eco's structural) form embodied in the cinema by the classical Hollywood paradigm.[4] If we consider classical narrative forms as being contained by the limits of the frame (as manifested in continuity, linearity and 'beginnings and endings'), then the perforation of the frame – the hidden beginnings and endings that Focillon speaks of – are typical of the neo-baroque. Classical systems remain centred, ensuring narrative clarity and symmetry of organisation and closure. A complete story is enclosed by each episode, and no serial effect is produced because no episode story branches beyond or reveals an awareness of events occurring in prior episodes. Nevertheless, seriality is implied in the repetition of characters and narrative patterns beyond single episodes. Diagrammatically, the first prototype may be visualised as a series of distinct narratives (the ellipses) that multiply themselves as the series progresses (Figure 5.1). Each episode's connection to the series is reflected in the partial containment provided by the open-ended rectangle, which then repeats itself as the next season of series is aired.

While Calabrese suggests that this first prototype dominated in the earlier period of the television series' history, more recently there has been a return to this formal structure – but with variations. The NBC shows *Law and Order* (1990–present), *Law and Order: Special Victims Unit* (1999–present), *Dragnet* (2002–present), *Law and Order: Criminal Intent*

(2000–present), *CSI* (2000–present) and *CSI: Miami* (2002–present) typify this structure (although, as I will suggest below, *Law and Order: Criminal Intent*, *CSI* and its spin-off series primarily succumb to the logic of the fourth prototype, while also occasionally crossing over into prototype 3). As is the case with the classical narrative familiar to the cinema, each episode places emphasis on goal-oriented characters, and a causal story structure that presents the viewer with a distinct sense of a beginning, middle and an end. In the case of *Law and Order*, for example, the show begins with the discovery of a murdered victim. Enter the 'Law' and the episode narrative goal: to determine who committed the crime and to see that justice is done. Enter 'Order', the driven district attorneys and their assistants who argue on behalf of the people, and who seek narrative closure by ensuring that justice prevails. Often, justice does not prevail, but happy endings are not always a prerequisite for narrative closure.

In *Law and Order* it is the accumulation of stories contained within distinct episodes that are important, which possibly explains the continued success of the show despite the frequent replacement of main characters (and the actors who play them) that have passed through the series. As is typical of prototype 1, little or no information about the main characters is provided to the viewer beyond its significance to the unravelling episode storyline. One the few exceptions is Detective Lennie Briscoe: in the twelve seasons this character has been in the show, the small amount of information the viewer has managed to glean about his personal life is that he served in the Armed Forces, he is a recovering alcoholic, he was investigated for corruption but was cleared, and that his daughter was killed by a drug dealer.[5] However, while the shows within this prototype 'frame' their narrative universes within the confines of the episode format (and ensure that the self-contained stories presented are devoid of diverging stories that leak beyond episode time) a neo-baroque polycentricism is reflected in the way further episodes persistently rupture this frame by endlessly multiplying it and reopening it in new story scenarios, and new crimes that must be solved in the following episodes. In a sense, that which emerges is the multiplication of classical narratives, narratives that, through their duplication and extension, create a dynamic and rhythmic interrelation and ultimate transformation into a neo-baroque logic.

Additionally, comparing 1950s and 1960s versions of this prototype to the more recent variation found in examples like *Law and Order*, it is clear that neo-baroque concern with open form is more rampant. Over the last decade, the addition to the schema involves the further rupture of the classical narration that typifies the first prototype – not only through episodic cadence, but also through a slippage of story-framing elements that occurs through the removal or introduction of additional characters. No longer are the main characters stable and consistent from episode to episode. In *Law and Order*'s thirteen-year history, a stream of district attorneys, assistant district attorneys and detectives have appeared in the show. This character exchange opens up the structure of the series further by suggesting the existence of narrative spaces outside the episode and series' reality. The revised version of the first prototype returns to the earlier form, but, in the process, initiates a neo-baroque motion that is even more fluid. The current variation of the first prototype abandons the stricter insistence on classical framing – a fact revealed in the serial-like rotation and replacement of characters/actors across the series, or in the way episodic closure is occasionally ruptured by also bleeding into other prototypes (as will be discussed below).

Furthermore, the character John 'Munch' (played by Richard Belzer) was originally introduced in *Homicide: Life on the Streets* (1993–99). Munch has opened the form of the first prototype further still. *Law and Order* and *Homicide: Life on the Streets* – both NBC series – began a number of cross-over episodes that usually commenced with a crime being committed in one show's reality, which then required collaboration between the New York and Baltimore crime fighters. Beginning stories in one show, then continuing them later in the week in the other is not only clever marketing (it increases the possibility that a viewer hooked on one of the series, but not the other, may become an avid viewer of the other NBC series as well), it also reflects a marked neo-baroque attitude towards space. The character who consistently appeared in these cross-over episodes was Detective John Munch, and when *Homicide: Life on the Streets* was cancelled in 1999, in addition to making cameos (as Munch) in television shows like *The Beat* (a Barry Levinson and Tom Fontana collaboration that followed in the wake of *Homicide* in 2000) and *The X-Files* (in an episode that retold an earlier adventure of the Lone Gunmen), Munch's character transferred from Baltimore to New York, becoming one of the main detectives in the new *Law and Order: SVU*.[6] While pre-1980s television series often indulged in cross-overs in order to introduce viewers to spin-off shows and their characters,[7] in the case of the more recent variation reflected in Munch's roaming tendencies (or Ellenor's in *The Practice* (1997–)), there are more radical formal repercussions in that actual story arcs develop, which abandon episodic closure for temporary serial development both within the one show *and* across other television shows that have their own distinctive story and character realities. As an example of the post-1980s variation of prototype 1, *Law and Order* reveals the rhythmic and polycentric organisation that is typical of neo-baroque aesthetics. While reflecting a classical preference for framing the narrative within the borders of episode time, the post-1980s variant of the first prototype is more prone to destabilise the classical closure that is more typical of the 1950s and 1960s: the neo-baroque delight with open form is more prominent.

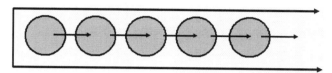

Figure 5.2 The Second Prototype – self-contained episodes, entire series has single narrative goal.

In the second prototype – early examples of which include *Zorro* (1957–61), *Ivanhoe* (1958–9) and *Gilligan's Island* (1964–7) – complete stories are contained within a single episode; however, the entire series is also constructed according to a single narrative progression that looks towards a final resolution. The form becomes slightly more open in that, while each episode is autonomous, it constitutes one episode in an entire series journey. In *Gilligan's Island*, for example, the series' narrative goal is to get the 'fearless crew' and passengers off the island and back home, suggesting an open form that gives each episode a sense of serial flow – one that leads towards one structuring goal. Each episode also consists of the various autonomous adventures of Gilligan and company, with few episodes referring to story events or character developments occurring in prior episodes. In the second prototype, the classical and baroque begin to intersect more forcefully: while a serial narrative structure is initiated, the open form of the baroque is conveyed both by the self-contained narratives that are resolved at the conclusion of each episode, and by the overall narrative goal of the series which implies (eventual) closure (even if, as was the case in *Gilligan's Island*, the goal of rescue was not to be achieved until the television movie was released nearly two decades after the series was cancelled). The episode connection to an overall series narrative is reflected in Figure 5.2 in the arrows that suggest each episode is both enclosed and continuing.

As is the case with the first prototype, there are fewer examples of this form once television moves into the 1970s. Already during the 1960s the drive of the television series is towards an increasingly more open format, one that moves steadily towards a seemingly chaotic 'madness' of narrative formation. For example, *I Dream of Jeannie* (1965–70) begins as a typical example of this second prototype. Jeannie's goal is to marry her master in the overall series progression, while each episode involves the singular, self-contained situations that Jeannie, Major Nelson and Major Healy find themselves in. The closer Jeannie gets to attaining her goal the more the episodic form begins to break down. Story arcs that continue across numerous episodes become more and more frequent (for example, the story arc dealing with the discovery of Jeannie's birthday, the one covering her master's pilgrimage to Bagdad, or that of the wedding itself). By the time *I Dream of Jeannie* reaches its final seasons, it slips into the logic of prototype three (see Figure 5.3).

Television shows today that still adhere to this format are most often found in game shows or reality television series like *Survivor* (2000–present), *The Bachelor* (2001–present), and *Big Brother* (2000–present). The overall series goal is clear – to be the final survivor (and win lots of cash), to be chosen as the bachelor's partner (or to have the option of winning lots of cash), to be last out of the Big Brother house (and win lots of cash). Each episode consists of formulaic tasks or rituals such as the struggle for reward and immunity in *Survivor*, and each series ends by eliminating contestants at the end of each episode (or, in the case of *Big Brother*, at the end of the week). *Star Trek: Voyager* (1995–2001) and *Monk* (2002–present) also contain elements of the second prototype. However, as is typical of television shows of the last two decades, there is a general tendency towards slippage between a number of prototypes. In the case of *Star Trek: Voyager*, for example, the series goal is reminiscent of *Gilligan's Island*: the fearless crew are lost in space, millions of miles away from their solar system, and the series goal is to find their way home. But *Star Trek: Voyager* also slips into the third prototype in favouring a more open structure that can allow the story to escape the limits of the episode. Similarly, the goal of Monk in *Monk* is to discover who murdered his wife and daughter, but, as will be revealed, the show also succumbs to the logic of the fourth prototype.

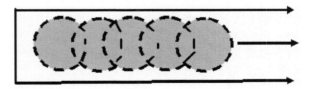

Figure 5.3 The Third Prototype – self-contained episodes, an
expanding series time, and character progression throughout the series.

In the late 1960s, the series and serial structure opened up further, following a movement away from self-contained episodes, to episodes that increasingly weave their stories across the series as a whole, producing a serial pattern familiar to the story arc. The movement is from a dominant closed order (prototypes 1 and 2), which contains elements of a more open, neo-baroque, to a dominant neo-baroque order, which contains elements of the classical. The initiating impulse of a more consistently neo-baroque open form is found in the third prototype that Calabrese suggests is marked by *Bonanza* (1959–73), especially as it developed in the late 1960s and early 1970s. As he explains, the innovative elements of this series lay in the relationship between episode time (which was closed, contained and concluded), series time (which was open, had no narrative goal and presented an infinite timeframe) and narrated time (which was also open in that characters developed and there was a greater flow and dependence on preceding episodes, thus reflecting features of the serial). Connections between episodes become more pronounced and, as Figure 5.3 suggests, narratives become more reliant on the stories of prior episodes. In *Bonanza* we find a reflection of what Calabrese states is the American television series' capacity to simultaneously produce an episodic, open, baroque form, and a closed, classical form. This combined state of classical within the baroque is typical of many contemporary entertainment stories.[8] As mentioned above, *I Dream of Jeannie* transforms into this prototype in the later seasons, as does *Get Smart* (which, early on, was more typical of prototype 1).

This form of neo-baroque seriality has continued to dominate and is found today in numerous cop shows like *NYPD Blue* (1993–present) and *Homicide: Life on the Streets*, investigative-focused series like *Crossing Jordan* (2001–present) and *Picket Fences* (1992–6), and science-fiction shows like *Star Trek: The Next Generation* (1987–94) and *Stargate SG-1* (1997–present). Even *The Simpsons* (1989–present), which has strong echoes of the first prototype (in its focus on self-contained episodes and, generally, its lack of character progression – let's face it, baby Maggie has not aged a day in the show's fourteen-year lifespan), crosses into the territory of this third prototype in its occasional 'serial' developments of some storylines – such as the death of Ned Flanders' wife and his subsequent search for a new partner, the continuing episodes that see Homer's brother appearing in the show, or the flowering romance between Principal Skinner and Edna Krabappel.

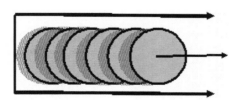

Figure 5.4 The Fourth Prototype – series as
variation on a theme producing a palimpsest effect.

Prototype 4 introduces yet another variation to neo-baroque seriality. Calabrese cites *Columbo* (1971–93) as the series (actually, a series of TV movies) that introduced the fourth prototype in the 1970s. The fourth schema relies on the technique of 'variation on a theme' and on the personality of the main character (in this case, Columbo, played by Peter Falk). There is no overall series story that closes the show's form and, like examples in the third prototype, the series could continue indefinitely. More recently, shows that have adopted this form include *Law and Order: Criminal Intent* (2001–present), *Monk* (2002–present), *CSI* (2000–present) and *CSI: Miami* (2002–present). Episodes build upon the model established in prior episodes. The episode narratives remain the same (a crime is committed in the beginning and the investigators solve it), yet different in that there are always slight variations in terms of the method of the crime, and in how the main characters expose the criminal. Unlike its predecessors *Law and Order* and *Law and Order: SVU*, *Law and Order: Criminal Intent* begins with a crime that more often than not reveals who the killer is. Enter Detective Robert Goren, played by Vincent d'Onofrio, and his partner Detective Alexandra Eames (Kathryn Erbe). The show is also increasingly becoming known by its adopted subtitle 'The Vincent d'Onofrio Show' for good reasons: viewers watch in avid fascination week after week as d'Onofrio surprises, teases and wins over the viewer through virtuoso performances that would do Columbo and Sherlock Holmes proud. The awkward and, at times, disturbing stances and head angles that disorient the suspects, the Holmes-like investigative deductions that lead him to expose the perpetrator, the episodes of sheer brilliance in which he stuns his diegetic audience with his encyclopaedic knowledge – all are presented week after week with subtle variations, twists and surprises, always making the viewer wonder 'what will he do next?'[9] A similar virtuosity is evident in *Monk*, but, in this case, the investigator is not only brilliant – he also suffers from an extreme case of Obsessive Compulsive Disorder. The tactic of outperforming and offering variations on a theme appears, in this instance, in the way Monk attempts to solve a crime while also trying to negotiate a world around him that is full of germs, chaotic events and people who insist on shaking hands.

CSI and *CSI: Miami* are slightly different in that the virtuosity comes from the stylistic properties of television production. The performance here is that of the special effect that offers astounding insight into the crimes. Crime-scene investigators Nick Stokes and Gil Grissom discuss what happens to a victim when he is shot through the heart, and there is a cut to a bullet being fired, the camera following its motion at a ferocious speed, then, it punctures human flesh and plummets towards the targeted organ, which we see pumping blood through arteries: as the bullet ruptures the heart, the flow through the arteries slows down then, eventually, comes to a standstill. The virtuosity comes from making visible to the viewer that which is invisible to the naked eye.

In the fourth prototype, each episode therefore functions as a self-contained fragment, but to recognize the variation the audience must have an understanding of how crimes were committed and solved in pre-existing episodes. Each variation of a theme repeats previous episode patterns in order to outperform them. Diagrammatically, the dynamic interaction between episode fragments and the series whole may be viewed as producing overlapping functions similar to prototype 3 (Figure 5.4). However, rather than episodes intersecting in ways that suggest narrative extension, the fourth prototype suggests a multi-layered structure that resembles a palimpsest. Each additional episode lays itself over prior episodes in an attempt to perfect on its predecessors and, partially at least, erase their presence through outperformance. An integral aspect of audience reception involves active participation in an aesthetic of repetition through the principle of variation on a theme. Integral to the strategy of 'variation of a theme' is the neo-baroque principle of virtuosity. Virtuosity and variation on a theme rely on the active engagement of an audience familiar with prior episodes in the series. In addition to simply repeating, virtuosity relies on varying and outperforming the characterisations, narratives, or performances of its predecessors. Through virtuosity these examples aim at creating their own centres and perfecting their forms while still maintaining a relationship to a multi-centred narrative universe.[10]

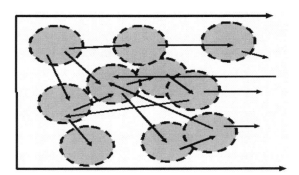

Figure 5.5 The Fifth Prototype – continuing
episodes and multiple narrative formations.

The fifth prototype, which is without doubt the most dominant serial form in television series today, has also become a significant form in contemporary entertainment media in general. It is characterised by dynamic narrative structures with multiple centres. As a prototype more typical of the post-1970s, however, closed narrative formations are unsettled more dramatically, taking the third prototype's form to extreme. Calabrese suggests that it was the television show *Dallas* that popularised this form. In its wake, *Dallas* has been followed by shows as diverse as *Hill Street Blues* (1981–87), *Miami Vice* (1984–9), *The X-Files*, *Millennium* (1996–9), *Star Trek: Deep Space Nine* (1993–9), *Ally McBeal* (1997–2002), *The Sopranos* (1999–present), *Alias* (2001–present), *Six Feet Under* (2001–5), *Buffy the Vampire Slayer* (1997–2003) and *Angel* (1999–2004). The episode borders of these series remain in continual states of flux encompassing aspects of all prior prototypes. They are the series as serial, in that throughout the entire series the viewer becomes embroiled in the changing lives and stories of multiple characters. These series therefore retain a sense of historicity and progress through the focus on characters that develop from episode to episode. Often, as with *The Sopranos* and *Six Feet Under*, the series time is potentially infinite with no overall narrative target in place. In the case of *The X-Files* traits of the second prototype are revealed in the show's respective goals of attaining the 'Truth'.

Additionally, throughout the fifth prototype no stable, singular, linear framework dominates (Figure 5.5). The shows are riddled with multiple narrative formations that stress polycentrism within the series itself. While one story may be introduced and resolved in a single episode, or across a series of episodes, other narrative situations may open up, extending the stories of multiple characters beyond a single episode and across the entire series. For example, while *Buffy the Vampire Slayer*'s 'Hush' episode dealt with a self-contained episode storyline in which frightening 'gentlemen' in suits arrived in Sunnydale and, in addition to ensuring that Sunnydale citizens lost their capacity to speak, some also lost their hearts – literally. While this story was introduced and concluded within a single episode, the serialised narrative dealing with Buffy and Riley's relationship and the revelation of their respective secrets (Buffy is the Slayer and Riley is an agent of the Initiative) wove its way through numerous episodes, coming to a head, ironically, in the 'Hush' episode that is about silence.

In examples of the last two decades, the episode fragment and the series whole co-exist and interact in ways that suggest more complex neo-baroque relationships, especially when compared to the interaction between fragment and whole that dominated in the 1950s and 1960s versions of the first and second prototypes. Episode and series borders are more readily ruptured, in the process creating a situation that requires that the viewer functions like a puzzle solver or labyrinth traverser: in order to understand the meaning of the whole, it is also necessary to piece together

and understand the relevance of the multiple and divergent story fragments that constitute the whole. For example, consider the convoluted,
multiple storylines that diverge and connect in *Alias*, which centre on
Sydney Bristow, an agent of SD-6, a top-secret division of the CIA, which
turns out not to be a division of the CIA (and the good guys) but of the
Alliance (the bad guys), the discovery of which then convinces Syd to
become a secret agent of the real CIA (under the command of the very
handsome Vaughan), and thus a double agent, which she later discovers her
father (Jack) also is, as was her mother (whom Syd believed was dead, but
who later turned up very much alive), though, as Syd discovers later, was
really working for the bad guys. Or was she? Add to this overall series storyline a combination of single episode storylines and (more frequently)
multiple episode story arcs that rely heavily on cliffhanger tactics, and we
have an extremely dense series of story scenarios that are mind-numbingly
difficult to make sense of if you have not been an avid viewer of the series
from its beginning.

   In addition to the complex seriality that extends across episodes and
seasons within series such as *Alias*, since the 1980s further transformations
have occurred within the fifth prototype that complicate the relationship
and articulation of story fragments and the series whole. Television has
begun to experiment with the serial, and the result has been some creative
scenarios that complicate narrative processes further still. The popular
series *24* (2001–present) is an interesting case in point. The title '24' places
a limitation and goal end point to the show, but the show returns each
season for a further 24 hours. In addition to presenting the multiple storylines that diverge and intersect and which are typical of the fifth prototype,
the variation of the split-screen technique also introduces a new aspect to
the serial. The show does not only reveal its serial story formations in a singular, linear sequence where one story action is followed by the other.
Often, up to four alternate storylines are on screen simultaneously. The
effect of seeing multiple events occurring concurrently, obviously, ampli-
fies the suspense and impels the spectator in his or her desire to ride the
conflict until resolution is ultimately attained, but it also shifts the presentation to a literal multi-linearity – a fact that highlights yet another articulation of neo-baroque polycentric logic, opening up narrative form in ways
that are more indicative of the hypertextual/hypermediated form familiar
to the computer screen.

   The show *Boomtown* (2001–present) experiments with multi-linearity
from an alternate perspective. *Boomtown* implements a storytelling device
that differs to other examples in this prototype. Drawing on elements of
prototype 1, each episode is self-contained in that the focus is on a single

crime (although, aspects of the main characters' lives slip ever so gently across episodes); however, it serialises its structure from *within* the episode: each crime is revisited from the perspectives of a combination of characters. In the fourth episode of season one ('Reelin' in the Years'), for example, the show begins with the arrest of a woman who, it is believed, killed a policeman twenty-six years earlier in a bank robbery. Two of the robbers were shot, one was later arrested, and twenty-six years later, Nora Jean Flannery (real name Sharon Lofton) was apprehended while going for a jog. We witness the arrest, first from the perspective of the patrol officers Ray, then Joel, Fearless and finally the suspect Nora Jean Flannery – each viewpoint being signalled by the inclusion of the characters' names onscreen as their version begins. In the second part of the episode, a series of characters retell their version of the day of the bank robbery twenty-six years earlier when the off-duty cop was killed. The tale begins with Kevin van Horn (who was wrongfully jailed for the murder), then details are added to the story through the perspectives of Andrea (a reporter), Paul (the dead cop's partner), Tom (patrol officer and son of Paul), Victor (the dead cop) and finally Sharon Renée Lofton (the killer), who insists she did not pull the trigger while the visuals show us otherwise. Revealing overtones of the fourth prototype's 'variation on a theme', the variations embodied in the retellings are now played out within the single episode.

Episodes such as those found more recently in the fifth prototype are indicative of a complexity that is driven by a concern with formal experimentation with the narrative possibilities of the series. The neo-baroque aesthetics that Calabrese assigned to pre-1990s television series has become more intense, revealing a dynamism that tests story boundaries to the extreme. When writing in the late 1980s, the five prototypes that Calabrese defined tended to develop from the 1950s in a sequential order from prototype to prototype (with points of co-existence). As has been argued, however, earlier prototypes have returned in the last two decades, revising their previous structural logic by embracing the formal properties of other prototypes, while still adhering to the dominant rules of their own system. Revealing a neo-baroque attitude to space, the co-existence of the prototypes creates greater slippage between previously distinct systems: episode stories continue into other episodes and across series, prototypes merge their rules with those of other prototypes, distinct television shows intersect their storylines with other television shows, and characters from one show traverse their series boundaries by travelling to other television series spaces, sometimes returning home or, sometimes, continuing on new journeys within an alternate narrative reality. All the while, the borders keep stretching as the series and serial continue to redefine their parameters. For

Deleuze, the labyrinthine complexity that characterises baroque form is visualised by the metaphor of the fold, or, rather, endless folds that double over one another in continuous motions. The world of the baroque fold is a world of 'converging series' and each fold expresses only 'one portion of the series' that converges into the next (Deleuze 1993: 50).

The neo-baroque example of the television series reveals a convergence of folds that continue to multiply. Given the increased emphasis on the cross-media development of the stories of shows like *Alias*, *Buffy the Vampire Slayer*, *Law and Order* and *Star Trek* into computer games, novels, comic books, theme-park attractions and fan fiction, the seriality inherent to television will need further revision. Cross-media narrativisations are, in some instances, becoming important disseminators of story information within the franchise as it disperses its form not only across the series of its own medium, but across multiple media. Eco's 'poetics of serial thought' must undergo yet another re-evaluation. But that's another story.

Notes

1. In fact, this cliffhanger ending was given some kind of logical closure. The same could not be said for the 1985 season of *Dallas*, when audiences were thrust into a convoluted narrative serial web the likes of which is yet to be outdone. So confused was this narrative that it has gone down in history as defying the spatio-temporal logic that a shared narrative reality should adhere to. Of course, I refer to the 1984–5 season of *Dallas*: Bobby Ewing had been murdered (and his alter-ego, Patrick Duffy, quit the show). The entire 1985–6 season continued without the popular Bobby, that is, until the final episode when, in the final scene, Pam Ewing, Bobby's wife, woke up and, cut to the bathroom, Bobby was revealed having a shower. As every TV-file knows, the next season began with the revelation that Pam had only *dreamed* that Bobby had died – in fact, she had dreamed the story events of the entire previous season. The only problem with this narrative revelation was that *Dallas* had also been responsible for further extending its narrative universe into another spin-off series in 1979. That series was *Knots Landing* (1979–93), and in the 'Bobby is dead' season of *Dallas*, the characters and storylines of *Knots Landing* had responded to the tragedy as if it were a real event. The narrative repercussions were, in the end, impossible to untangle in order to give them any semblance of an agreed upon reality.
2. To distinguish the current articulation of the baroque from its earlier variation, I opt for Calabrese's preference of the term 'neo-baroque' (Calabrese 1992: 14).
3. Calabrese discusses the five televisual serial prototypes in his chapter 'Rhythm and Repetition', ch. 2 (Calabrese 1992).
4. Classical formal traits have also been acknowledged as features that dominate

the cinema of the classical Hollywood period of c. 1910s–1950s. For Bordwell, Staiger and Thompson, characteristics of this cinema's classic aesthetic norms included a narrative structure that reflected closure through its cyclical nature, which shifts from equilibrium, disequilibrium and narrative conflict, to the re-establishment of equilibrium and a return to a status quo (see Bordwell and Thompson 1993) and (Bordwell et al. 1985).

5. A similar minor revelation of character pasts slips into the episode reality of *CSI*, for example, in the occasional mention made of Catherine Willow's past life as a stripper. Other similar serial narratives emerge but are never permitted to overtake the self-contained episode story.

6. Other such cross-overs occurred between *Ally McBeal* and *The Practice*, *Law and Order: SVU* and *The Practice*, *Boston Public* and *The Practice*. Unlike Dick Wolf's *Law and Order* dramas, David Kelly's productions favour a more overt serial form familiar to the third and fifth prototypes.

7. For example, *The Danny Thomas Show* (1953–65) introduced audiences to *The Andy Griffith Show* (1960–8); *The Beverly Hillbillies* (1962–71) crossed over with *Petticoat Junction* (1963–70), and *Green Acres* (1965–71); *Adam 12* (1968–75) with *Dragnet* (1967–70); *Happy Days* introduced Laverne and Shirley from *Laverne and Shirley*; *The Six Million Dollar Man* (1974–8) and *The Bionic Woman* (1976–8); and *Soap* (1977–81) and *Benson* (1979–86).

8. Calabrese rejects Focillon's evolutionary model of distinct systems, stating instead that the classical and baroque are found throughout the history of art, co-existing with one another, with one system often dominating over the other (Calabrese 1992).

9. *Law and Order: Criminal Intent* also slips out of the fourth and into the third prototype on occasion, particularly in the way the show taunts the viewer with Goren's past and family history.

10. The strategies of the fourth prototype have also become a feature of blockbuster film sequels.

Bibliography

Bordwell, David and Thompson, Kristin (1993), *Film Art: An Introduction*, New York: McGraw-Hill.

Bordwell, David, Staiger, Janet and Thompson, Kristin (1985), *The Classical Hollywood Cinema: Film Style and Mode of Production to 1960*, London: Routledge.

Buci-Glucksman, Christine (1986), *La Folie du voir: de l'esthétique baroque*, Paris: editions Galilée.

Buci-Glucksman, Christine (1994), *Baroque Reason: Aesthetics of Modernity*, London: Sage Publications.

Calabrese, Omar (1992), *Neo-Baroque: A Sign of the Times*, New Jersey: Princeton University Press. (Originally published as *L'Eta Neobarocca*, Editori Laterna 1987.)

Deleuze, Gilles [1988] (1993), *The Fold: Leibniz and the Baroque*, trans. Tom Conley, Minneapolis: University of Minneapolis Press.

Eco, Umberto (1984), *Semiotics and the Philosophy of Language*, London: Macmillan.

Eco, Umberto (1989), *The Open Work*, Cambridge, MA: Harvard University Press. (Chapters 1–6 originally published in 1962.)

Eco, Umberto (1992), 'Foreword', in Omar Calabrese, *Neo-Baroque: A Sign of the Times*, New Jersey: Princeton University Press, pp. vii–x. (Originally published as *L'Eta Neobarocca*, Editori Laterna 1987.)

Focillon, Henri [1934] (1992), *The Life of Forms in Art*, London: Zone Books.

Hagedorn, Roger (1988), 'Technology and Economic Exploitation: The Serial as a Form of Narrative Presentation', *Wide Angle* 10(4), 4–12.

Jameson, Fredric and Masao Miyoshi (1998), 'Notes on Globalization as a Philosophical Issue', in Fredric Jameson and Masao Miyoshi (eds), *The Cultures of Globalization*, Durham and London: Duke University Press, pp. 54–77.

Jay, Martin (1994), *Downcast Eyes: The Denigration of Vision in Twentieth-Century French Thought*, Berkeley: University of California Press.

Ndalianis, Angela (2004), *Neo-Baroque Aesthetics and Contemporary Entertainment*, Cambridge, MA: The MIT Press.

Wyatt, Justin (1994), *High Concept: Movies and Marketing in Hollywood*, Austin: University of Texas Press.

CHAPTER 6

Serial Narrative and Guest Stars: *Ally McBeal*'s Eccentrics

Greg Smith

A prime-time serial narrative elaborates the continuing ebb-and-flow of relations among a core group of characters. Although individual characters may come and go (as the series exhausts its need for them, or as actors move on to other opportunities), the primary group of characters remains fairly stable. By using the network of familiar characters, the makers of the series rely on the emotional power of our connections to those characters, thus enacting the thematic tensions of the series in their most dramatically weighted form. Events on a serial have power because they happen to characters in whom we have invested a considerable amount of time.

But the prime-time serial cannot take care of all of its narrative business by staying solely within the tightly bound world of core characters. The prime-time serial needs guest stars. What narrative function do these guest actors play? *Ally McBeal* provides a case study in dealing with this larger question, demonstrating how such guest appearances provide conflict in ways that the core ensemble cannot. In addition, this essay articulates how *Ally*[1] balances guest stars with recurring characters to make its political argument about eccentricity. By making its case about eccentric behaviour, instead of politically loaded differences such as race, *Ally McBeal* frames its argument in ways that seek to bypass resistances to questions of difference. It marshals our allegiances to long-running serial characters and balances them with the more targeted rhetoric provided by guest stars to create a complex appeal to audience attitudes.

Three Cross-Dressers, Three Strategies

Most dramatic and comic television narratives eventually rely on guest stars to provide conflict.[2] Non-serial dramatic shows (particularly those dealing with police officers, detectives, or lawyers) build the guest perfor-

mance into the basic structure of the series. The outsider creates the conflict in these shows; without him or her there would be no case to solve,
prosecute, or defend. Situation comedies do not necessarily rely so heavily
on the guest appearance. Conflict defines the 'situation' in a sit-com, and
frequently these conflicts come from within the established sit-com
'family.' On *The Cosby Show* one of the children will try to sneak some mis-
behaviour past the Huxtable parents, causing the crisis that the wise
mother and father must solve. But a long-running sit-com must re-
energise itself with fresh characters because eventually the options for conflict among the principal characters are exhausted. Sometimes the answer
for a sit-com is to add another recurring character: a new child on *The
Cosby Show*, a wife for Robert on *Everybody Loves Raymond*. Other sit-
coms enliven the relationships by having guest characters drop by (a
primary character's sister, an old friend from high school), thus giving the
Friends someone new to react to. Because characters in these series essentially return to their initial states at the beginning of each episode, these
non-serial prime-time shows eventually rely on the conflicts provided from
outside the carefully established ensemble.

Daytime serials, with their more laid-back pace, are more likely to rely
entirely on their primary network to provide conflict (Allen 1985). Prime-
time serials, usually airing only once a week to an audience that expects
more rapid narrative progression, demand more plot more often than a
small group of core characters can dependably produce. The sheer quan-
tity of conflict required to keep a prime-time audience interested often
necessitates that a prime-time serial be replenished by guest stars.

Ally McBeal, like other 'professional' serials (such as *ER*, *LA Law*, and
The Practice), uses the structure of the individual case to provide narrative
payoffs for single episodes. The legal case provides a clear binary narrative
event that provides a bit of closure within the serial whole. The accused is
found guilty or not guilty, both in our eyes and in the jury's, thus bringing
to a halt the conflict brought about by the guest star while continuing the
character negotiations within the primary cast. *Ally McBeal*, with its
strong continuing storylines of character development, almost never shows
a case that extends over more than one episode,[3] while *The Practice* (a show
oriented more towards the actual case outcomes, focusing less on the serial
growth of characters) is more likely to use cases that last several episodes.
Each serial must determine the appropriate balance of long-term serial
character growth and short-term narrative payoff to keep its audience's
interest.

Guest stars are useful to a prime-time serial particularly because of
their transitory nature. If a network of serial characters must handle the

continuing ramifications of narrative actions, then the advantage of guest players is that they *don't* have to deal with these consequences. A guest character can create a serious conflict and then depart, thus satisfying the series' need for drama without requiring a full commitment of the show's resources. If an issue is of serious dramatic import to a continuing character, then the serial tends to give those tensions full rein, exploiting our investment in the character over time. Not every dramatic conflict must be played out for a lengthy period, and guest characters can pose issues that are of vital importance to them without burdening the serial with a continuing narrative obligation.

As a way to introduce the relative narrative functions of guest and recurring characters, I will examine three *Ally* characters who all open up similar challenges to the show's articulation of sexuality. By looking at three transgendered characters who exist for different lengths of time on the series, we can better see the kinds of purposes that guests serve.

An individual episode of *Ally* entitled 'Boy to the World' (episode 1: 10) can present a young transvestite (Stephanie, played by Wilson Cruz) in trouble with the law, raising issues about eccentricity/difference without getting fully caught up in issues about homelessness, runaways and prostitution. A guest star's appearance almost necessarily opens up more concerns than can be closed down by a single jury decision within an hour's screen time, and therefore the narrative structure of using guest performers must simplify and shortchange complex issues. Of all the possible themes raised by the plot of 'Boy to the World', the episode activates the meaning that is most central to the show's overall concerns: the notion that eccentricity/difference is seen as 'deviance'. Ally defends Stephanie on her third charge of prostitution, which means that the gentle spirited youth could face prison. Ally befriends the fragile runaway and suggests that they use an insanity defence, arguing that Stephanie's transvestite fetishism is a pathology. Stephanie refuses to choose the practical defence, arguing that she left her home in Ohio because people called her 'sick', and so she doesn't want to label herself a 'freak' in an official court. Stephanie would rather choose prison than to call her behaviour deviant.

Stephanie's poverty and her position as a sex worker provide narrative urgency to her case, but the dialogue emphasises the emotional scars caused by a provincial culture that labels cross-dressing as deviant. The episode itself works hard to make sure that it doesn't argue that impoverished prostitution is some kind of worthy individual lifestyle choice, nor does it argue that transvestitism actually *is* insanity, but instead that it could be used as a strategy to exonerate oneself legally. And yet the show's psychologist agrees that Stephanie is 'messed up', and everyone expresses concern in serious, hushed tones about her plight. The overt signs of Stephanie's 'messed-up' state are her poverty and her illegal actions, though the focus of the dialogue is on her choice to cross-dress, so it's easy to confuse whether the episode condemns her transvestitism or her unemployment as the source of her trouble. In an hour, it's difficult for the show to make sure both that the situation is dire and that transvestitism is not responsible for the direness of those circumstances.

Ally negotiates that the case will be continued without any legal finding for a year, conditional on Stephanie being employed. Ally offers to employ her at her law firm, and she is accepted into the slightly akilter world of Cage and Fish. Here Ally acts as saviour to halt Stephanie's decline, but to do so is to make Stephanie potentially a part of the primary cast. Given the focus of the series on sexual politics in the workplace, it would be difficult for a transvestite office worker to stay in the background for any length of time, placing transgendered sexuality as an unavoidably central issue for the show. Since *Ally* devotes itself primarily to the difficulties of heterosexual romance, this new emphasis would be tangential, and so by the narrative logic of the serial, *Ally McBeal* must excise Stephanie. Although she has been employed, Stephanie returns to the streets where a sexual pickup goes awry, and she is killed violently. Unfortunately, the needs of the serial narrative to remain focused on its thematic core causes *Ally* to rely on one of the oldest conservative narrative strategies for dealing with deviance: killing the character. The core characters are free to move on without her, carrying only the memory of the lesson she taught about the dangerous discourse of deviance.

Consider how *Ally* depicts other transvestite characters and the issue of deviance/tolerance. The show's fourth season introduces a recurring guest character: Cindy McCauliff (Lisa Edelstein), a closeted crossdressing client. When Mark (James LeGros) pursues her romantically, Cindy is both drawn to him and afraid of his reaction when he discovers her 'secret'. Finally she pulls him close to her during a slow dance, thus revealing her penis, and Mark initially recoils in shock. He regroups and declares that he wants to continue to have a romantic relationship with her. This is a remarkable moment in the history of prime-time portrayals of sexuality: an avowedly heterosexual character choosing to stay in a same-sex romantic relationship because he 'can't see [her] as anything other than a woman' (episode 4: 3 'Two's A Crowd'). To Mark, the gender Cindy chooses is more important than her physical sexual characteristics.

Soon afterwards, Mark discovers that he has difficulty following through with his bold declaration. Even normally tolerant John cannot support him, and he recommends that Mark and Cindy visit a therapist who specialises in couples facing 'distinct challenges' in 'getting them to accept each other [and also] gaining acceptance for them as a couple in the society at large'. They visit the therapist's group therapy session along with several other couples: a young man and an elderly woman, an obese woman and a small bald man, a dominatrix and a very prim-looking man, and male Siamese twins (joined at head) with an average-looking woman. Here the episode clearly emphasises the obvious discrepancies between the couples as the camera pans among them, encouraging us to view them as society is wont to do: as a freak show. In this moment of comic spectacle, *Ally* positions us as outsiders judging these incongruous couples, thus duplicating for a moment the politics of othering by reducing these couples to their externally observable differences.

After having built up sympathy for Cindy by providing us with access to her conflicted feelings over a couple of episodes, the camera abruptly turns its harsh gaze on her, grouping her with other 'freaks'. In this moment, we see the potential cost of maintaining this relationship given society's norms because the camera briefly reminds us how easily we would judge such an unusual couple. Cindy flees this group encounter, refusing to accept herself as one of those aberrant persons, which leads to the breakup of her relationship with Mark. Mark's politics lead him toward a bold coupling, but he learns that his romantic feelings cannot go where his well-meaning politics intend for him to go (episode 4: 4 'Without a Net'). By placing our sympathies with Cindy over several episodes, then suddenly othering her as a freak, the show pits the liberal instinct towards tolerance against the personal forces of sexual attraction in order to illuminate the problems posed by difference. This use of a continuing guest character allows for a more subtly nuanced depiction of this tension.

Cindy is one of several characters who have extended stays on the show while they date a principal character. When the firm hires Clare (a former client) to serve as Richard's secretary, it 'promotes' her from a continuing guest role to a central member of the core ensemble, and in so doing it demonstrates yet another argument about the acceptance of difference. Clare is played by Barry Humphries as a variation on his cross-dressing portrayal of Dame Edna Everage. *Ally McBeal* treats Clare as a true oddity: one look at Clare's bizarre appearance is enough to send a narcoleptic minister (Carl Reiner) into unconsciousness (episode 5: 2 'Judge Ling'). This blue-haired, stocky, ebullient, garishly dressed woman quickly demonstrates her tendency to shock people verbally as well as visually. She blurts out inappropriate sexual comments, which eventually leads to her being accused of sexual harassment (she invites one fellow worker to 'share a hot dog under her canopy') (episode 5: 13 'Woman').

Clare's cross-dressing figure could potentially pose some of the same difficulties we noted in 'Boy to the World'. Here again we have an attention-getting transvestite who is hired by the firm, so once again we have the possibility of derailing *Ally*'s focus on heterosexual romance in the workplace. Stephanie is so destabilising that she must be eliminated in one episode; on the other hand, Clare's oral frankness and her eccentric passion for frankfurters is accepted into the oddball-centred world of *Ally McBeal*. The key difference here is that Clare is a *female* character, not a transvestite. The cross-dressing by the actor who plays Clare is never overtly mentioned. Clare is an avowedly heterosexual character who expresses desire for men and pursues them.[4] The fact that the actor playing Clare is a biological man in drag obviously queers the character in ways that set up a host of sly, winking jokes. For instance, just before Clare begins to lip-synch for Nelle singing 'I'm a Woman' (Clare's self-admitted theme song), Elaine looks downward at Clare and advises her to 'keep it tucked in', much to Clare's astonishment (episode 5:13 'Woman').

We should acknowledge that Clare represents a milestone in the history of transgendered imagery: a transvestite actor playing a 'real woman' in a prime-time ensemble. Certainly this achievement is a mixed bag. Unlike most previous examples of cross-dressing, Clare's narrative purpose cannot be simply reduced to her transvestitism (by comparison, we get very little information about recurring character Cindy McCauliff except for her transvestitism). Clare avoids television's tendency to present drag as being funny in and of itself, but she is the butt of more sly jokes. She also becomes a figure of 'noble othering', dispensing wise advice from her liminal position, serving a similar function at times to the Wise Old Black Person or the Sage Indian Shaman stereotypes. Because Clare joins the ensemble as a continuing principal cast member, the depiction of tolerance here can be much more fully elaborated than in Cindy's case (in which tolerance is raised as a political option, only to be closed down by romantic difficulties) or Stephanie's example (where the destabilising transvestitism must be quickly expunged). A single-episode guest raises more issues about tolerance than can be dealt with fully. If a character has a more extended stay on the show, the serial can weave together Othering moments with empathic appeals. If an eccentric becomes part of the primary cast, then a certain amount of tolerance becomes necessary, though (as we see in Clare's case) she can be made liminal through a variety of strategies. In the example provided by transvestite characters, *Ally McBeal* shows how the serial can use the narrative capabilities of single guest appearances, continuing guest roles and primary characters to raise a variety of issues about tolerance.

Physical Difference and the Trade-offs of 'Eccentricity'

This strategy of overtly disavowing Dame Edna's cross-dressing gives us hints about the way that *Ally McBeal* treats difference. One central focus for the show is the status of the eccentric in modern society. Positioning the show as being about 'eccentricity' instead of a more specific category such as 'race' is a clear ploy to separate the issue of difference from its current political baggage. Although there still remains much work to be done in achieving real world racial tolerance, on television the topic of accepting racial difference has been repeatedly portrayed by the vaguely feel-good politics of mainstream media. Blatantly racist characters in current-day media are hissable, melodramatic villains, making it difficult to portray the politics of tolerance to hip contemporary audiences without preachiness, and therefore fictional media present many of their arguments about difference in disguised form (horror films detail invasions by 'aliens', for instance, or superheroes discuss tolerance for 'mutants'). In a media era that constantly needs new material to fill 500 channels, the danger is that arguments for tolerance will feel so sanctimoniously familiar that they will be heard as yesterday's news.

Ally McBeal chooses to bypass the more familiar frames for discussing difference by creating a world where such differences are not significant. *Ally* is admittedly a fantasy in which race does not exist.[5] Renee's status as a black woman never affects her professional activities, nor are black judge Seymour Walsh's (Albert Hall) decisions ever questioned on racial grounds. Although Ling's vilification owes much to the history of the Dragon Lady stereotype in Asian imagery (Tajima 1989; Hagedorn 1994), again the racial difference poses no overt problems when she and Richard are in a relationship.[6] In a series that looks to explore the difficulties of modern romantic relationships, race would seem to be an obvious source of conflict, and its absence is conspicuous on the show (Patton 2001: 229–60).

This absence is partly explainable in terms of the show's focus. By narrowing its case law and its characters' personal crises to those dealing with our changing expectations about what men and women are, *Ally McBeal* mines its primary material in remarkably rich fashion (it is almost impossible to envision a sexual harassment scenario that has not been dealt with during the five seasons of the show). Since it would be difficult to deal with both race *and* gender in this level of detail, one could argue that *Ally* should not be expected to handle racial difference with

the same aplomb that it does gender.[7] It is a matter of necessarily choosing an emphasis.

This is not to say that *Ally*'s strategy of ignoring race is apolitical, nor
is its politics uninformed. It is an extension of an earlier tactic from *LA
Law*, David Kelley's first series. When I watched *LA Law* I recall being
struck by the appearance of a black judge whose race on the bench was
not mentioned as significant to the plot. Upon further consideration, I
realised that the obvious point being made was that we should not expect
that a black character necessarily exists only to address black issues. *LA
Law* consistently placed black judges on its fictional benches until eventually I stopped mentally labelling them as 'black judges' and simply
thought of them as 'judges'. The conspicuous absence of the mention of
race was, in this particular instance, a powerful political tool to acclimat-
ise the viewer to accept African-Americans in a position of judicial
power.

Politics necessarily involves matching particular tactics to the needs of a
specific time and place. There are no global strategies that apply equally
well to all scenarios: a strategy that was effective in the 1980s might not work
in the year 2000. And so one could certainly argue that the Kelley tactic of
not naming race has lost its effectiveness by the time *Ally McBeal* airs. And
yet *Ally McBeal* attempts a more elaborated version of Kelley's earlier argument for tolerance. Instead of displacing questions of race on to 'aliens' or
'mutants', *Ally* reframes the question as being about 'eccentricity'.

'Eccentricity' is a more general notion allowing us to discuss a broader
range of people than the more concrete categories of 'race' or 'sexual orientation', just as the cooler term 'difference' allows academics to bypass
the particularities of colour to discuss broader patterns of discrimination.
On *Ally* people are discriminated against because they don't fit into set
business norms or established romantic expectations. Sometimes these
distinctions are based on bodies (obesity, baldness, or simply being 'funny
looking'); sometimes they are behavioural (the desire to fly with wings, a
foot fetish); at other times they are concerned with identity politics
(homelessness, dwarfism). The issues are the same as the romantic tolerance of *Guess Who's Coming to Dinner* (Kramer 1967) or the workplace discrimination of *Philadelphia* (Demme 1993), but reframing these issues as
eccentricity can help a jaded audience that has seen one too many sancti-
monious pleas for tolerance, encouraging them to revisit the issues with
fresh perspective.

Certainly there are dangers in the political choice of changing race or
difference into 'eccentricity'. 'Eccentricity' can make social difference seem
freely chosen, as if an individual chose to be fat or to blurt uncontrollably due

to Tourette's syndrome, and thus eccentricity at times threatens to reduce identity to the less politically potent concept of 'lifestyle' (as postfeminists have noted about the current de-fanging of feminist politics in the media) (Dow 1996; Faludi 1992; Press 1991; Lotz 2001). Eccentricity also can tend towards 'cuteness' as opposed to the more disturbing barriers of difference. In addition, what eccentricity gains in generality, it loses in specificity, and many alternative voices ground their challenge to mainstream media silences by rooting their expression in the particularity of individual experiences of discrimination. Again, no political tactic is one-size-fits-all; I merely wish to acknowledge the complex set of advantages and disadvantages of *Ally*'s eccentricity strategy.

We can clearly see the advantages and limitations of the eccentricity strategy by examining guest characters who are physically Othered. In many of the guest roles, the problem that brings discrimination has to do with physical appearance. In one particular case, the legal claim is clearly race presented in a disguised version; a woman whose skin has permanently turned orange sues because she is discharged from her job, and Billy argues before the court, drawing on racial discrimination laws to further his case (episode 2: 7 'Happy Trails'). In other cases, however, the guest's physical appearance causes more complicated claims. In 'The Oddball Parade' (episode 3: 14), a graphic design firm becomes successful partly because of the work of a set of 'weird'-looking employees: a man who claps and repeats words compulsively, an obese woman, a transvestite and a man whose face 'scares children'. When the company becomes more successful and moves to an open studio where the employees can be seen by clients, the owner fires these long-time employees because they were not 'commensurate with the image' of the firm. In such cases, the customers can be blamed for the firing:

John:	Don't you consider it a prejudice to judge somebody on looks?
President:	I wasn't doing it. The clients were.
John:	How do you not foster that bigotry when you respond to it in this way? Who cares! Eccentricity could be a selling point. It goes with distinction, individualism.
President:	Is that what I'm supposed to say? Look at the distinctive defensive tackle wearing a dress? . . . Do you have any idea how hard it is to survive in today's market? . . . Clients make quick decisions. They choose companies that instill them with confidence. These four people, they couldn't do it, as wonderful as they are, and as president of my company I had a responsibility . . . It isn't always about product; it's about selling. That's business: selling, selling, selling. (Episode 3: 14 'The Oddball Parade')

If business depends on the customer's trust in the company's employees, then a whole host of personal factors may become relevant to their jobs.

Blaming the customer's judgments for the company's hiring and firing is an old standby for racial discrimination, and in these cases *Ally* extends the logic of discriminatory arguments so that we may see them still at work in the age of the kinder, gentler corporation. The logical extension of practices that blend business and appearance is to consider the conflict between personal expression and job performance. *Ally* raises the argument that a modern business employs the worker's looks as well as his or her physical or mental labour, just as Arlie Hochschild has argued that certain jobs pay for 'emotion work'.[8] *Ally* forces us to recognise the impasse between the politics of liberal acceptance and the blurring of product and image, although most modern businesses pledge overt loyalty to both principles without acknowledging any potential conflicts.

These *Ally* cases about tolerating eccentric appearance in the workplace are easier for audiences to accept because we understand the legal precedents for enforcing official, public tolerance. *Ally* pushes the issue further, however, when it interrogates whether individuals should necessarily accept eccentrics as lovers. In these episodes, guest stars pose a more personal question about whether the politics of tolerance extends from the public sphere of employment to the more private concern of sex and romance.

In one episode a woman meets a man through an online dating service, and she falls in love with him during their phone conversations, stating that physical appearance did not matter to her. When she finally meets him in person, she discovers to her surprise that he is a dwarf, and she breaks off the relationship, causing him to sue for emotional damages. This improbably forced setup allows *Ally* to concentrate purely on the issue of the romantic partner's height. Like Stephanie (the tragic transvestite discussed earlier), the dwarf risks a trial in hopes that the official voice of the court will declare that his difference does not make him a 'freak' (episode 4: 18 'The Obstacle Course').

An episode such as this one is narratively set up to ally our sympathies with the rejected man, hoping that he will find love or at least justice. *Ally McBeal* acknowledges that extending one's romantic love to someone you don't find attractive is more easily done in the movies and on television than in real life. In an episode when an obese man breaks off his engagement to perform an Ally-like act of impetuous romanticism and ask Ally if she would date him, she refuses him purely on grounds of lack of attraction, though she initially denies this reason:

Renée: Why did you automatically dismiss the idea of dating him?
Ally: Didn't think he was my type.
Renée: You ruled him out instantly because of looks.
Ally: No, I knew he was in questionable health. It isn't that simple. A person gets a vision of how a date might go and I couldn't picture it. [Ally immediately imagines getting in a car. The overweight man gets in the other side, and the car tips over on to its side.]
Renée: Sad thing is, in a movie we'd both be rooting for the gal to date the guy. (Episode 1: 6 'The Promise')

The show acknowledges the power of popular narrative to encourage us to extend our sympathies towards the less attractive romantic underdog, but it simultaneously admits that this choice is easier to make from the comfort of a cinema seat or a living-room recliner. Such narratives typically depend on giving the underdog a faux unattractiveness, making minor cosmetic alterations (such as wearing glasses) on a glamorous Hollywood star. Such facile obstacles disappear, thus rewarding the wise lover for seeing deeply and transforming the person through a loving choice. By using the same narrative logic that it uses to champion acceptance of eccentricity in the workplace, *Ally* makes us acknowledge that we should be open to a full range of romantic possibilities, but it does not let us live comfortably with that romantic utopia. On *Ally* the unattractive guest performer does not become a more easily loved beautiful swan. The fat man and the dwarf, however sympathetic, remain the same physically, thus forcing Ally and others to acknowledge the awkward difference between their political acceptance and their romantic inclinations. A well-intentioned left-leaning person may argue for acceptance for all in the workplace but still hold very specific prejudices about potential lovers, according to *Ally*. In an era of touchy-feely narratives of acceptance, *Ally* reminds us that all acceptances are not equally easy.

The potential dangers here are myriad for reasserting old social prejudices, and *Ally McBeal* certainly has multiple difficulties in presenting its guest weirdos. First of all, the show pokes vicious fun at the oddballs, forcing us to make harsh external judgements that would seem to undermine its attempt to gain the viewer's tolerance. By making a visual spectacle of its guest eccentrics, *Ally* can potentially reiterate long-standing social judgements against certain kinds of bodies. The show sometimes attempts to bypass our histories of prejudice by presenting novel physical or behavioural oddities (the orange-skinned woman, for example, or a man who hits happy people) (episode 1: 23 'These Are The Days'). This allows us to examine the notion of eccentricity with a certain level of abstraction, since we are not accustomed to thinking about these particular characteristics. But *Ally* also deals with judgements about more familiar identity politics, including the previously mentioned attention to transvestitism. Perhaps most importantly, given the public controversy about actress Calista Flockhart's thinness, the show returns several times to images of over-weight people. The lawyers talk an overweight, bald millionaire client into getting a prenuptial agreement before he marries an attractive younger woman, and the man's personal history repeats the parental warning heard in the case of the online dwarf. The obese man says, 'When I was seven my mother put me on a diet, said if you're fat no girl would ever love you' (episode 4: 17 'The Pursuit of Unhappiness'). *Ally* temporarily lends us the perspective of someone who has received such harsh social judgements, making sure that the person has compensating virtues that should theoret-ically outweigh his body issues.

And yet weight creates a seemingly unassailable barrier to the supreme goal on *Ally McBeal*: finding one's 'soulmate'. In a previously mentioned episode, a fat man (Harry Pippen, played by Jay Leggett) on the verge of marrying an obese woman asks Ally for advice because his fiancée does not inspire his romantic ardour. After Ally advises him to follow his passion, he breaks off the impending wedding, causing the large jilted bride to confront Ally: 'People like me and Harry don't get the partners of our dreams. Sometimes when you hold out for everything you end up with nothing. Remember that the next time a fat man asks you for advice' (episode 1: 6 'The Promise'). Ally concurs and changes her advice to the large man, encouraging him to settle for companionship. For the first time, Ally advises someone to drop out of the quest for a soulmate, arguing in essence that a separate system exists for those not fortunate enough to be within the con-ventional realm of attractiveness. *Ally* forces us to examine the claims of popular culture that 'love is all around' and confronts us with the idea that romance is not conducted on equal grounds. Unfortunately, it does so by labelling fat as the quintessential example of an admittedly unwarranted but still powerful limitation on achieving one's romantic dreams.[9]

The more widely held the difference depicted (such as being over-weight) on *Ally McBeal* is, the more difficult the issue is to handle within the fantastic world the characters inhabit. *Ally* simply does not know what to do with a serious real world problem like homelessness. Homeless guest characters appear on *Ally* to disturb her comfortable class position through anti-social action, but these disturbances are always made safe by revealing that the character is not truly a street person. As Ally passes one such beggar, he lashes out:

For God's sake don't look at me, corporate hollowed-out . . . Walk by me like I don't exist. I exist, lady! You don't have to give me change, you can say no,

but I exist! I am not beneath an answer . . . Rich single lonely heart lawyer
. . . Bet this is the longest conversation you've had with someone not dressed
in Prada or Calvin Klein. (Episode 3: 9 'Out in the Cold')

Later we discover that this 'street person' who pegs Ally so ruthlessly is
really an insurance agent masquerading in order to collect information
about homelessness in America. Just as Hollywood tends to cheat in its
portrayal of physical unattractiveness, *Ally McBeal* cheats in the way it
depicts homelessness. One side effect of emphasising 'eccentricity' over
'difference' is that real world problems can become trivialised.[10] The show
overall seeks to create a more generalised argument for tolerance, but in so
doing, it trades away the raw particularity of familiar, threatening difference such as homelessness.[11]

It is not surprising, therefore, that one of *Ally*'s preferred eccentricities
is dwarfism (or at least characters who function as dwarves). One recurring 'little person' on *Ally McBeal* is lawyer Oren Koolie, a precocious ten-
year-old with a hormone deficiency (played by 3' 2" Josh Evans). Koolie
uses his short stature to legal advantage, deploying tantrums to elicit
larger settlement offers, and thus he is part of a continuing tradition of
guest characters on *Ally* who use their obvious difference to their professional advantage. 'Little people' are relatively safe eccentrics for *Ally* to
portray, since the difference dwarves pose is obvious and yet clearly not
due to any potentially blamable action on the individual's part. They exist
in real life (unlike, say, orange women) but in such small numbers that they
are rarely seen in broad society (unlike the obese or the homeless), making
it easier for them to serve as the butt of politically incorrect physical
humour. Dwarves on the show convey a dependable sense of strangeness
with little of the potential fallout of portraying more politically powerful
minorities.

Another byproduct of the emphasis on 'eccentricity' is that it opens the
category of difference to be used by the dominant: heterosexual white
people. Sectors of white (male) America have voiced well-publicised protests about the 'preferential treatment' given to minorities. This 'backlash'
against affirmative action and other civil rights mechanisms recognises the
rhetorical power of claiming the status of 'victim' and bemoans the white
inability to use the same moral claims to advance their own cause (Faludi
1992). By framing its argument in terms of 'eccentricity', *Ally McBeal*
widens the category of the oppressed to include an enormous range of
unusual appearances/behaviours, including people who sweat profusely,
who are inappropriately happy, or who have foot fetishes (episodes 1: 19,
2: 17 and 4: 17).

In almost every case, the eccentrics who guest star on *Ally McBeal* are white.[12] The political liabilities of the eccentricity strategy here are clear: by extending a primary tool of the subordinate group for use by the dominant, the show potentially evacuates the political effectivity of discussing actual differences. By making the prejudices against transvestites, the homeless and sweaty people appear to be interchangeable, the show lumps together sexual mores, economic/class oppression and social distaste as if they were all the same thing. In helping us to see that the battle for tolerance is not solely about race, class, gender and sexual orientation, *Ally McBeal* risks blindness to the very categories of identity that started the discussion of tolerance.

Guest Delusionals

Eccentricity is a perennial favourite subject of David Kelley's, one he has pursued on other television series, thus allowing us to distinguish different strategies for using eccentric characters. *Picket Fences*, for instance, depicted a small town full of eccentrics (similar to *Twin Peaks* and *Northern Exposure*).[13] While *Twin Peaks* extended David Lynch's uncovering of the horrific underbelly of the placid image of the small town, *Picket Fences* (more like Joshua Brand's and John Falsey's *Northern Exposure)* gave us a more benign, whimsical version of rural oddballs. To do so, both *Picket Fences* and *Northern Exposure* use a time-honoured strategy of placing a 'normal' couple at the centre of the drama, thus providing audiences with an emissary into this odd community. We can view the community weirdos in *Picket Fences* from the perspective of the most 'normal' persons in the cast (the ostensible stars of the show), the town sheriff and doctor (Jimmy and Jill Brock, played by Tom Skerritt and Kathy Baker). While this tactic has its advantages (the normal couple can model for us the correct tolerant attitude for accepting unusual behaviour), it also has its disadvantages. By keeping the 'normal' couple central and the eccentrics at the margins, *Picket Fences* makes the oddballs the object of our gaze without having to take on their perspective.

Ally McBeal takes a bolder step because it makes an eccentric the centrepiece of the show. The series asks us to take on a self-doubting, hallucinatory woman as our primary locus of identification instead of the 'normal' people (Billy and Georgia), who are tangential. Being forced to take on the perspective of an overtly delusional character could be frighteningly off-putting, given the norms of mainstream media. In addition, unlike most serials and ensemble dramas, *Ally McBeal* is primarily concerned with its protagonist (as the title would indicate), and thus this accentuates the difficulty of having a central eccentric. *Ally* makes little attempt to present a realistic world, but instead bends its construction around its protagonist's perspective.

Part of *Ally*'s argument about tolerating eccentricity, therefore, depends on placing an oddball as its protagonist. But how can the serial make her perspective seem more reasonable and less off centre? One way is through judicious deployment of guest stars. One of the major purposes of the guest character on *Ally McBeal* is to depict someone even more eccentric than *Ally* is. Over time Ally's perspective begins to look more balanced, not because she alters her attitudes towards romance or towards fantasy but because she seems sane by comparison.

Guests can show us a road that Ally has not taken; they can depict the consequences of more radical stances than Ally's, just as recurring characters do on the show (Richard, for example, embodies Ally's greed for money and professional status, while Elaine gives fuller rein to Ally's sexuality). As John notes, the primary lawyer characters remain safely within the boundaries of more appropriate behaviour, leaving the guest stars to venture further into uncharted territory: 'We look at [our eccentric clients], and we think, "How pathetic." Well, maybe we're the pathetic ones. They're out walking planks; we stay tucked inside ready to represent them when they fall' (episode 2: 18 'Those Lips, That Hand'). Because of their brief tenure on the show, guests may push these pathetic/admirable/outlandish tendencies further because they do not have to gain continuing sympathy on other episodes, as recurring characters do. Guest stars provide the basic narrative structures that make Ally's eccentricity seem more acceptable over time.

In the previous section we mostly examined guest characters whose physical appearance makes them stand out, but *Ally* presents an even larger range of characters whose mental stability is in question. This provides a useful context for us to judge our central character, who herself is prone towards hallucinations and stubbornly held delusions. Rather than tracing a long character arc in which its protagonist slowly grows out of her dysfunctions, *Ally McBeal* depicts a woman who refuses to give up her most outrageously eccentric qualities, even when they threaten her professional career.

Early in the first season, Ally is hauled before a disciplinary board that questions her sanity after she gets into a fight in a supermarket over a can of potato chips. As the legal panel discusses Ally's case, more and more odd behaviours come into question. When Billy accuses Ally of being 'off balance', she defiantly snaps back, 'Who wants to be balanced? Balanced is overrated!' (episode 1: 5 'One Hundred Tears Away'). Ally even clings

to her most apparently pathological quality: her tendency to see hallucinations of pop singers, dancing babies and others. When an imaginary Al
Green begins to intrude into her work, causing Ally to confuse reality with
fantasy, she begins to consider taking medication to control her visions,
but she decides against it. 'One of the reasons I don't try to control [my
hallucinations] is because I like it. It's magical. I feel nourished by them
spiritually, emotionally' (episode 3: 3 'Seeing Green'). Instead of taking
advantage of the possibility for character growth through the course of a
serial narrative, Ally remains unrepentantly committed to the very qualities that would initially seem to be her greatest faults. The series pins
much of its hopes for reclaiming Ally's 'normalcy' not in her own personal
evolution but in the parade of seemingly more mentally unbalanced guest
performers.

Since comparisons are necessarily relative, if *Ally* populates its world
with characters more delusional than its protagonist, it can make her seem
more acceptably mainstream. Such characters tend to embody a particular
aspect of Ally's mental make-up, showing us the logical conclusion of each
individual eccentricity. For instance, we noted that the world of *Ally
McBeal* is warped around its protagonist's idiosyncratic sensibility, but
what if the law firm literally organised itself around her hallucinations
instead of Ally venturing alone into the realms of fantasy? *Ally McBeal*
provides an instructive comparison in a charismatic senior citizen named
Marty Brigg (Orson Bean), whose elaborate fantasies about pygmy hunts
both terrorise and delight the inhabitants of a nursing home. At first it
appears that he spins his stories as a means of enlivening the institutional
dreariness. He therefore refuses to admit publicly that he fabricates these
tales: 'If [the other residents] heard me deny, there'd be no game to go
along with. They need me to believe. I'm the one who delivers them to that
other world' (episode 3: 12 'In Search of Pygmies'). Eventually, however,
it becomes apparent that he actually believes in and sees the pygmies,
causing him to be thrown out of the home because of the chaos he causes.
Ling (who befriends him) offers him a place to live, but just as *Ally McBeal*
could not handle the addition of Stephanie (an unstable young transvestite
runaway) to the firm's staff, the show has no place for a live-in character
who is more hallucinatory than Ally. The narrative, therefore, is forced to
kill off this particular guest.

This episode causes us to consider the possibility that Ally's fantasies
serve to enliven the potential tedium of the law firm, just as Brigg's do for
the nursing home. Furthermore, Ally's dogged belief in her romantic day-
dreams makes it possible for others in the office (and, by extension, in the
audience) to believe in romance as partly or fully as they/we can. Brigg,

however, shows us what a workplace would be like if it were organised around fantasies. By leading his fellow patients on pygmy hunts, he becomes a destabilising force that must be excised, and this shows us what might happen to Cage and Fish if that workplace more fully embraced her hallucinations.

The focus of these legal arguments is less on the actual client's plight and more on the relevance of the client's circumstances to Ally and company. When Ally defends a man so in love with his terminally ill wife that he chopped her hand off as a keepsake, *Ally McBeal* seeks to redeem the impulse behind perhaps the most outrageous example of eccentric behaviour on the show. Ally does not lend a token defence for her client, but instead she embraces his rationale, championing him as an instructively dedicated believer in passion. She attacks Renée (the prosecutor on the case) for not being open enough to see the lesson posed by the defendant's outlandish act: 'You're so jaded that you can't even conceive of the idea that someone might be that madly in love.' Renée retorts, 'Only you can interpret mutilation as love.' When Ally makes her closing argument, she barely even mentions the case, focusing attention instead on the impact of the case's issues on her own life. She answers Renée's charge that Ally is a 'hopeless' romantic:

> Sometimes I think hope is the only thing I've got going. The thing that I hope for most, I'm embarrassed to admit, is emotional dependence. Probably why my friends think I'm crazy. Who would actually want that kind of weakness? But I do. I want to meet fall in love with, and be with somebody, that I can't live without. I envy a little what [the defendant] had. Of course it isn't normal what he did. I could never see myself doing something like that, as I'm sure nor could you. As for the love that made him do it, I pray that some day I'll know some of that madness. The D.A. can't make room for the possibility that love can be this powerful, and that makes her a little hopeless. We all want to be madly in love, don't we? He was, and I suspect still is. (Episode 2: 18 'Those Lips, That Hand')

Ally clearly distances herself from the particularity of the client's eccentric act, liberating the issues raised by the case from their origins. Again, the importance here is not on the eccentric act itself but on the rhetorical argument embodied in the guest delusional's act.

The legal system asks jurors to perform a balancing act. On the one hand, the court must abstract the details of a case and judge the potential precedent-setting impact of its decision on future court cases. On the other, it must examine the particularity of the case, determining the appropriate punishment for the specific circumstances. *Ally McBeal* leans towards the abstracting function. By positioning its guest characters as 'eccentric' (and not necessarily clear-cut members of legally protected categories), it asks us to extend the comfortable notion of tolerance to a broader set of less comfortable behaviours and appearances, thus re-engaging our jaded sensibilities with the difficulties of tolerating Others. While arguing for broader tolerance of its guest eccentrics, *Ally* simultaneously asks us to look past them to examine the possible impact of these characters' choices on the principal characters' lives.

The structure of a non-serial series encourages lead characters to 'learn lessons' from the guest star's situation, but then we return in the next episode to the same basic configuration of main characters as if no learning had taken place. This structure trivialises the moral assertion of the individual episode, creating a Sisyphean narrative trek for the primary characters. The serial, however, allows characters to change across time, but it cannot alter its network of characters so radically that the show loses the appeal that first attracted viewers.

Ally's negotiation of these complexities is distinctive. The central character holds steadfastly to her core beliefs (e.g., romantic love), even when those beliefs are so eccentric as to appear pathological (e.g., the positive value of fantasy). *Ally McBeal* asks for a serial change in the viewer's attitudes, encouraging us to consider the pros and cons of accepting eccentricity in a variety of personal and professional arenas. Both guest and recurring characters share the load in encouraging us to make rhetorical comparisons to the protagonist, and over time we are asked to endorse Ally's peculiar way of being in the world as a better option than the ones provided by other eccentrics. The show does not demonstrate Ally changing over time as much as it asks *us* to revisit our judgements of her in light of the new contexts provided by a series of guest characters.

Ally McBeal provides a case study in the intricate ways that a prime-time serial narrative can weave together a complicated political argument out of the strands provided by guest stars, recurring characters and series regulars. Changing the politically loaded concept of difference into a potentially more acceptable notion of eccentricity is only possible through deploying guest stars. *Ally* is distinctive among prime-time serials because it does not change its protagonist's central values (thus relying on the serial's tendency for character growth); instead it normalises her by parading a series of even odder characters through its plot-lines. Guest stars are necessary to generate the conflicts required in a prime-time serial; paying attention to the way those characters are used is necessary to understand the construction of the show's political argument.

Notes

1. Throughout this essay, I will use '*Ally*' as shorthand for the television series and 'Ally' (without italics) to refer to the titular character played by Calista Flockhart.
2. Horace Newcomb notes that *Bonanza*'s drama mostly depended on the conflicts provided by those who entered the Cartwrights' lives (Newcomb 1987: 617). Fred E. H. Schroeder argues that the guest villain is the key to serial television (Schroeder 1976: 270–1).
3. The exceptions are the cross-over episodes between *Ally* and *The Practice* on 27 April 1998 and the case in which Jenny makes a nuisance suit against the phone companies at the beginning of season five. Thus season five begins with two narrative tasks that *Ally* never tried before: a lengthy case and the introduction of four entirely new recurring characters (Jenny, Glenn, Raymond and Coretta).
4. Clare becomes engaged to Jerome, played by folk singer Loudon Wainwright, who in real life is father to Rufus Wainwright, an openly gay musician (episode 5:17 'Love is All Around').
5. Series creator David E. Kelley said, 'We are a consciously colorblind show. In the history of the show, we have never addressed race. The reason is simple. In my naive dream, I wish that the world could be like this. Since Ally lives in a fanciful and whimsical world, there is not going to be any racial differences or tensions. All people are one under the sun' (Braxton 1999).
6. For an overview of Asian stereotyping in mainstream film, see Xing (1998: 53–86), Marchetti (1993), and Bernstein and Studlar (1997).
7. In several episodes, *Ally* does examine class, but this distinction serves largely as a barrier to romantic relationships, as would be expected in this series. Ally's difficulties with Victor (Jon Bon Jovi) have much to do with the difference between their jobs (lawyer vs. plumber), and John and Nelle's relationship ends largely because he discovers her unapologetic class snobbery.
8. Arlie Russell Hochschild, *The Managed Heart: Commercialization of Human Feeling*, Berkeley: University of California Press, 1983.
9. For an interesting take on the cultural meanings of fat, see Kipnis (1996).
10. Examples in the intentionally outrageous dialogue are easy to find, such as Ally saying, 'Sometimes I'm tempted to become a street person, cut off from society, but then I wouldn't get to wear my outfits' (episode 1: 5 'One Hundred Tears Away').
11. Similarly, scholars have argued that third-wave feminism (or postfeminism) softens the political edge of feminist politics by reducing feminist aims to a 'lifestyle' that women are free to choose or not.
12. In the case in which graphic artists sue for being fired because of their unusual appearances, one (a linebacker-sized cross-dresser) is black (episode 3: 14 'The Oddball Parade'). We briefly see a black bride appear before Judge Ling

to complain that her 'perfect' wedding was ruined by an ex-boyfriend who objected during the ceremony, leaving her 'damaged' (episode 4: 18 'The Obstacle Course').
13. For a fuller discussion of *Picket Fences*, see Robert J. Thompson (1996). For more on *Northern Exposure*, see Williams (1994).

Bibliography

Allen, Robert C. (1985), *Speaking of Soap Opera*, Chapel Hill: University of North Carolina Press.

Bernstein, Matthew and Studlar, Gaylyn (1997), *Visions of the East: Orientalism in Film*, New Brunswick: Rutgers University Press.

Braxton, Greg (1999), 'Colorblind or Just Plain Blind?', *The Los Angeles Times*, 9 February, Fl.

Dow, Bonnie (1996), *Prime-Time Feminism: Television, Media Culture, and the Women's Movement since 1970*, Chapel Hill: University of North Carolina Press.

Faludi, Susan (1992), *Backlash: The Undeclared War against Women*, London: Vintage.

Hagedorn, Jessica (1994), 'Asian Women in Film: No Joy, No Luck', Ms. 4(4), January/February, 74–9.

Hochschild, Arlie Russell (1983), *The Managed Heart: Commercialization of Human Feeling*, Berkeley: University of California Press.

Kipnis, Laura (1996), *Bound and Gagged: Pornography and the Politics of Fantasy in America*, New York: Grove.

Lotz, Amanda D. (2001), 'Postfeminist Television Criticism: Rehabilitating Critical Terms and Identifying Postfeminist Attributes', *Feminist Media Studies* 1.1, 105–21.

Marchetti, Gina (1993), *Romance and the Yellow Peril: Race, Sex, and Discursive Hollywood Strategies in Hollywood Fiction*, Berkeley: University of California Press.

Newcomb, Horace (1987), 'Toward a Television Aesthetic', in Horace Newcomb (ed.), *Television: The Critical View*, 4th edn, New York: Oxford University Press.

Patton, Tracey Owens (2001), 'Ally McBeal and her Homies: The Reification of White Stereotypes of the Other', *Journal of Black Studies*, 32(2) November, 229–72.

Press, Andrea (1991), *Women Watching Television: Gender, Class, and Generation in the American Television Experience*, Philadelphia: University of Pennsylvania Press.

Schroeder, Fred E. H. (1976), 'Video Aesthetics and Serial Art', in Horace Newcomb (ed.), *Television: The Critical View*, 1st edn, New York: Oxford University Press, pp. 260–72.

Tajima, Renée (1989), 'Lotus Blossoms Don't Bleed: Images of Asian Women', in Diane Yen-Mei Wong and Emilya Chchapero (eds), *Making Waves: An*

Anthology of Writings by and about Asian American Women, Boston: Beacon, pp. 308–18.

Thompson, Robert J. (1996), *Television's Second Golden Age: From 'Hill Street Blues' to 'ER'*, Syracuse: Syracuse University Press.

Williams, Betsy (1994), '"North to the Future": *Northern Exposure* and Quality Television', in Horace Newcomb (ed.) *Television: The Critical View*, 5th edn, New York: Oxford, pp. 141–54.

Xing, Jun (1998), 'Cinematic Asian Representation', in *Asian America through the Lens: History, Representations, and Identity*, Walnut Creek, CA: Altamira Press.

CHAPTER 7

The Representation of Youth and the Twenty-Something Serial

Sarah Cardwell

In a sense, the underlying purpose of this chapter is to posit a television category or genre that is not yet officially recognised: the twenty-something
serial. This will be achieved through exploring the connections and developments visible in three of its most notable examples: *This Life* (BBC2,
1996–7), *Queer as Folk* (Ch4, 1999–2000) and *Teachers* (Ch4, 2001–present).
I shall argue that the twenty-something drama is one that can be defined by
its possessing a combination of textual features – thematic, stylistic and
tonal – as well as by its intended and actual audience of 'twenty-somethings'. Interestingly, these programmes seem to address not just a twenty-
something audience but a particular generation of them: Generation X.
Beginning in the mid-1990s with *This Life*, and moving through *Queer as
Folk* to the recent *Teachers*, one can sense formal developments and related
shifts in tone. Such changes suggest not just the growth of the genre but also
a maturing audience – one whose average age mirrors that of the central
characters (in their mid-twenties in *This Life*, and crossing over the significant boundary into 'thirty-somethings' in *Teachers*).

Very little has been written about these serials, and even less about the
notion of a twenty-something serial. Karen Lury's recent study of 'youth
television' (2001) is concerned with television targeted at 'Generation X'
(born in the late 1960s and early 1970s), broadcast between 1987 to 1995.
This essay can therefore be seen as picking up the trail where Lury leaves off,
in the mid-1990s, and considers the television serial dramas pitched explicitly and emphatically at that same generation, who were reaching their mid-
twenties by this time. Whilst there has been considerable work undertaken
from a sociological perspective on youth audiences and the media, young
adults in their twenties are ordinarily regarded as part of the adult audience
and not considered separately. This is a reasonable assumption; however, in
contemporary society, those in their twenties face particular experiences that
are peculiar to their age group, and these programmes recognise this. They

thematically, symbolically and expressively present the problematic tensions that characterise this age group's experience, and indeed this particular generation's identity.

Generation X and Television

Although the term 'Generation X' is somewhat contentious, there is common agreement upon the age range of the group to which it refers: the generation of young people born in the mid-1960s and the 1970s, after the 'baby boomers'. Rob Owen, author of *Gen X TV*, cites two dictionary definitions, '"the generation of persons born in the 1960s and 1970s, the children of the Baby Boomers, often variously regarded as apathetic, materialistic, irresponsible, lacking purpose, etc." and "the generation born . . . after 1965"' (Owen 1997: 2).[1] Whilst Generation X is sometimes regarded as including all those born between 1961 and 1981 (for example Howe and Strauss 1993), the core group of interest for Owen is between 1965 and 1975; Lury similarly limits her focus to those born in the late 1960s and the 1970s. This suggests that Generation X can be narrowed down to those born in the period from the mid-1960s to the late 1970s.

Lury sets out the specific social, economic and cultural contexts that shaped this generation's experiences (Lury 2001: 2–11). In the British context, Generation X might be defined as a new 'lost' generation, caught as they were in their early adulthood between Thatcherite and Blairite Britain. These young people thus experienced one of the most important identity-defining periods of their lives – their twenties – during a time of indefinite character, which may explain the vague rumblings of discontent and uncertainty, sometimes misunderstood as apathy or lethargy, that were associated with them, and which were captured in literature such as Douglas Coupland's *Generation X*. There was a sense amongst Xers that, being born too late to be mature adults during the 1980s, they had missed out on the intense experiences (good and bad) of the Thatcherite eighties (thus they often regard that previous era with a mixture of nostalgia and disdain); simultaneously, they were one of the groups almost wholly overlooked in Blair's new vision of Britain, which seemed focused on families (with most changes in tax credits and benefits being targeted at this group), and on the younger generation – children and the under-twenty-fives (through an emphasis on education, training and youth employment).[2] Stuck in the middle, deemed too apathetic to vote or engage fully in public life, the generation 'in between' was seen to lack a sense of identity, self-recognition and wider purpose.[3] This was doubtless exacerbated by the huge increase in the number of graduates, which was not matched by a similar increase in truly 'graduate' jobs. It is this 'overlooked' generation, especially those in the middle classes, who were addressed, in turn, by *This Life*, *Queer as Folk* and *Teachers*, as they moved through their mid- to late twenties towards their thirtieth birthdays. Writing as one of that group myself, I can attest to the importance of these programmes in representing and validating a sense of generational identity in a televisual landscape that until recently seemed uninterested in exploring the particular concerns of this generation.

It must be recognised that 'Generation X' is not a straightforward sociological or historical label for one age group, and that the 'media', broadly conceived, have played a dominant role in establishing the term and its referent. The name itself is taken from Coupland's novel *Generation X*, although it should be noted that Coupland took the title from a sociological text, *Class*, written by Paul Fussell; Fussell included a final category in his delineation of class: category 'X', which included, 'people who wanted to hop off the merry-go-round of status, money and social climbing that so often frames modern existence' (Coupland 1995). Fussell's Category X crossed all generations; it was Coupland who attached this term to a particular generation.

Owen acknowledges not just the literary origins of 'Generation X' but also the continuing role played by other media in establishing and sustaining it:

> Who are the members of Generation X? The media stereotype is white, middle-class kids who grew up in suburbia, went to college and are searching for a career, but end up working at The Gap. In reality, a generation is more than a demographic unit, but because television and the media love to group people in target markets, Generation X often appear to be only white middle-class twentysomethings. (Owen 1997: 2)

Owen subscribes to the notion that Generation X constitutes a definite generational group, whilst emphasising that its name and identity is to a considerable degree a media construction. In particular, he regards television as fundamental in shaping the identity of Generation X:

> Why write about television and Generation X? That's pretty easy. The two were made for one another. Would the stereotype of Generation X exist if TV had not been invented? Probably not. Would television exist without Generation X? Yes, but its programming would certainly look different. (Owen 1997: xi)

Owen implies that there is a mutually sustaining relationship between Generation X and television, one created from childhood:

[I]t's tempting to define Generation X as simply an age group, but that classifi-
cation ignores the fact that Xers are all members of one TV nation . . . the first
group for whom TV served as a regularly scheduled baby-sitter . . . the first to
experience MTV . . . the first generation to grow up with VCRs and multiple
remote controls . . . the most media-savvy generation ever. (Owen 1997: 5–6)

Lury similarly proposes that an intimate relationship exists between television and this generation, which manifested itself particularly in the late
1980s and early 1990s. Schedulers and advertisers found a media-literate
and desirable target market in Generation X; twenty-something audiences,
in return, were offered programmes that spoke to them more directly than
ever before. Generation X might have been 'created' by the media, but it in
turn shaped television. In the late 1990s this connection between television
and Generation X persisted, giving rise to texts such as *This Life*, *Queer as
Folk* and *Teachers*. These serials were pitched at Xers, who were in their late
twenties and early thirties when the programmes were broadcast.

Television with Attitude: The Twenty-something Serial and Generation X

The serials explored in this essay exhibit some stereotypical views of young
adults, yet they also offer and assert an appealing twenty-something identity for the 'lost' generation caught in their early adulthood between
Thatcher's and Blair's Britain, and excluded in several senses from either
regime. This identity is constructed in various ways: through an explicit
rejection of older generations, particularly those closest in age to the
drama's central characters; through the expression of certain attitudes to
life, work and relationships; and through directorial stylistic choices. In
this way the serials offer a coherent and flexible identity to a generation that
is often accused of lacking distinctive identifying values and features. They
do so in a characteristically reflexive manner, presenting and expressing the
problematic tensions that characterise this particular generation's identity
(or their search for identity – often over-dramatised as an 'identity crisis').

Owen suggests that there are key traits of content, structure and attitude
that define American 'Gen X TV': the representation of 'friends as family',
serialised storylines and a foregrounded employment of music (Owen
1997: 10). The British twenty-something serials discussed herein are
somewhat different, but they share an emphasis on 'friends as family', and
in this they are differentiated from thirty-something serials, which tend to
focus on couples who are slightly older and who are having families of their
own. Parents are ubiquitous in thirty-something serials; in twenty-
something serials, they are almost non-existent (as all three examples in

this essay reveal). Lury notes that Generation X, more than any generation before them, tend to undertake 'abrupt changes of life plans' (Lury 2001: 4) in response to their environment, a trait that some might regard as fickleness; this tendency is also well represented in the examples herein. At the level of explicit content, then, these programmes present familiar life choices and events to a twenty-something audience. Beyond this, the programmes convey particular narrative, thematic and stylistic concerns, using dialogue, space, *mise-en-scène*, colour and music to represent and construct the voice(s), spaces and culture of a generation.

The changing tone of this genre from the mid-1990s to the early 2000s also expresses the 'attitude' perceived to typify its target audience's generation. 'Coupland has said that Generation X is not a chronological age but a way of looking at the world. True, but most of the people who look at the world in this Gen X way (cynically, ironically, sarcastically) fall into the twentysomething age group' (Owen 1997: 10). A media-literate generation, Xers are said to be particularly fond of 'irony, postmodernism . . . poking fun at the establishment . . . and self-consciousness' in television drama (Owen 1997: 10). Lury offers a more intricate account, which characterises the attitude of these viewers as ambivalence, defined as 'the co-existence of two opposite emotions': she notes the presence of an 'aesthetic sensibility' of 'cynicism and enchantment' which defines this group's relationship with television, and which is 'also an attitude that young people have adopted more generally' (Lury 2001: 10).

Lury, in contrast with Owen, is keen to emphasise that this 'youthful attitude' is not necessarily restricted to those born within the narrow birth years of Generation X, 'Generation X emerged as an identifiable part of the population who could be recognized not simply by their age – which could be anything from 15 to 34 – but more precisely by their consumption patterns or . . . more intuitively, through their "attitude"' (Lury 2001: 21). Qualifying this, she notes that 'youth in this [her] study is not determined by age, but relates to a historical and mediated construction of "youth" or "youthfulness" as an attitude, or a series of traits, habits, and beliefs' (Lury 2001: 126). This conception of youthfulness is one that also underlies my analysis of the programmes dealt with here, as is one further feature of Xers' attitude noted by Lury: their high level of 'self-reflexivity' or self-awareness (which, as she observes, is often misunderstood as being simply cynicism):

This quality of self-reflexivity is the most obvious and the most consistent element of many of the programmes I have described. Although the self-reflexivity of many of the programmes may seem to imply a distancing between the viewer and text, I think that what my evidence suggests is that it may actually be a way of binding the viewer closer to the text. It reveals how the viewer can be (re)enchanted. (Lury 2001: 130)

It is important to recognise that traces of this attitude are found not just in the viewers of these serials but also within the texts themselves, bestowing a particular tone upon later examples of the twenty-something serial (*Queer as Folk* and *Teachers*), especially. The stylistic innovations seen in these serials have profound effects upon their tone. In particular, what has sometimes been described as a 'postmodern' tendency within television can be seen as something more particular: a shift in style and tone within programming aimed at this 'young' audience. As John Corner notes, citing Lury's work on 'cynicism and enchantment', and referring specifically to comic aspects of youth television (such as those seen in *Teachers*):

[Youth television has] seen great changes in the last decade. The comic modes currently on offer here both reflect elements in adult programming and also signal emerging tendencies in comic sensibility. A distinctive play-off between 'enchantment and cynicism' . . . can be found within many new programmes, together with an increased tempo and sharp disjunctions of sequence and mood. Across most areas of television comedy, the use of irony has become more common. Combined with the more widespread employment of pastiche and hectic, if not manic, forms of projected sociability, this has been seen by some critics as part of a decisive shift towards more postmodern forms of pleasurable viewing, although much of a more traditional character still retains popularity. (Corner 1999: 97–8)

The stylistic features he notes – of pastiche, increased tempo and disjunctions – as well as their impact upon and interrelation with tonal qualities such as humour and irony, are clearly present in the serials addressed here. To focus on such thematic, stylistic and tonal attributes is a much more productive and responsive way of approaching 'youth' programmes than the more common approach of assimilating them within the genre of soap opera,[4] especially because a decisive move away from the conventions of soap opera towards a more hybrid form is evident through *This Life* to *Queer as Folk* to *Teachers*.[5] Twenty-something dramas combine these qualities in a particularly concentrated way that appeals to Generation X viewers.

The Voice of Youth: Starting out in *This Life*

This Life garnered an eclectic mix of viewers, and achieved far wider recognition, acclaim and notoriety than was initially expected. However, the programme was primarily pitched at the twenty-somethings it depicted, and the rapid development of the programme on a traditionally 'minority' channel into a cult serial suggests that it offered these viewers something rather different from that which had gone before. Defining a new audience group as it did, one major task for *This Life* was to distinguish itself from existing examples of the most closely related genre: the thirty-something serial. As one might expect, then, *This Life* was at pains to distinguish the 'youthfulness' of its themes, characters and attitude, and to place some distance between twenty-somethings and other generations.[6]

This is achieved both explicitly and implicitly. Explicitly, characters in all three serials (*This Life*, *Queer as Folk* and *Teachers*) take up disdainful and derogatory attitudes towards the generation that precedes them (and the over-fifties are almost entirely absent). Thus in the first series of *This Life* we are encouraged to take Joe's point of view when he scornfully ridicules his middle-aged boss's Porsche, pointing out that it is 'so eighties', and undermining the older man's attempts to behave in a carefree and youthful manner (his boss remains unrepentant and unaffected). There is an air of youthful rebellion in the characters' dismissal of this older generation, tangible in Anna's frank assertion: 'I'm going to say something really blasphemous now. The Beatles were crap.'

Inter-generational relationships are presented as doomed: in *This Life*, Milly's affair with her older boss causes the breakup of the pivotal relationship between her and Egg, and the consequent collapse of the central group of characters. In *Queer as Folk*, Stuart's relationship with the fifteen-year-old Nathan is not presented as damaging, but it is shown to be ultimately unfulfilling; more significantly, the breakup of Vince's relationship with his older boyfriend provides the key motivation for the final, celebratory sequence of series one (as I explore later). Inter-generational relationships challenge the autonomy and unity of the twenty-something age group and are consequently depicted as threats to the central characters' friendships and relationships.

The use of voice(s) is important to *This Life*. There are both implicit and explicit references to 'the voice of youth' – a voice that is clearly defined, and is in some senses exclusive (it clearly excludes and mocks those thirty- and forty-somethings who attempt to appropriate it), but is not monolithic. Echoing the programme's youthful attitude, evident in its straightforward and relaxed presentation of sexuality, drugs and inter-personal relationships, youth is allied with a voice that is progressive and egalitarian (which compares interestingly with the later *Teachers*). After Anna's interview at the law firm central to the story, her prospective employers discuss her suitability, including within the remit of their discussion the fact that she has 'great legs': 'Never underestimate the importance of legs,' warns one of the men on the panel. A question is directed to Miles, one of our protagonists, 'And what does the voice of youth say?' The voice of youth responds accordingly, 'I think she'd be a good barrister.' Thus youth is implied as reasonable, intelligent and politically liberal (whilst managing to avoid the stifling dullness of 'political correctness').

The voice of youth is also expressive, readily conveying thoughtfulness and passion, and a high level of self-awareness and reflectiveness. In the opening sequence of episode one, each protagonist speaks directly about his or her philosophy of life and about what he or she has learned. Egg reflects that there are no simple answers in life, 'That much is clear by now'; his words 'by now' emphasise the present moment, the importance of recognising what is past, reflecting upon it, and engaging fully in the present. His philosophy arises from 'common sense' and experience, and is expressive of the apolitical stance often attributed to Generation X; this is affirmed later by Warren, 'You can't change out there [gestures towards the outside world]; you can in here [taps his head].' This is a solipsistic philosophy, one well-suited to a post-Thatcherite, pre-Blairite world in which this generation feels broadly overlooked and insignificant. Twenty-somethings here are resourceful, intelligent, thoughtful and engaged, but they are keen to reject the truisms of earlier generations and they embrace the present over the past, whilst hoping to defer the future (this latter trait is the defining feature of the protagonists in *Teachers*).

Lez Cooke offers one of the first scholarly critiques of *This Life*, focusing on how the serial was innovative in style and content, and formed part of a new, 'upmarket, youth-oriented' strand of programming. He classifies *This Life* generically as 'a "lifestyle" drama, in which the social lives of the characters were the main dramatic interest' (Cooke 2003: 179). On the matter of style, he accurately notes that:

> For these dramas a faster tempo and such stylistic innovations as hand-held camerawork, elliptical editing, unusual shot transitions, montages, fantasy sequences and surreal inserts contrive to introduce something new into British television drama, a new form for a new post-modern audience, an audience that has not been reared on studio naturalism and which is impatient with the slow narrative development and 'realist' *mise en scène* traditionally associated with British television drama. (Cooke 2003: 178)

However, Cooke appears to overlook an important aspect of the 'new postmodern audience': its constitution in terms of age or 'youthfulness'. Although he notes that the writer of *This Life*, Amy Jenkins, was 29, and that the characters were of a similar age, he seems uninterested in the notion of the twenty-something drama, exploring *This Life* and *Queer as Folk* relatively separately, and focusing on style and on the ideological implications of content (for example the representation of gay issues). This seems to neglect the significance of both programmes as twenty-something dramas in the same vein.

Where are we Going? Hitting Twenty-Nine in *Queer as Folk*

I would not wish to argue that *Queer as Folk* is not a 'gay drama', for that would be absurd. However, to regard it as *only* a gay drama is to overlook other of its important thematic concerns. *Queer as Folk* is not reducible to gay drama, and its divisions and borders are drawn not just in terms of sex-uality but also in terms of age. Most saliently, if one considers the endings of both series (one and two), it is clear that the primary theme of these scenes is age, and not sexuality (the latter is taken for granted, the former constitutes the central problematic of the narrative). In this way it is strik-ingly comparable with *This Life*. The advertising for *Queer as Folk* clearly demonstrated that the intended audience was not just a gay one but a young one, and the programme reflects this not just in its explicit content, its themes and concerns, but also in smaller details of image and sound. [7]

At the end of series one, Vince makes a spur of the moment decision to dump his considerate, attractive older boyfriend, Cameron, and return to Stuart's somewhat unsatisfactory but enduring friendship. Age is centrally important to this sequence. Vince decides to finish the relationship because Cameron patronises him over the phone, chiding Vince in an affectionate, paternal manner that he resembles a little boy who never tidies up his room. As we cut between Vince standing in the road, talking on his mobile, and Cameron sitting waiting in a trendy restaurant, the stark differences between the two environments are highlighted. Vince, wearing a bright-scarlet shirt, stands next to the red mini given to him by Cameron; Cameron sits in a minimalist bar area, with blue as the dominant colour, surrounded by straight, older couples. Resolving to finish the relationship, Vince uses the excuse of poor reception on his mobile ('I can't hear you. You're breaking up . . . we're breaking up') to end the call and, locking the car keys in the abandoned car, he takes off for the Village in search of Stuart, running through the streets with a new sense of vigour and purpose, joyfully explaining to bemused bystanders the importance of his journey. He justifies his choice of Stuart over Cameron in terms of endless youth, 'Unrequited love: it's fantastic. It never has to change, it never has to grow up, and it never has to die!' When he finds Stuart, they neither speak, nor kiss, nor touch one another: they leap to a podium and dance together in a childlike and exuberant fashion. Thus Cameron's cool and collected maturity is counterposed with Vince and Stuart's joyful embrace of playfulness. The older generation is literally dumped, in preference for a love that never has to grow up, age or die. Vince and Stuart's attitude to growing up could not be clearer, and the sequence captures this wonderful spirit of resistance, affirming youthfulness as an ideal state of mind.

Series two foregrounds age even more explicitly, as well as reaffirming the importance of free, youthful spaces (such as Canal Street), and the characters' freedom to move between and define those spaces for themselves. Stuart and Vince are twenty-nine, and each of them experiences his own fears and crises regarding his impending thirties. The final scene of this final series reveals Stuart 'handing over' Canal Street to teenager Nathan: he hands over his mobile phone, the equivalent of his 'little black book', and his language becomes poetic and melodramatic, as he embarks on an eloquent eulogy to Canal Street, warning Nathan to take care of it for future generations. Finally, he and Vince depart the scene in a bizarre, surreal finale, as Stuart's familiar black jeep turns into a 'time machine' vehicle reminiscent of one of Vince's favourite *Doctor Who* effects, and they are 'transported' at super-speed to the American mid-west. The playfulness of the programme thus extends to a play with genre, in which realistic depictions give way to symbolic and mythic ones. Here, we see the mixture of enchantment and cynicism proposed by Lury: the scene is captivating, beautiful, playful and colourful, yet Vince's curbing of Stuart's excessive dramatic tendencies – 'don't be so camp' – adds a knowing, ironic, 'cynical' note to the scene.

This finale is clearly different from *This Life* in its departure from realistic depictions of time and space, and its flamboyant character. However, the endings of the two have something striking in common. There is a fascinating tension within the serials, relating to how youth is regarded by others. On the one hand, the voices, spaces and culture of youth are regarded as potentially politically progressive, even radical; on the other hand, the serials seem ultimately unable to deal with the characters' apparently liberated lives and the possibilities that their youth appears to open up. *This Life* ended after two series, despite a storm of protests from viewers. *Queer as Folk*, similarly, went into a second series, but this series only contained two episodes as Russell T. Davies, the writer, refused to write any more. They were both, therefore, suddenly curtailed, despite being popular. The programme-makers in each case argued that greater character and narrative development was impossible. So *This Life* ended in chaos, the characters' lives in tatters, *Queer as Folk* with a curious genre-bending finale which lifted the characters out of 'reality' and into the realm of myth. Thus neither narrative could ultimately contain the possibilities of youth, perhaps suggesting that the strong generational identity epitomised in the characters was of no lasting value; the programmes either condemned the characters to misery and destruction, or avoided the question altogether by escaping into the fantastical. Here at least, in the end, the lost generation remains just that.

There appeared to be a sense, then, that the serials had nowhere to go. Perhaps the blame cannot be laid at the door of programme-makers who lack inspiration regarding the future of Generation X. Perhaps instead this is a consequence of the genre: if the programme is based on young people, and the particular nature of their lives, where can it go? Twenty-somethings become thirty-somethings, and if the serial is dependent upon their age for its central narrative tensions, the age of twenty-nine (that of Stuart and Vince) is extremely tricky. Does a twenty-something serial become a thirty-something serial simply because its characters reach their thirtieth birthdays? This is neither generically nor commercially feasible, as was recognised in the decision not to prolong either series. In both cases the possibility of ageing was anathema to the programmes.

Queer as Folk therefore foregrounds for its ageing audience a key narrative tension that was first seen in *This Life*: the necessarily transient nature of youth. *Teachers* tackles this head on, making it its central underlying concern.

The Hatching of Egg: Forever Young in *Teachers*

The playfulness perceptible in *This Life* and *Queer as Folk* becomes one of the most prominent characteristics, indeed, a defining trait, of *Teachers*, and the starting point for this is the central group of characters. A clear comparison is drawn between the protagonists, a group of late twenty-somethings (and early thirty-somethings) who work together in Summerdown comprehensive school, and their pupils. The teachers are neither high-achieving careerists such as those depicted in *This Life*, nor the trendy, city-types presented in *Queer as Folk*; rather, they are relaxed to the point of lethargy at work, cynical about their careers and anyone who is 'too keen', and uninterested in or failing at their personal relationships. They show most enthusiasm when engrossed in drunken discussions of inanities. Their hobbies outside the classroom include lolling around in the staffroom, smoking behind the bikesheds (having confiscated the cigarettes from pupils), and hanging out at the bowling alley, or in the local pub – a dreary, unfashionable place from which pupils are informally banned ('you stay out of our pub, we'll stay out of yours'). In short, these are twenty-somethings who stalwartly refuse to 'grow up' and conform to the norms of adult society.

One significant continuity between *This Life* and *Teachers* is the presence of Andrew Lincoln. Lincoln played 'Egg' in *This Life* (a name which stuck with him long after the programme had ended) and in *Teachers* he plays Simon, who at first seems to be a reprise of Egg.[8] In *This Life*, Egg was the character who really lost his way. Disillusioned with law, he dropped out to become a writer, but discovered he lacked the self-discipline required of his new career and meandered from one whim to another for the rest of the series. One could imagine Egg ending up as Simon, a new teacher who drifted into teaching because he liked reading English literature and was unable to think of anything else to do.

The first episode of *Teachers* begins with Simon's twenty-seventh birthday, and his symbolic refusal to cut up his 'young person's railcard', to which he is no longer entitled. His similarity with his pupils is established as we see him cycle to school, weaving in and out of the traffic, with his rucksack on his back. It is clear from the first series that Simon is at a transitional stage in his life: he cannot cope with being seen as a 'role model', and has a problem dealing with the discovery that his new girlfriend is the ultimate authority figure, a police officer (as he sees her put on her uniform for the first time, he hopefully asks whether she is a stripper-gram). His father is in the process of re-establishing himself within a new 'ready-made' family, with his younger girlfriend and her baby daughter, and complains of Simon's 'lack of commitment'. The sight of his father playing the role of 'family man', wearing an apron and feeding mush to a dribbling toddler, is too much for Simon to bear, and he finally moves out. Simon is thus clearly established as a focus for twenty-somethings who have no desire to settle down and do the family thing, and his playfulness and vitality, alongside his world-weary cynicism, captures the 'cynical enchantment' of the generation who avidly watched *This Life* and *Queer as Folk*, as they settle into post-university jobs and careers but wish to hang on to the freedoms and childlike qualities of youth.

The themes and style of the programme are integrated, with playful touches being introduced through ludic elements of style. Each new day is marked by the appearance of the name of the day (Monday, Tuesday . . .) somewhere in the *mise en scène* – in a re-formed car aerial, on an advertising hoarding, or under the duvet that is thrown aside as Simon stumbles from his bed. Distinctions between reality and fantasy are frequently undermined through distortions of sound and image. The entrance into a room of Jenny, the frosty English teacher, is accompanied by the sound of a chilling wind; the noise of Simon's father's sexual antics with his girlfriend are heard by Simon through the walls of his bedroom, and exaggerated to the extent that the house shakes, the walls and ceiling start to crack, and possessions tumble from the bookshelves in the room. Whilst these are obviously expressive of Simon's overfertile imagination, and are primarily for comic effect, other such distortions are more subtle, and lead to more complex defamiliarisation. Simon and his girlfriend, Maggie, attend an uncomfortable dinner party at the house of his colleague Susan and her partner, Peter. Representing the only young couple who are 'settled' and living together, Susan and Peter offer a broadly negative picture of such grown-up relationships: the tension between the couple reveals frustration and disillusionment, and this tension is magnified by odd framing, confusing editing, which ignores point-of-view shot conventions, and distorted sound.[9]

The effect of this is that Simon's emotional point of view is prioritised, and the sources of his stress are highlighted: all those things that relate to his fear of getting older, settling down and being in a committed relationship. However, it would be wrong to dismiss Simon as immature and unreflective. He makes an interesting and important distinction when he attempts to define his problem with his being a teacher, 'I hate "being" it, not doing it.' Indeed, although he cares little for the form-filling, exam coaching and political correctness of present-day school teaching, and cares too greatly what his peers might think of him, his genuine love of English literature and poetry are emphasised. Simon does not lack empathy with and enthusiasm for what he does – he is an anti-authoritarian afraid of turning into the kind of older authority figure he sees around him (as he says to his pupils, 'We're all still fighting the same system from within'). His fear arises from a lust for life and for fun, and a particularly youthful insecurity, not from apathy or malevolence.

There is some pathos in *Teachers*, and perhaps the first series sustained this element best.[10] Primarily, though, and in keeping with the greater amount of comedy in the programme, it celebrates friendship and fun, and the ability to live fully in the present. It valorises light-heartedness, playfulness, even silliness, and expresses *joie de vivre*. But *Teachers* is not superficial or naive, and being 'in the know' is valued. Knowingness is conveyed mostly through irony, such as when Simon asks for patience from his friends as he is 'trying to manufacture sincerity'; further, irony is presented as being a tonal trait that defines this generation's communications (confusion arises when in the first episode Simon asks his pupils to clarify whether they are 'being ironic' as he assumes they cannot be serious). Knowingness is even present in stylistic elements of the programme, as viewers are expected to appreciate its intertextuality. Visual motifs such as the repeated surreal background images (oversized penguins, children with machine guns, dwarf catering staff) echo previous education-themed texts such as *Gregory's Girl* (1981) and *A Very Peculiar Practice* (1986–8), and the soundtrack – a mixture of 1980s–90s pop songs that are a source of nostalgia for the audience – also creates an often sharp running commentary on the storyline.

In keeping with *Teachers'* cutting, unsentimental humour, it is interesting to note the change in the 'voice of youth' in *Teachers*, compared with *This Life*. The twenty-somethings here are open to others, but are not egalitarian in the way that their predecessors were, and there is a strong strand of anti-political correctness here, such as in the wounding observations made directly to characters about their size (fat teacher Lindsay), colour (black secretary Liz) and ugliness/abnormality (cross-eyed secretary Carol and various odd-looking pupils). Their outspokenness and honesty is depicted as childlike directness, and esteemed as such.

This does not mean that *Teachers* is ideologically reactionary. Some episodes, such as that in series three in which Kurt is confined to a wheelchair, humorously explore and critique widespread attitudes to and prejudices about issues such as disability, whilst puncturing the pomposity of politically correct directives, exposing their contradictions, oversights and excesses. Further, by presenting characters who are youthful and playful, and who are not caught up in the concerns of marriage and family, the programme creates an equality between its characters, levelling them. Irrelevant of gender or race, for example, they are shown to exhibit shared interests and fears; friendship across those differences is affirmed. The common experience of a generation overcomes superficial differences of colour and sex. *Teachers* is affirmative, youthful and rebellious.

One might ask, finally, what these twenty-somethings are rebelling against. Twenty-something serials do not just portray and appeal to twenty-somethings: they depict the concerns of this generation as arising in particular from their age, and one of the central tensions present here is that which is perceived to be the looming black cloud of the characters' thirtieth birthdays. Coupland entitled one of his chapters in *Generation X* 'Dead at 30, buried at 70' (Coupland 1995: 34), and this fear of losing the lust for life at thirty is an explicit theme of *Teachers*. Whilst *This Life* and *Queer as Folk* dealt with the thirty-something problem by escaping before it occurred, *Teachers* deals with it by ignoring it. Running the risk of appearing childish, *Teachers* shows that twenty-somethings need not change simply because they become thirty-somethings; it reassures its viewers that they can continue to play well past that dreaded thirtieth birthday. It accepts the advantages of being older than school pupils, but rejects unnecessary responsibilities, asserting that this is the best place to be: between young and old. The teachers have privileges and power over the schoolchildren, and exuberance, liveliness and freedom over their elders. 'Thirty-something' themes explored in *Cold Feet* and the American series *thirtysomething*, such as settling down, marriage, divorce, children, family life, career crises, and so on, are rejected, glossed over or treated only as sources for humour, disparagement or disdain here. This is no doubt the key reason why many older viewers dislike *Teachers*, and why the twenty-something audience who grew up with *This Life* and *Queer as Folk* find it refreshing. What simpler and greater image of eternal, youthful happiness can there be than that of friends Brian and Kurt, at the end of a night out, putting behind them all the stresses placed upon their friendship by Brian's brief attempt at a romantic relationship, as they play, exhibiting great earnestness and attention, with their home-made light sabres (rolled-up newspapers) on a bridge above the city.

Notes

1. These definitions are taken from *Webster's New World Dictionary*, November 1995, and *Random House Webster's College Dictionary*, 1996, respectively.
2. Generation X were not the only generation to be overlooked in the early days of Blair's government: senior citizens are another prime example.
3. This derogatory image of Generation X led to them being referred to as 'slackers', after Richard Linklater's 1991 film *Slacker*.
4. Twenty-something dramas are most often regarded as soap operas: Rachel Moseley (2001), for example, defines teen drama as a subgenre of soaps and Lez Cooke (2003) classifies *This Life* alongside soaps, too. This is done primarily on the basis of content: the programmes' focus on interpersonal relationship and character-based action.
5. The increased use of irony, disjunctions in mood and tone, and new comic forms is evident in other programmes that appeal to twenty-something audiences, such as *The Office*, *I'm Alan Partridge* and *Marion and Geoff*. These programmes also demand a new kind of audience engagement that can be correlated with Lury's 'enchantment and cynicism' (see Cardwell 2003 on *The Office*). However, as these programmes do not primarily explore the lives, experiences and concerns of Generation X, I have excluded them from this study.
6. This sense of a divide between the 'baby boomers' and their offspring, Generation X, is created by several factors. There is the age-old tradition of inter-generational conflict, which is easily visible on the many websites hosted by members of Generation X, where one finds numerous postings that rail against the 'mess' that the previous generation left behind. There are also more modern commercial factors as well: it is advantageous for advertisers to create clearly defined, demarcated, target groups, and this is most easily done by distinguishing between groups and playing one off against another.

7. One of the television advertisements for *Queer as Folk* included interviews, recorded after the broadcast of the first episode, of young people enthusing about the serial; also included was a woman in her fifties or sixties saying that the programme was 'disgusting' and shouldn't be shown. The latter inclusion was of course a witty way of confirming that the target audience for the programme was varied in sexuality but not so varied in age.

8. Simon's character left *Teachers* during the second series, but returned for occasional episodes in the third series.

9. Thirty-something Peter's lack of understanding of Simon and his peers (including Susan, Peter's wife) is made apparent when he refuses to engage in one of Simon's silly 'what if' conversations, stating that he refuses to join in, because the conversation is 'ridiculous'. Susan and her husband Peter separate later in the first series.

10. In the first series, the tone is complicated by pathos, and I would argue that a darker, more contemplative tone is achieved. Two key factors contribute to this: Brian's eagerness to teach in a classroom, ever frustrated, and contrasted with his colleagues' laissez-faire attitudes to the classroom jobs they take for granted, and Simon's relationship with Maggie and friendship with Susan, both of which he fails to value. Although we engage with Simon, we cannot fail to see the unhappiness he unwittingly causes others through his self-absorption, and so whilst we laugh at his antics we also recognise the sharp pathos in his situation.

Bibliography

Cardwell, Sarah (2003), 'The Rise of the Television Mockumentary: From Familiar Genres to new Forms', *Anglo Files* no. 129, September, 30–41.

Cooke, Lez (2003), *British Television Drama: A History*, Oxford: Oxford University Press.

Corner, John (1999), *Critical Ideas in Television Studies*, Oxford: Oxford University Press.

Coupland, Douglas (1995), Interview cited on 'Stephen's Generation X site' http://users.metro2000.net/~stabbott/genxintro.htm

Fussell, Paul (1983), *Class: A Guide through the American Status System*, New York: Summit Books.

Howe, Neil and William Strauss (1993), *13th Gen: Abort, Retry, Ignore, Fail?*, New York: Random House.

Lury, Karen (2001), *British Youth Television: Cynicism and Enchantment*, Oxford: Oxford University Press.

Moseley, Rachel (2001), 'The Teen Series', in Glen Creeber (ed.), *The Television Genre Book*, London: BFI Publishing, pp. 41–3.

Owen, Rob (1997), *Gen X TV: 'The Brady Bunch' to 'Melrose Place'*, New York: Syracuse University Press.

CHAPTER 8

Violence and Therapy in *The Sopranos*

Jason Jacobs

Melfi: Tell me about the Soprano temper.
Tony: The thing is – it's bad for business. Clouds your judgement . . . We forget that in the old days, the ones that came over, that started this thing – they didn't get mad. They just smiled and nodded and made sure you got it later. That's the whole beautiful point.[1]

You just can't help yourself [2]

The first scene of *The Sopranos* episode 'Amour Fou' shows Carmela (Edie Falco) and Meadow Soprano (Jamie-Lynn Sigler), wife and daughter of New Jersey mob boss Tony Soprano (James Gandolfini) looking at paintings in the Brooklyn Museum of Art.[3] The first shot after the title sequence shows a close-up of Carmela's hand holding a handbag, with a large ring prominent on her finger. The camera pulls back revealing the open space of the gallery as Carmela walks between black sculptures towards her daughter. We can hear music that is not part of this world, but appropriate to the rarefied setting; it is an aria, 'Sposa son disprezzata' sung by Cecilia Bartoli.[4] In long shot, as Carmela reaches Meadow, we hear her ask, 'Do you have a tampon?', before there is a cut to a close-up of the couple as she says, 'I'm spotting.'

This opening shot is a good example of the art of *The Sopranos*. There is a deep richness in the choices that are made here, in the points of comparison and contrast, and in the ranges of feeling that are evoked. The shot contrasts the close-up of Carmela's hand with the subsequent evolution of the image into a wide one, so that the detail of the ring is immediately contextualised: as Carmela's and within the wider space of the gallery. The ring is a private possession that can be carried everywhere; by placing the ring and its owner within the context of the museum, a public space with priceless works of art that are for anybody who wishes to view them, the shot compares two kinds of display, two kinds of possession: that of personal wealth derived from organised crime and that of legitimate publicly owned art. The ring itself is a giant oblong sapphire surrounded by diamonds, large enough to obscure the knuckle of Carmela's ring finger. It is a ring that signifies excessive wealth that is in inverse proportion to taste. But however big it is on Carmela's finger, it is dwarfed, as she is, by the size of the room and the life-size human sculptures that populate it, posing a direct contrast between things of beauty and the ring. Their motionless gestures are contrasted with Carmela's steady movement towards Meadow; in particular the most prominent sculpture in the foreground is one of Rodin's full-figure nude studies of Pierre de Wissant (for his later *Burghers of Calais*): the figure holds his right hand towards his head as if in intense despair – it is a striking pose of anguished introspection.

The ring has narrative weight too. Tony gave it to her as a birthday gift despite being in the middle of an affair with Mercedes car saleswoman Gloria Trillo (Annabella Sciorra).[5] Carmela accepted it with pleasure despite being told by a psychiatrist to leave him because her life of luxury is funded by 'blood money'.[6] So the ring is a visible sign of her continuing complicity in Tony's crimes; and insofar as the ring denotes possession, her complaint to the psychiatrist about Tony's infidelity (his 'fucking whores') begs the question of her moral position in their relationship. Her narrative arc in season three is precisely concerned with her attempt to reconcile the bad feelings generated by this complicity and her desire to escape responsibility for her continued enjoyment of the comforts and benefits of staying married to the mob.

At the same time, there is the extradiegetic music. The aria describes the pain and longing of a wife who is outraged by her husband's behaviour but still in love with him: 'And yet he is my heart, my husband, my love' ('E pur egl'è il mio cor/il mio sposo, il mio amor), and finally 'my hope' ('La mia speranza'). Bartoli's superb breath control extends the second syllable of 'speranza' so that it becomes a richly layered cry of exquisite pain and yearning. Her voice is supported by a plaintive piano, whose slow notes chillingly evoke the sad inevitability of loss. Juxtaposed with the image of the ring and then the gallery the music seems congruent with both setting and character.

One does not need to know that the music is about a wife who has been betrayed, or that the singer is Cecilia Bartoli, or that the sculptures are by Rodin in order to grasp what is happening in this shot.[7] It is a song that conveys profound sadness and hurt, but it is also a classical song about yearning, in contrast to the Lost Boys' song, 'Affection' that plays over the credits at the end of the episode, which, although equally direct, belongs to the world of the legible popular music. So the song at once 'fits' Carmela but is as distant from her as the world of sculpture and art seem to be. In this scene things of great beauty are being measured against the everyday, so that Carmela's first words are surprising not so much because of their content as because of their context. The rarefied world of the art gallery and opera are contrasted with the inconvenience of not having a tampon when you need one.

The music continues in subsequent shots. After expressing concern that her mother should get a medical examination, Meadow gives Carmela a tampon, and she walks back through the sculptures in long shot. We then we get a slow pan across some paintings being consumed in another part of the museum to rest on Carmela and Meadow looking at a portrait by Rubens. Time has passed and we are in another part of the gallery. 'Imagine having your portrait painted', says Carmela. 'She's just some wife of a rich merchant. That's how Rubens made his money,' Meadow replies. Again we get the contrast between art and physical necessity which reflects upon Carmela's position as the wife of a rich man. The objects in the gallery are being recruited to narrative demands.

After some discussion about Meadow's grades, Meadow announces that she has split with her boyfriend Jackie Aprile Jr (Jason Cerbone) and walks away. Carmela follows Meadow into another room in the gallery; something off screen catches her eye, and her mouth opens slightly. Her slow walk towards the off-screen object is coloured by the resumption of the 'Sposa son disprezzata' piano, as the camera pans to follow her movement. We then cut to a medium shot of Carmela's face looking in awe and wonder at a large painting. A reverse cut shows us it in more detail: Jusepe de Ribera's *The Mystical Marriage of St Catherine*, which depicts the infant Christ held by his mother, with Catherine beneath them kissing his hand. As Meadow reads out the title Carmela realises with emotion and awe, 'That's the baby Jesus.' 'She's marrying a baby?' says Meadow; to which Carmela responds, 'We all do. [Wiping tears] I shouldn't be sarcastic.' We get a closer shot of the painting as Carmela continues to stare in wonder as she says, 'Look at her. The little baby's hand against her cheek. She's so at peace. A beautiful, innocent, gorgeous little baby.' She continues to stare as we hear Bartoli stretching that syllable. Then Carmela says, 'Come on, let's eat' and the scene ends.

It is difficult to think of a scene in *The Sopranos* like this that is so far away from the brutal violent world of the mob that is frequently shown to us. And yet there is a connection between Carmela's tears and the wider theme of personal responsibility that is critical in the show. There is no question that Carmela's tears are genuine; but as she wipes them away the ring is prominent again. What is the cause of her sorrow? We are asked to measure the depth of this sorrow against the music we hear and images that we see.

Where non-diegetic music is often used to reinforce a particular reading, mood or tone, here it is used both to colour the scene and to open up, rather than confirm, possible readings. Is Carmela's sadness of that epic deep quality we hear in Bartoli's voice, or is it a product of more everyday anxieties. The music could be used to lock down a particular reading of Carmela but like many of the strategies of the show, this layering simply expands the range of possible readings. Where music could be used to insist on a particular reading, here it extends the range of contrast: it asks us to compare the depth of feeling and sadness in the song with Carmela's response to the painting. Her unexpected vaginal bleeding could be a sign of menopause, ovarian cancer or pregnancy; hence her response to the painting and the baby has two possible meanings. Perhaps her tearful appreciation of the infant Christ, 'the innocent, gorgeous . . . baby' signals her intuitive understanding that the spotting means the end of future pregnancy; equally, a real pregnancy would allow her to justifiably remain with Tony, since she could not contemplate divorce when raising a small child. But there is more. As is usual for the period, Ribera's infant Christ possesses adult features juxtaposed with his toddler-sized torso and limbs. This rhymes with Carmela's astute comment that 'we all do' (marry babies). Her comment signals that the impulsive, instinctual desires of infants may linger in the adult men that women marry.

So what we see in her apparently unbidden aesthetic response to the painting is layered with narrative significance. The sensual response to art is compared to other involuntary bodily responses – the bleeding, the tears, the desire to eat. The scene illustrates the way in which *The Sopranos* can use contrast – say between the expression of feeling and its motive – and comparison – say between the high art trappings of the museum and the necessity of bodily needs in subtle and revealing ways. Later in the episode we are asked to measure what seems like a strong aesthetic response to the beauty of a painting with Carmela's tearful response to a television commercial for dog food. 'What is the matter with me?' she asks herself. Carmela is looking for an external event that will let her off the moral hook. Paradoxically the event is literally internal. The vaginal bleeding she noted at the start of the episode prompts her to visit a priest who is training to be a psychologist, Father Obosi (Isaach De Bankole). In confession she voices her worries that she has ovarian cancer or may be pregnant. Carmela repeats Dr Krakower's assertion that her life is a lie and that she should leave her husband. Obosi reminds her that in Catholicism divorce is out of the question (unless he is abusive: Carmela: 'Not to me.'). Obosi offers her a way out: 'learn to live on the good side [of Tony]: there is a point inside yourself, an inner boundary, beyond which you feel culpable. You've got to come to an awareness of where that line is and forego those things that lay without it.' Later, after an examination clears her of ovarian cancer she has dinner with the other mob wives. When the discussion turns to Hilary Clinton and the humiliation suffered because of her husband's infidelities, Rosalie Aprile points out that, 'She stuck by him. Then she did her own little thing.' This seals Carmela's decision to remain with Tony. The episode ends with her reading a training book for real-estate agents; she has found the point beyond which she 'feels culpable' and no longer wears the ring.

This detailed examination of the opening scene of this episode illustrates the profound attention to detail and character that *The Sopranos* continually exhibits. At the time of writing *The Sopranos* is currently shooting its sixth and final season since premiering in 1999 on HBO. During its five seasons it has offered an emphatically realist account of organised crime in a fictional New Jersey mob family. Its central character, Tony Soprano, is a successful mob boss with a problem – his panic attacks and general depression require him to visit a therapist. Acts of brutal violence are therefore contrasted with moments of reflection and introspection. As several commentators have pointed out, the concentration on those characters associated with, but not active within, the mob, is part of the show's innovation in combining the melodrama of the domestic with the traditions of the gangster genre (Lavery 2002). In this way an epic canvas is combined with an intimate one.

Since the show is emphatically character-based we might expect as the seasons continue to achieve a more comprehensive account of them; but in fact, as in the case of Carmela, the serial form – which could be used to gradually uncover and reveal character – is used instead to continually confound a settled view of any one of them. In a perceptive essay Martha P. Nochimson argues that, 'more than can ever be true of the characters in a film as the script is developing, the characters in a television series take on a life of their own, season by season revolving to reveal what has been under the surface of their original identities and relationships'. She goes on:

> We increasingly see Tony from a variety of perspectives, each of which has a truth equal to his, granting the viewer a prismatic, inconclusive view of all the characters. American mass culture has been profoundly hostile to ambiguity and nuanced ethical perspectives, but these are the essence of televisuality by virtue of what serial television does to narrative structure. (Nochimson 2003)

Several other writers have commented on this and on the ways in which the serial form can offer the breadth and comprehensiveness that the narrative fiction movie would find difficult. Nevertheless there are distinctions to be made. While it is true that over the season we find out more information about the characters and their histories, this is not the same thing as coming to understanding and insight about their motives and desires. Whereas the classical gangster genre has a rise and fall arc and therapy typically seeks to resolve or relieve psychological and emotional problems, in *The Sopranos* there is little development.

Tony, for example, remains much the same throughout (apart from his spell of chronic depression in season one) and never questions the means by which he 'puts food on his family's table'. Of course if too much change is achieved then the formula is broken. But *The Sopranos* is emphatically realist in its depiction of the quotidian details of gang life both at work and at home. In that sense it resembles a nineteenth-century realist novel. Unlike *The Godfather* or *Goodfellas* it is also grounded in the present day of New Jersey. This rooted contemporary realism allows the show to incorporate into its narrative structures commentary on the contemporary world.

This is not to claim that the show does not change. Indeed, as the seasons progress there is a particular aspect that rises to increasing prominence. This is the issue of impulsivity. Like Carmela's tears, the show asks us to consider the relationship between the structure and traditions of the mob, the decline of the American family, with the unstructured, unregulated world of instinct, desire and impulse. It is the latter that therapy seeks to address – uncovering the structures and patterns of impulse in order to better manage them.

It is Tony Soprano's loss of control over his body – his panic attacks – that begins in the pilot episode, and is a continuing issue in most of the seasons, which means he is forced to attend therapy whether he likes it or not because his existence as a capable leader appears under threat. This immediately raises the issue of the connections between his criminal activities and his medical condition. In doing so the early seasons of *The Sopranos* made explicit its interest in contemporary definitions of criminality and the contemporary therapeutic culture. In having one of the characters as a therapist *The Sopranos* was able to explore issues of personal responsibility, impulse control and criminality. According to the show's creator, David Chase:

Certainly I think [*The Sopranos*] describes American materialism. American . . . psychobabble. The victim society that we have, that we're developing.

The society of non-accountability. You know, the rugged Yankee American guy, who doesn't really seem to exist anymore. So in that sense it's an American phenomenon. But then I go to Europe and I hear the same things. That it's a welfare state and half the people are on the dole and nobody takes responsibility, you hear the same thing all over. (Fellezs 2002: 167)

It is somewhat odd that Chase's clear hostility to 'psychobabble' and the issue of accountability has been little remarked upon, but it is one that resonates with contemporary discursive contexts around crime and criminal behaviour.

In the past criminals were considered to be a minority, an other outside the norms and rules of decent society; nevertheless there was a prevailing optimism that such behaviour could be overcome through better education and the widespread dispersal of culture. As Andrew Calcutt notes, traditional ideas about criminality began from the assumption that 'the criminal is above all a calculating individual' (Calcutt 1996: 39), and even those who saw criminality as a product of breeding noted this was confined to a minority. Criminal behaviour was understood in sharp relief to commonly shared moral values. By the end of the nineteenth century, with capitalism clearly not spontaneously resolving criminality, theorists such as Émile Durkheim began to develop theories of *deviance* that self-consciously avoided the moral dimension to the understanding of criminal behaviour: 'Deviance, in short, is a de-moralised concept of crime and anti-social behaviour' (Calcutt 1996: 46). Gradually during the twentieth century, capitalism, rather than being seen as an inevitable solution to criminal behaviour, was beginning to be seen as its cause. Were criminals pathological or the society that produced them?[8] Crime was not seen as an aberration of American values but as an expression of them. As Calcutt notes, this was the beginning of a moral relativism in response to crime, one that had many celebrating the 'resistant' nature of criminal subcultures in response to bourgeois conformity.

More recently criminality has been pathologised and rather than seeing criminals as a product of society or beyond it there is a strong tendency to attribute criminal potentialities to the population as a whole, in the sense of 'in those circumstances' anyone would do the same thing. As James Nolan has observed, conventional morality has shifted from a sense of right and wrong to one of health and illness. He points to various cases from the 1990s where therapeutic discourses were employed in public defence of criminals: the Lorena Bobbitt acquittal because of temporary insanity, the Lyle and Eric Menendez mistrial after the defendants claimed they were victims of family abuse. Nolan goes on:

Recent therapeutic defence strategies have also been based on such patholo-gies as overindulgence in junk food (the so-called twinkie defence), too much television watching, alcoholism, PMS, and postpartum depression. (Nolan 1998: 77)

The medicalisation of crime effectively redefines criminality. According to Nolan's analysis of drug-related crimes, 'Where once drug offences were seen as legal infractions that needed to be punished, they are increasingly viewed as illnesses that need to be treated' (Nolan 1998: 100). If criminal-ity is a sickness then the issue of individual responsibility is diminished. When Canadian politician Svend Robinson admitted to stealing a diamond ring worth $50,000 in April 2004, he claimed that he was under consider-able emotional stress at the time and received considerable public sympa-thy. As Tana Dineen points out, echoing Nolan, the event was:

a modern ritual in which we obviate crime and guilt by recreating them as aspects of mental illness . . . Psychological notions have become our new moral reference points. Having substituted 'health and illness' for 'right and wrong', we have developed a common therapeutic language that provides the sole route to caring and forgiveness. (Dineen 2004)

Rather than being held responsible for our failure to control our impulses and behaviour we can expect to receive a pathological label. In terms of the Mafia it is clear that many of the characters in *The Sopranos* occupy what the *Diagnostic and Statistical Manual of Mental Disorders, Fourth Edition* (DSM-IV) describes as Antisocial Personality Disorder. This illness is characterised by:

a pervasive pattern of disregard for and violation of the rights of others . . . failure to conform to social norms with respect to lawful behaviours . . . impulsivity or failure to plan ahead . . . irritability and aggressiveness, as indicated by repeated physical fights or assaults . . . lack of remorse, as indi-cated by being indifferent to or rationalizing having hurt, mistreated, or stolen from another. (American Psychiatric Association 2000: 301.7)

The medicalisation of criminal behaviour is reflected in the changing depiction of the gangster on screen. In earlier gangster films the individ-ual criminals – such as Tom Powers in *Public Enemy* (1931) – were pro-pelled by personal ambition coupled with a capacity for remorseless brutality that underscored their success. As Gilberto Perez points out in his excellent discussion of the development of the gangster genre, such figures are supplanted in the modern gangster movies by a depiction of col-lective and ultimately corporatised organised crime, where the individual and his impulses are more of a threat to money-making than its dynamic motor (Perez 1997).

The Godfather (Coppola, 1972) for example, has no instances of murder that could be called impulsive. The killing of Michael Corleone's (Al Pacino) enemies at the end of the film, for example, is clearly planned and choreographed with deadly effectiveness. Michael and his father's (Don Vito Corleone (Marlon Brando)) cold-blooded strategic thinking is contrasted with that of Sonny Corleone (James Caan), who follows his temper rather than his intuition. Sonny's impulsivity is associated with excessive testosterone/masculinity, and it is his temper that is the means by which he is lured to his death by the Barzini family. In the first half of *Scarface* (DePalma, 1982) Tony Montana's (Al Pacino) ambition to rise to the heights of gangsterdom is consolidated by his controlled and fearless aggression. But once his rise to power is complete we see this character losing control over himself. In part this is because of his pathological jealousy of any man who comes close to his sister Gina (Mary Elizabeth Mastrantonio) which eventually leads him to kill his partner and friend Manolo Ray (Steven Bauer) when he discovers them together. He refuses to be complicit in an assassination attempt that would have involved killing a woman and child, instead executing the assassin Alberto (Mark Margolis) in a fit of righteous temper, an act that seals his fate. In *Goodfellas* (Scorsese, 1990) murderous impulsivity is embodied in the figure of Tommy De Vito (Joe Pesci). Whereas other killings in the movie, such as those committed by Jimmy (Robert De Niro), can be read as a response to anxiety or for self-protection, Tommy's behaviour threatens to disrupt the structure of organised crime itself. He kills a young boy, Spider (Michael Imperioli), who dares to tell him to 'go fuck yourself', an act that bewilders his partner Jimmy (Robert De Niro), who asks 'What's the matter with you? Are you a sick maniac?' Tommy also kills Billy Batts (Frank Vincent) over what seems little more than a personal slight. Because Batts was a 'made' guy and part of a crew he was protected; Tommy is later executed for the killing, since as Henry Hill's (Ray Liotta) voice-over explains, the only way to kill a made guy was by arrangement (a sit-down) and with a good reason. The inability to place loyalty and solidarity to the Mafia family above personal hurt is clearly self-destructive in this case. Whereas the killing of Spider is an inconvenience to the mobsters, the murder of Batts threatens to undermine the criminal structure whereby higher-up guys are protected by the traditions and rules of the mob family.

The distinction and blurring of these two kinds of violence – the planned hits and those spontaneous outbursts of violence – are central to

The Sopranos' modernisation of the genre. The second kind and the implications for the solidarity of the group become increasingly prominent as we get to the later seasons of the show. As David Chase has remarked:

> The whole system, the whole hierarchy is set up to prevent violence being done to guys who are higher up. There's rules against made guys shooting another made guy. It kinda makes sense. I mean it's an attempt by criminals with limited impulse control to have some kind of structure.[9]

The contrast between the two kinds of violence is not explicitly established until season three, although traces can still be detected in earlier seasons. The murders in season one are all planned hits: there is the attempted assassination of Tony,[10] the successful hits on Mikey Palmice (Al Sapienza),[11] Brendan Filone (Anthony DeSando),[12] and the execution of FBI 'rats' Jimmy Altieri (Joseph Badalucco Jr) and Febby Petrullo (Tony Ray Rossi).[13] Even those planned hits retain some element of infantile temper tantrums: when Mikey Palmice is hit by Paulie Walnuts (Tony Sirico) and Chris Moltisanti (Michael Imperioli) in the woods the ferocity of the gunfire is, at least on Paulie's part, provoked by his irritation after walking into poison ivy.

In season two some of the planned hits can be seen as the product of generational inexperience, with two 'young punks' trying to make their mark, Sean Gismonte (Chris Tardio) and Matt Bevilaqua (Lillo Brancato Jr), who attempt to kill Chris.[14] Their motive is that they are 'nobodies', and in killing Chris they hope to win respect from mafia captain Richie Aprile (David Proval). Chris kills Sean during the attack and Tony hunts down and executes Matt. The climax of the season comes with the elaborately planned execution of FBI rat Pussy Bonpensiero (Vincent Pastore) by Tony, Paulie and Silvio on board a hired boat.[15]

However, the most stunning instance of impulsive killing comes towards the end of this season. In 'The Knight in White Satin Armor',[16] Richie Aprile and Tony's sister Janice (Aida Turturro) are engaged to be married, but Richie fails to get support for his planned assassination of her brother and is losing money; as a result the large house and grand wedding they've planned is looking unlikely. Worse, Junior Soprano (Dominic Chianese) has told Tony of Richie's plans and Tony, after consulting his *consigliore* Silvio Dante (Steven Van Zandt), has agreed to have him killed. This never happens: while arguing with Janice in the kitchen Richie punches her in the mouth. He sits down, and begins to eat his dinner: 'What you lookin' at? You gonna cry now?' Janice comes back with a gun and shoots him in the chest, then again in the head as he lies wounded on the kitchen floor.

Compared to many other instances of violence in *The Sopranos*, Richie's punch was a minor one. There is no history of abuse between them – indeed for a character so nasty to others, Richie's treatment of Janice is particularly considerate up to this point. There is no doubt that Richie deserves little better, but the scene challenges us to think of Janice as his victim. Clearly this resonates with well-known instances of wives who have killed their husbands after suffering domestic abuse for years. But Janice's action is better understood as one that combines impulsivity with an instinctive strategic insight. Richie is no good to her as a future boss, as an economic support and now it seems he may embark on a career of abuse. Janice calls her brother and Richie is cut up and disposed of.

In the third season this dangerous quality of impulsiveness is embodied in Ralph Ciferetto (Joe Pantoliano), whose erratic and violent behaviour is coupled with his desperate ambition to be promoted to a captain. Ralph's brutal killing of his girlfriend Tracee, by beating her head in, is an emblematic moment in this respect.[17] Ralph's scary temper is complemented by violent outbursts from other characters, notably Mustang Sally's (Brian Tarantina) savage beating of an Aprile relative with a golf club for nothing more than speaking to his girlfriend;[18] and Paulie's killing of the Russian mobster Valery (Vitaly Baganov), again provoked by little more than a personal slight.[19] Finally there is Jackie Aprile's disastrous attempt to rob a card game which ends in his execution.[20]

In season four there are the planned-but-aborted hits on Johnny Sack (Vincent Curatola), Ralph Ciferetto and Carmine Lupertazzi (Tony Lip); but the season is dominated by the increasingly erratic behaviour of Tony himself, culminating in his killing of Ralph over the death of a horse. Whereas Tony's impulsivity had never threatened the solidarity of the mob, here his killing of a mob captain is directly counter to the rules that should protect made mobsters from individual vendettas.

In season five the issue of impulse control is made central and embodied in the arrival of Tony's cousin, Tony Blundetto (Steve Buscemi). After getting out of prison, Blundetto attempts to go straight and set up a massage business. But after fortuitously finding ten thousand dollars and then losing it on gambling he is provoked into attacking his future employer.[21] He subsequently returns to the mob, a decision that seals his fate when Tony is compelled to assassinate him in order to maintain the loyalty and support of his mafia family.

Often the failure to control oneself is associated in *The Sopranos* with the younger inexperienced characters. In 'Amour Fou' the twenty-something son of a former mob-boss, Jackie Aprile, hopes to rise up the ladder of the mob by robbing a card game. His plan goes awry from the get-go. After telling his friend Dino (Andrew Davoli) to call Carlo (Louis

Crugnali) (who has a shotgun), they return to the Aprile house (because Dino's mobile does not work) where *Basic Instinct* is playing on the TV. 'Have they shown my favourite part yet?', says Jackie as the two of them sit on the sofa to watch. This is no procrastination but simply two guys distracted by the TV. The image fades to black as they watch. Later we see them eating a pizza and watching MTV, where Jackie tells Dino once again to call Carlo, 'Do you want to spend the rest of your life with your head up your ass?' The robbery itself is a disaster. Arriving outside with Carlo, Dino and their driver Matush (Emad Tarabay), Jackie has second thoughts.

> *Dino:*   What's the matter.
> *Jackie:* I don't know. You sure you wanna do this?
> *Dino:*   Why? Don't you?
> *Jackie:* Fuck it, let's go down the shore.
> (Pause)
> *Dino:*   Let's do it before the crank[22] wears off.

Whereas the point of the robbery was to achieve status and recognition, now Jackie is determined not to be recognised. He tells Dino to do the talking because 'Eugene . . . will recognise my voice.' Instead of courage and determination, the group appear ill prepared and nervous – that Dino suggests they do it while still under the influence of drugs implies that without it they would not have the inner resolve or courage to carry it out.

On bursting into the card game we discover that both Chris, Albert Barese (Richard Maldone) and Furio Giunta (Federico Castelluccio) are playing – all of them part of Tony's crew. Initially the group seem in control, telling the players to hand over their money and possessions. Christopher and the other mob guys seem calmer, however, than the robbers themselves (Chris and Furio advise them to 'Take it easy'). Jackie in particular is irritated by the dealer, Sunshine's (Paul Mazursky) incessant commentary: 'This is a low-level game, guys, all you're gonna get here is practice . . . Victory has a hundred fathers but defeat is an orphan.' Jackie tells him to 'Shut up, stop fucking looking at me', forgetting that his voice will give him away, as it does, to Christopher. When another mob guy suddenly enters Carlo panics and lets off a shot; immediately we cut outside to see Matush speeding away in the getaway car. As Sunshine continues to voice his adages ('If you can keep your head while those around you can't . . .') Jackie begins to shoot him repeatedly in the chest (a total of seven times) and a shoot-out ensues with Christopher killing Carlo, and Furio being wounded in the thigh by Jackie.

Dino and Jackie run outside to discover their getaway car gone. Jackie hijacks a car and zooms off leaving Dino in the road. Chris and Albert execute him on the spot (shooting him a total of eight times in the head). Jackie's impulsive actions, shooting an unarmed man at close range merely because he irritated him, make him a poor candidate for a mobster. His failure to command group solidarity because of his own indecisiveness and his selfish desire to protect himself evidenced by the brutal way he leaves Dino to his fate indicate a stupid boy way out of his depth.

In part the Dino and Jackie characters are stock elements in a *Sopranos* season. In the first season it was Chris himself and his partner Brendan Filone (Anthony DeSando) who played the role of young parvenus looking for shortcuts to the top; Christopher is so obsessed with being recognised as a mobster that he steals a wad of newspapers that mention him by name, and is affronted when Brendan is described as a major figure after he is killed. The unregulated energy of the young men who wish to make it as mobsters has a destabilising effect on the solidarity of the mob providing narrative conflict. Chris remains the source of the youthful, unregulated impulse. He survives not because he is smarter than the others, but, in part, because he is related to Tony, who tutors him to abandon his hopes of being a screenwriter. This desire in itself suggests a recognition that there might be something more glamorous than being a mobster; nevertheless the fact that he is a hostage to his impulsive nature is underlined in season four when he becomes a fully fledged heroin addict.

In the scene that follows the shoot-out, Chris himself throws a tantrum in front of Tony. Angry at the effrontery of Jackie's action he tells Tony, 'Little motherfucker – he's goin' Tony, he's goin' big time . . . If I see him I'm doing him tonight!' When Tony tells him not to, Chris refers to the rules of the mob: 'Because he's Jackie Aprile's kid? You not gonna let this go – you can't! – he took a shot at me, he tried to kill Furio – we're *made*.' Tony reminds him that this risks exposure but Christopher calls Tony a hypocrite: 'You preach all this wise-guy shit and the only ones who have to follow the rules are us.' But Tony's long-term strategic thinking is correct. After Christopher says 'I loved you', Tony grabs him by the collar and says, 'What happens I decide. You don't love me anymore that breaks my heart, but it's too fuckin' bad. Because you don't gotta love me. But you *will* respect me.'

Dramatically such instances of the failure to control one's temper allow for sudden and novel shifts in the narrative. But they are also part of a wider project of the show to understand the relationship between the therapeutic impulse to cultivate the Self, to express one's feelings, and the necessity of adult solidarity in the (mafia) group in order to maintain the system of organised crime. In this way therapy and violence are not

opposed but interlinked. For example, in 'Season 5, episode 13' Melfi tells
Tony to 'own his feelings', but in doing so Tony realises that he has to
assassinate his cousin, Blundetto, in order to maintain the loyalty and
structure of the mob he rules. It is one of the frequent signals that the show
makes that therapy makes Tony a more efficient mob leader rather than
instilling a solid moral compass.

By framing the show as presenting therapy in relation to the mob, for
whom adult solidarity is a matter of life and death, the relationship of the
Self to the group is acutely posed. Contemporary therapy is concerned
with the cultivation of the Self defined as the inner self: it seeks the relief
of emotional problems through adjustments in the inner world of the individual (Furedi 2003: 144). This is why Melfi's treatment of Tony is
doomed since many of Tony's problems are not amenable to being
reframed as internally caused; Tony exists in a network of organised crime
that constantly throws up new problems, issues and temptations. He
cannot achieve self-understanding without threatening the future of his
mafia leadership. Leadership demands sensitivity, controlled aggression,
strategic intuition and an ability for the theatrical gesture. Tony's hypersensitivity to moods, gesture and emotional landscapes is both a strategic
advantage, allowing him to 'read' the intentions of mob friends and
enemies and the source of his frequent existential angst.

Indeed it is precisely the concentration on individual introspection and
its relativist consequences that Tony objects to repeatedly in therapy. In
'Amour Fou' Melfi tells him that his mistress, Gloria – another one of her
patients – is attracted to him 'like a moth to the flame', and raises the idea
of 'mad love', an intense all-consuming but destructive desire. For Melfi,
such couplings confirm her ideas of repetition compulsion, the need to
repeat what is familiar even if it is harmful. But Tony does not compre-
hend her clinical clarity; he must come to his own understanding through
action rather than reflection.

One of the claims of therapy is that impulses and compulsions, moods
and sadnesses, rages and depressions are structured and patterned. Its aim
is to clarify and identify such patterns the better to manage them. But this
presupposes that the structure is buried in the past, ossified, waiting to be
chipped away and discovered. But patterns and structures of the human
mind are not fixed, like a script, in childhood; they are constantly available
to change and modification. Melfi's attempt to identify the structure of
Tony's attraction to women who are psychologically similar to his mother
fails. It is Gloria Trillo who, for her own erotic and suicidal reasons, intuitively grasps this and it is she who, in a cathartic violent argument, enrages
Tony so that he comes to realise the truth. In a therapeutic world that

encourages us to 'express our feelings' the one emotion that is deemed to require control is anger. And yet it is precisely rage and anger that clarifies for Tony his relationship with Gloria.

In 'Amour Fou' there are several scenes that illustrate this, building up to the climactic violent fight between Gloria and Tony. We see them in bed at Gloria's house enjoying a post-coital conversation; Gloria attempts to tell Tony about her unhappy relationship with her family, but frequent cuts to Tony 'listening' show that he is more interested in forming smoke rings with his cigar. Gloria tries a more direct appeal by turning up the radio that is playing 'Affection' and doing a striptease show before jumping on him.[23] This scene illustrates Gloria's intuitive understanding that Tony can be reached only through direct, elaborate theatrics. Later they have a strong argument about the possibility that Tony's former girlfriend has slashed Gloria's tyres. Again, Tony is difficult to reach.

It is by chance that Carmela is at the Mercedes showroom when Gloria is there to offer her a lift home. During the journey home Gloria quizzes Carmela about her family. Carmela's ring is prominent here but also her inability to stop boasting about her family's achievements, particularly Meadow's attendance at Columbia University. 'At least your daughter doesn't have to latch on to a man for success,' Gloria tells her in a barbed attack. When Tony finds out about this he confronts Gloria at the car showroom and ends the relationship. Later when Gloria phones him in hysterics he visits her late in the evening at her place.

This climactic scene is depicted as a violent form of psychodrama in stark contrast to the sterile therapy sessions. Her house is a small cottage, with wood panel floors and walls. It is cosy and dark. Annabella Scioria's performance as Gloria Trillo is outstanding. She mixes a smart, self-assured persona, with a coquettish, girlish thrill. When she gets what she wants, before others know she is going to get it, we see a girlish smirk of triumph flicker across her face. This happens twice, once in the underground parking lot, and again when Tony confronts her in the Globe motors showroom after he discovers she has given Carmela a lift home. In this scene she again gets what she wants – Tony to attempt to kill her. At first Tony attempts to connect with her despair.

Gloria: My life's a trip to nowhere.
Tony: You bring it on yourself. [Tenderly] Look. It's over. I mean we had our 'mo-fo' or whatever. And it was great. [He touches her cheek and she nuzzles his hand with it.] And now it's time to put it to bed.

Gloria is seated on the floor near the staircase as Tony towers over her, but her savage reply is spat out with provocative intensity:

> *Gloria:* What you think you can treat me like some fucking stupid *goombah* housewife? You think I'm gonna let some fucker shit over me just because he buys me a ridiculous gaudy fucking ring?

Again the ring functions as a sign of Tony's economy of compensation and love; she directly challenges both his crudity and taste, and Carmela's mute complicity in accepting. The provocation works and Tony slaps her viciously, 'Do you think my life's a fucking picnic?'

> *Gloria:* Oh, poor you. [She gets up and approaches Tony] You've got a fucking dream life compared to mine. Nobody cares if I'm alive or dead.

At this point we see Tony moving away from her towards the door with an odd look on his face.

> *Tony:* I didn't just meet you. I've known you all my life. My mother was just like you. A bottomless black hole.
> *Gloria:* Oh, the mother now. I surrender, burn me at the stake.

In her theatrical manner Gloria achieves what Melfi fails to do, allowing Tony to understand the similarity between Gloria's melodramatic self-pity and his mother's pathological depression. As he goes to leave, Gloria threatens to tell his wife and call his daughter at Columbia; a violent fight in the kitchen area ends with Tony on top of Gloria with his hands around her throat. Tony's enormous frame is contrasted with the slight build of Gloria:

> *Tony:* Now you listen to me. You go near my wife or my family and I'll fuckin kill you, you understand me? I'll fuckin kill you.
> *Gloria:* [choking] Kill me, kill me you cocksuck – [spits in his face] Kill me –
> *Tony:* You fuckin bitch! [squeezes harder]
> *Gloria:* Kill me. Kill me. Kill me. Kill me. Kill me. [Tony lets go and leaves] Kill me. Kill me. Kill me. Kill me.

In the next scene with Melfi she encourages him to think about what it was about Gloria that reminded him of his mother. Tony: 'Look I don't want to fuck my mother, I don't care what you say.' 'Not fuck', replies Melfi. 'Win her love . . .' But where does this insight get anybody? Tony's response is a very practical one – to threaten Gloria using one of his hoods Patsy Parisi (Dan Grimaldi) to stay away from him or die. Tony understands that the clinical insights of therapy do little to solve the problems he is faced with day by day. Tony grasps the world better than Melfi because he understands that there is no understanding that would settle the problems the world continually throws up to him. At one point, to Tony's bewilderment, Melfi – like a true nihilistic postmodernist – quotes from Yeats' 'Second Coming': 'The falcon cannot hear the falconer . . . the centre cannot hold.' But how does this bleak view of the present and the future help us from day to day? As Tony often quips, 'How do people find the time?'[24] After Tony kills Ralph in a violent rage he dreams about a car journey with Ralph, Melfi asks him what he thinks the dream means:

> Why don't you just tell me? We have to go through this exercise every time? What about impulse control? I've been sitting in this chair for four fucking years and still nothing's been done about that. And it leads me to make mistakes at my work. What good did you do me with that?[25]

Melfi talks of their achievements, claiming that there has been 'significant relief' in the areas of panic attacks and depression, and Tony mocks her, 'Oh yeah, my mum would come over a pot roast . . . All this fucking self-knowledge – what the fuck has it gotten me?' When Melfi replies that there must be other sources of pain and truth worth exploring, Tony is derisory: 'Pain and truth – come on! I'm a fat fucking crook from New Jersey.'

The complexity of the shadings of character, the shifts in tone, between the brutal, the despairing and the comic are unlike anything else on television. In fact *The Sopranos* is redolent of Philip Roth's trilogy of novels – *American Pastoral* (1997), *I Married A Communist* (1998) and *The Human Stain* (2000), also set in New Jersey, in their detailed attentiveness to the losses and gains of the past sixty years of American life, the impact of detraditionalisation and the weakening of adult solidarity. Roth's novels are also deeply concerned with the possibilities and deceptions of realising the human in contemporary life. In another literary connection David Chase has remarked that Flaubert's *Madame Bovary* was an influence: 'all those characters, the horrible life, and yet there's something strangely funny about it'.[26] In his introduction to *Madame Bovary*, Geoffrey Wall notes that it is, '[t]he tense alternation of feeling, of pathos and irony, of intimacy and estrangement, that makes up the sweet and sour pleasure of *Madame Bovary*' (Wall 2003: xxvi). Like Emma, Tony is a fascinating mixture of popular culture, ambition and submission to impulses and appetites that society does not sanction. And like her, Tony intuitively – but not intellectually – understands that the world is a deeper and richer place than can be encompassed by the sterile categories of society and the therapy that it sanctions as a panacea. Tony may not understand himself but he understands the world better than Melfi. Who would envy her insight? In this way the show challenges us to consider a mob leader as a better human being than his therapist. Tony is the most interesting thing in her life.

Critical to *The Sopranos'* appeal in this respect is the performance of James Gandolfini – it is difficult to imagine another actor who can be at home in a domestic as well as a mob setting.[27] His massive bear-like frame appears to embody a breadth of human dimensions, its failures, excesses and aspirations. Gandolfini is able to display tenderness, cruelty, brute force, hypersensitivity, charm, hatred, despair and rage, and in doing so opens up a further dimension to screen acting: the ability to invite simultaneous pathos, pity and terror. At times he is baby-like, whining about his food, or his needs, at other times he is the dominant cigar-puffing Alpha Male surveying his mob and blood families with arrogant satisfaction. And then he can play the victim, what he calls 'the sad clown', a self-pitying despairing Everyman lost in a threatening, dangerous and incomprehensible world. What is engaging about Tony is his defence of human agency and responsibility even as he hypocritically calls his own work 'putting food on my family's table' and exhibits little or no guilt about his crimes, except perhaps in the very legible dreams he experiences.[28] Throughout season five Tony is explicitly associated with a wild bear that invades the Sopranos' garden; in the final episode we see in slow motion a form emerging from the trees that turns out not to be the bear but Tony.

A frequent motif is the shot of the haggard, just-woken Tony lumbering down his driveway to pick up the morning newspaper, or, in 'Amour Fou', scooping cereal at the breakfast bar in his dressing gown, as Carmela reads the paper. 'I think it's shocking that the English government didn't tell anyone about mad cow's disease.' 'Maybe they didn't want to create a stampede,' he quips. Minutes later he has Gloria by the throat at the Mercedes showroom. *The Sopranos* challenges those who see this as a contradiction instead of what it is, being human. In that sense *The Sopranos* represents the return to humanist values and classical realism that the 1980s and 1990s postmodern television sought to undermine. However brutal and unpleasant Tony is at times, he stands as the last humanist in a world of relativist chaos. Unlike Carmela, he is not prone to doubt about his actions (although he questions some of his decisions).

There is something marvellous in the fearsome ambition, singularity of purpose and leadership that Tony embodies, a quality that is sorely lacking in contemporary popular culture with its insistence on flawed victims and rejection of heroism. In 'Christopher' he berates Silvio for buying into the victim culture; Tony may be inarticulate but it is an expressive, wonderful inarticulacy. Tony should be imprisoned for his brutal ugly crimes, but one can only hope that he is never 'cured'. To borrow from the end of Roth's *American Pastoral*, what on earth is wrong with Tony Soprano?

Notes

1. Tony Soprano talking about his temper to his therapist Jennifer Melfi in 'Cold Cuts', season 5, episode 11.
2. A3, 'Woke Up This Morning' (from their 1997 album, *Exit on Coldharbour Lane*); a version of this track is used for the title sequence of *The Sopranos*, although that version does not contain these lyrics.
3. Season 3, episode 12.
4. This aria comes from Vivaldi's first opera *Ottone in Villa* (1713), a lurid and complex melodrama.
5. 'The Telltale Moozadell', season 3, episode 9.
6. 'Second Opinion', season 3, episode 7. The psychiatrist is called Dr Krakower (Kracauer?), a Jew who bears a passing resemblance to Freud himself.
7. The scene was filmed on location in the Brooklyn Museum of Art and the Rodin sculptures we see are part of its permanent collection.
8. See for example Fritz Lang's wonderful *You Only Live Once* (1937).
9. David Chase, DVD commentary for 'Whitecaps', season 4, episode 13.
10. 'Isabella', season 1, episode 12.
11. 'I Dream of Jeannie Cusamano', season 1, episode 13.
12. 'Meadowlands', season 1, episode 4.
13. 'I Dream of Jeannie Cusamano', season 1, episode 13.
14. 'From Where To Eternity', season 2, episode 9.
15. 'Funhouse', season 2, episode 13.
16. Season 2, episode 12.
17. 'University', season 3, episode 6.
18. 'Another Toothpick', season 3, episode 5.
19. 'Pine Barrens', season 3, episode 11.
20. 'Army of One', season 3, episode 13.
21. 'Sentimental Education', season 5, episode 6.
22. 'Crank' is slang for amphetamines.
23. 'Affection' by The Lost Boys; the main lyric is, 'Give me some affection/Why's it so hard?'
24. For example, see 'Employee of the Month', season 3, episode 4.
25. 'Calling All Cars', season 4, episode 11.
26. Museum of Television and Radio Seminar, Los Angeles 2000. Available for viewing at the Museum of Television and Radio, New York and Los Angeles.
27. The only other contemporary actor who combines menace, build and charm is Michael Madsen – but it is extremely difficult to imagine that actor playing a domesticated husband.
28. See 'Two Tony's', season 5, episode 1.

Bibliography

American Psychiatric Association (2000), *Diagnostic and Statistical Manual of Mental Disorders, Fourth Edition*, Washington, DC: American Psychiatric Association.

Calcutt, Andrew (1996), 'Uncertain Judgement: A Critique of the Culture of Crime', in Suke Wolton (ed.), *Marxism, Mysticism and Modern Theory*, London: Macmillan, pp. 40–60.

Dineen, Tana (2004),'Don't Blame me, Blame my Stress' *Spiked*, www.spiked-online.com

Fellezs, Kevin (2002), 'Wiseguy Opera: Music for *Sopranos*', in David Lavery (ed.), *This Thing of Ours: Investigating 'The Sopranos'*, London: Wallflower Press, pp. 162–75.

Furedi, Frank (2003), *Therapy Culture: Cultivating Vulnerability in an Uncertain Age*, London: Routledge.

Lavery, David (ed.) (2002), *This Thing of Ours: Investigating 'The Sopranos'*, London: Wallflower Press.

Nochimson, Martha P. (2003) 'Tony's Options: *The Sopranos* and the Televisuality of the Gangster Genre', *Senses of Cinema*, http://www.sensesofcinema.com/contents/03/29/sopranos_televisuality.html

Nolan, James (1998), *The Therapeutic State*, New York: New York University Press.

Perez, Gilberto (1997), *The Material Ghost: Films and their Medium*, Baltimore: Johns Hopkins University Press.

Wall, Geoffrey (2003), 'Introduction', *Madame Bovary*, London: Penguin, pp. xvii–xxxvii.

CHAPTER 9

Television, Horror and Everyday Life in *Buffy the Vampire Slayer*

Eric Freedman

Television introduced the conflicted nature of domestic space as at once private and public in the 1950s, as the television industry invested itself in (and profited from) the very anxieties that were directed towards the new technology. These anxieties were linked both to the role the new medium might play in shaping everyday domestic life and with external situations and reactions along broader cultural indices. One obvious source of this anxiety was the ease with which the new medium could bring global and national news events into domestic space. Consequently it is not surprising that science fiction and horror found their place on television, as these particular genres are often the site at which cultural and technological anxieties seem to intersect. 'Implicating the "other" in family life, postwar American horror has become increasingly marked by a thematic recognition that the social world can no longer be conceptualized and dramatized as an opposition between private and public spheres' (Sobchack 1996: 145). With the movement from film to television, horror and science fiction genres have literally invaded the domestic sphere and opened up the family room to the horrific world outside of this traditionally private and safe domain. At the same time contemporary Hollywood horror is frequently marked by its spatial relocation to the American landscape and its temporal relocation to the present and also focused on the 'other' within the nuclear family and specific social groups, particularly teenagers. With the advent of cable and satellite broadcasting the replaying of these tensions as postmodern pastiche in contemporary television programming has been a tactic taken on by a television industry regrouping to capture a teen marketplace. What follows here is an investigation of this phenomenon via the recently emergent Warner Brothers television network in order to link political economy to traditional studies of gender.

The pursuit of the teen market has centred on the teen body. Within the televisual landscape of reconfigured serial horror, science fiction and fantasy, the teen body is figured as both fantastic and real. Several contemporary programmes within this history and frame of reference – among them *Buffy the Vampire Slayer* and *Smallville* – exist within the broad conceptual terrain of genre and seriality and they provide examples of how the fantastic and the real via genre and form are linked to ideology, myth and commerce. Within this frame of reference Buffy Summers' body articulates a spectacular form of capitalist realism played out in the familial and familiar realm. By 'reading' Buffy's body, among others, this chapter explores the manner in which the teen body is attached to a political economy whose values it serves to celebrate and promote, and considers the specific connection of this body, owned and operated by the WB, and laid alongside that of *Dawson's Creek* and others who live together on the young net (which hit the airwaves in 1995, the same year as UPN), to contemporary national consumer-goods advertising.[1]

'From the 1960s onward, family life and social life have continued to converge, partly in response to a number of institutional shifts; within this chronology, horror (as well as science fiction and fantasy) has been transformed into a generic form that includes elements of the family melodrama – a genre whose own representations are driven by an opposing realism' (Sobchack 1996: 146). *Buffy the Vampire Slayer* and the other genre-linked WB programmes do not mark the first intersection of horror and melodrama on television; programmes such as *Tales of Tomorrow* (1951–3) and *Dark Shadows* (1966–71) also clearly extend melodrama into the realm of the fantastic, while even more firmly grounded realist serials have incorporated the aura of the fantastic into far-flung subplots, exploring both horror and sci-fi within suburbia (consider, for example, *General Hospital*'s nuclear weapons subplot in which Luke and Laura are instrumental in saving the world from certain destruction by a madman set on global conquest).

The double coding of bodies such as Buffy Summers, bound by the expectations of both the fantastic and the quotidian, is made possible by the narrative economies of the serial form. At the same time, the liberatory discourses that circulate around such programmes as *Buffy the Vampire Slayer* claim a progressive politics of gender and sexuality. However, as horror and science fiction converge with the everyday in teen melodrama, the serial form demands the playing out and repetition of loss and recuperation, empowerment and disempowerment, and closes off particular prospects for the negotiation of identity. What then are the limits of these probable readings?

Generic Convergence

Although horror, science fiction and melodrama have somewhat distinct generic codes and have different historical cycles (of peak production), the three genres can nonetheless combine in specific cultural contexts in the service of common social directives. Vivian Sobchack notes that:

> Engaging in urgent and dynamic exchange, whose goal is ultimately conservative, the three genres attempt to narratively contain, work out, and in some fashion resolve the contemporary weakening of patriarchal authority and the glaring contradictions that exist between the mythology of family relations and their actual social practice. In all three genres those contradictions are most powerfully condensed and represented in the problematic figure of the child. (Sobchack 1996: 147)

Citing the work of Dudley Andrew, Sobchack claims the privileged figure of these texts as a site in which the narrative problematic coalesces as a primary agent that can 'transform the trouble in the text' (Sobchack 1996: 147). Clearly the ready alignment of these genres with questions about the limits of family makes them fertile ground for teen-centred plot-lines pitched at teen audiences, a demographic engaged with the very questions at the heart of such narratives. And the ensemble dynamic of *Buffy* and *Smallville* does not necessarily contradict the claim for a central agent, but rather allows multiple points for investment and the extension of the central 'trouble' across multiple plot-lines; ensemble casting fosters greater permutations of each narrative's central problematic (or enigma) and plays into the very demands of the serial structure. Horror, science fiction and fantasy fit readily into the highly coded landscape of melodrama for adolescent viewers, for individually and together the generic elements of each form work towards expressing the anxieties of inbetween-ness – a metamorphosing body caught between childhood and adulthood. In this landscape, developing sexual awareness is often expressed without punishment. In fact, the protagonist's struggle with normalcy, with his or her insider/outsider status, is commonly related as the unending quest for the very pleasures of normalcy (the goal is to fit in and experience the mundane tribulations of everyday life in rural or suburban America), a position that the protagonist cannot occupy in a stable fashion. Moreover, this conflict is enacted on familiar ground – the home, itself a site of struggle, an arena in which teens are confronted with the binary possibilities of dependence and independence, and in which rebellion is a normal state of affairs.

Genre cycles – the resurgence of certain generic forms at particular historical moments – can be read as an index of more general cultural conditions; as well, individual generic forms evolve in relation to a number of broader artistic and social conventions. For example, the investment in horror and its reshaping and relocation in the late 1960s can be read as indicative of industrial shifts (in culture industries such as film and television) as well as cultural shifts. Gregory Waller suggests that post-1968 US horror can be understood as an extended dramatisation of such specific issues as:

> Fluctuations in 'key economic indicators' and attempts to redirect domestic and foreign policy; Watergate and the slow withdrawal from Vietnam; oil shortages and the Iranian hostage crisis; the rise of the New Right and the Moral Majority; and the continuing debate over abortion, military spending, and women's rights. (Waller 1987:12)

Waller suggests that the genre can be interpreted as, 'An index to and commentary on what have often been identified as the more general cultural conditions of our age' (Waller 1987: 12). The focused recombination of specific generic forms for perceived markets on the WB is a simple commercial strategy. However, the rise of one particular paradigm such as the teen-orientated series within a given cultural moment indicates an industry engagement with viewer response that specifically invokes the broader social and political climate. It is too great an undertaking for me to consider the dominant project of generic recombination since the mid-1990s, but any attempt at political categorisation must situate the products of television alongside those of other media forms, such as film and multimedia gaming. Following Robin Wood's lead, I speculate that as any new generic synthesis achieves a point of stability, reflected in the coherency of both its codes and its ideological machinery, it cannot help but become regressive; nonetheless, the progressive and reactionary text (as well as reading strategies) seem to be mutually dependent; the negotiation for dominance is driven by factors that exceed the text. It is my goal to examine the mechanisms by which such negotiation can be delimited (Wood 1986: 191).

Seriality and Televisual Flow: Style as Substance

Using a model suggested by Robert Allen, my examination of the serial text as social phenomena is grounded not simply on content analysis but more significantly on aesthetics; yet the formal codes I turn to first are of a specific variety. Allen suggests that the paradigmatic structures of serial television are the point of complexity and engagement; while the syntagmatic dimension (the linear axis of story) is rather formulaic (a survey of serial programmes reveals quite a limited number of plot variants), the paradigmatic recombination of character relationships and settings can be quite nuanced (Allen 1983: 103). And while setting is commonly under-utilised in serial narratives, it is nevertheless an important visual code. True to form, as Sarah Kozloff notes, setting is typically privileged only in the opening montage sequence of any serial programme, and thereafter the body of the narrative action unfolds on sets that 'are not particularly evocative or individualized' (1987: 75). Yet rather than ignore setting in favour of character, setting merits further scrutiny as a complex textual code, especially as it seems to work against at least one of the assumed codes of seriality (the prolongation of events) while reinforcing many of the genre's other key structures; indeed the montage sequence operates as a doubly purposed hermeneutic act, introducing the semiological complexity of both the specific programme (revealing and reviewing the central conflicts and enigmas) and the genre itself (as a shorthand guide to serial television's textual strategies, the genre's rituals are laid out in compressed form). And the montage sequence is no longer simply an appendage to a programme body; rather, it has taken on a degree of independence as a commercial trailer.

The WB has developed a standard format for advertising its shows in its interstitial bumpers; the formula is applied across the network's programmes and daily line-ups. While the nuances of this strategy shift from season to season, the WB adheres to a number of distinct conventions. As one example, the WB advertises its autumn 2003 Wednesday line-up with a literal 'The WB Wednesday' sign composed of theatrical lights on a fixed armature; the sign stands in what appears to be a neutral studio backlot, and its illuminated facade resonates with the antiquated codes of Hollywood glamour. The stars of the evening's featured programmes are posed not as characters but as celebrities and each is photographed in direct address, framed by both a photo-style computer-generated matte as well as the voice of an off-screen male narrator. The bumper does not engage with the specific generic codes of its advertised programme, but rather trades these in for the neutral signifiers of celebrity and event programming. Yet this trading in signs is made possible only by the viewer's familiarity with each show's cast. The pleasure consigned to the bumper is one of recognition, and by extension the viewer is being rewarded with what seem to be extra-textual cues; the viewer is given a glimpse at a backstage persona (the actor out of character), however performed this may be, and the direct address and positioning of the actor, outside of the show breeds familiarity. The viewer is meant to feel a kinship with the actor, who, alongside fellow actors, has willingly dropped out of character. To draw a theatrical parallel, the cast steps out in front of the curtain. The WB has codified self-effacement in the bumper (breaking the fourth wall), if only to draw out and reward an attachment that will allow the subsequent fantasy to unfold unfettered by self-reflexivity.

Much work is being performed in what otherwise reads as a straightforward advertisement for the programme that follows. The 'look' itself is a particularly significant gestural detail; each of the actors is presented in the process of directly addressing the camera and notably there are no reverse shots. We are provided instead with a liberal series of jump cuts that may feature each actor from multiple vantage points, or simply string the actors together in sequence. The look is an open-ended invitation, an act without closure. The serial programme also privileges the act of looking. Characters routinely gaze at each other in an unspoken dramatic exchange. While the reverse shot may be provided in the body of the narrative, the act is one of infinite repetition, a visual corollary for longing and what are commonly unresolved or long-delayed romantic attachments. Not surprisingly, this grammatical tactic is often the featured element in billboard and print advertisements for these programmes; reduced to a single-image frame, the two-shot is the form of choice. The cross-promotional print campaign for *Smallville* and Verizon Wireless features a two-shot of Lana and Clark as its header. The banner is a composite image that positions Lana behind Clark, their bodies intersect, their eye-lines match, but they face in opposite directions. The exchange is anxiously unresolved; although the two looks seem to be directed at each other, the spatial dislocation of their bodies makes closure a logistical impossibility. Both desire and tension are given form through this static reference to televisual symbolism; the tactics of seriality itself are similarly charged.

Segmentation of narrative has been the standard form of television construction and contemporary series privilege the title sequence. John Ellis sees this as a critical variant on the standard of segmentation:

> There is a high degree of autonomy for the title sequence, since it is repeated every time the programme format is used and usually provides a highly generalised, gestural conception of the programme it advertises, unlike the material used to showcase individual programmes. A strategy increasingly used with American series is to combine the two forms, so that the standard title sequence integrates shots from the individual programme in a highly enigmatic or incoherent way. (1982: 119–20)

Many WB programmes adopt a parallel titling strategy: individual episodes begin with one scene of narrative action which is followed by the opening credit sequence; in turn, the credit sequence is commonly followed by the first commercial break before the viewer is returned to the show's already unfolding narrative. While the serial narrative's function is the extension of a story arc, the title sequence works in reverse by collapsing it. Yet this contraction is not quite the opposite of the protracted narrative, for key narrative moments are provided to the viewer in a montage of non-sequiturs. The plot fragments are presented out of sequence; episodic and seasonal moments are presented in a new order that foregrounds not only the individual plot points but also their significance as metaphors for the overarching themes of the programme. These plot points are commonly chosen for their immediacy, the degree to which they can be instantly recognised as particular narrative instances with decided importance – moments of significant character development, dramatic development, or more generalised thematic attachment.

The title sequence for *Smallville* plays out these relations. It establishes the programme's characters, sketches out their significant relations, and replays the show's origin myth, the ground zero of all subsequent dramatic conflict, and includes images crafted specifically for the opening credits. Images produced specifically for the title sequence are not without a narrative push: the show's characters are not pulled entirely out of the universe of *Smallville*; rather, they are foregrounded yet immersed in the fictional environment and thus seem bound to a particular narrative moment even if it cannot be located in a particular episode. And all of the images found in the title sequence are subjected to a new formal logic that freely re-crafts and reorganises moments into a new spatial and temporal framework. The effects deployed in the title sequence, from subtitling to compositing and graphic manipulation, not only mark out the performance of excessive style, but, as John Caldwell suggests, are far from ideologically neutral, working as 'attempts to create visual analogues of feelings, products, surfaces, artifacts, and material pictures – representations of the stuff of mass culture itself' (1995: 152).

The credit sequence has evolved since the show's pilot, with several significant redesigns. The pilot episode does not have a credit montage; rather, subtitles are inserted into the diegesis after the first narrative sequence. By the second episode, however, a distinct credit montage was introduced, and as with the pilot's subtitles located after an introductory narrative sequence. The montage sequence evolved during subsequent seasons, as characters were added or dropped, as clips from later episodes were added to the mix, and as several composite shots were reworked. The sequence displays the programme's narrative catalyst and then in a form of rapid exposition defines the individual characters and sets them in dramatic relation to one another. The composite images position each cast member (in foreground close-up) against a character-defining backdrop. Each background has narrative import. In the second season credit sequence, Clark is bound to the meteor shower, which marked his arrival on Earth. Lana is seen visiting her parents' gravesite (her mother and father were killed by a falling meteorite during the shower) and it is here that she has her first-intimate conversation with Clark that binds both of them as orphans and kindred spirits. Lex and his father are both superimposed on signifiers of wealth, power and privilege. Peter is bound to his own agricultural roots as well as the Kent family (and will become the first to be trusted with Clark's secret identity). Chloe is connected to her academic pursuits and her role as the editor of the school newspaper and a writer for the yearbook. Clark's parents are attached to their homestead and farm, suggesting virtue in its attachment to the nation and the land. Martha is positioned inside the home yet in view of the threshold, across which hangs an American flag. Jonathan is profiled in a low-angle shot that silhouettes him against the sky and alongside the weather vane mounted atop the Kents' home, pronouncing him a directional signpost and trusted stalwart.

The title sequence also replays central plot points, further defines individual characters, and sketches out the web of interpersonal relations. The season two credit sequence includes the following images:

- Lex strikes Clark with his car, and the vehicle careens off a bridge into the water below.
- Clark rescues Lex from his submerged vehicle (the crash and rescue are conjoined moments from the series premiere that establish the central enigma for Lex; in subsequent episodes Lex attempts to unravel Clark's miraculous survival).
- Clark and Lana watch the sunset together (a critical two-shot, for if the secret at the heart of the narrative is Clark's hidden identity, the central extended narrative question is not simply '[when] will his secret be revealed?' but also '[when] will he get the girl?').
- Chloe explores a darkened interior with her flashlight in hand (the shot establishes her investigative instincts and her journalistic sensibility, marking her subsequent pursuit of mystery).
- Clark hangs from a scarecrow post in a field (a homecoming hazing ritual found in the series pilot, that also marks Clark's body with the legendary 'S' and provocatively posits him a martyr).
- Martha holds a young Clark in her arms and Jonathan is by her side (the Kents have just found the boy after the crash of his space ship).
- Lana stands on a roadway watching three twisters in the distance.

- Clark is hit by a speeding bus that collapses around his body.
- Clark is hit by a mace that breaks apart as it impacts his body.
- Lana is thrown by an explosion.
- Clark is struck by lightning (this caps a series of action shots that have a narrative function, foregrounding Clark's superhuman abilities and underscoring Lana's vulnerability; a generic function, foregrounding the supernatural and establishing a principle dynamism; and a purely televisual function, foregrounding the nature of the visual effects embedded throughout the series).

The title sequence introduces the show's cast; it also sets the serial in motion, sketching out subplots and character relations mapping Clark as a central figure on to the lives of each of the other residents of Smallville. It introduces the fundamental premises, iconography and enigmas, and situates the players within the community of Smallville and in relation to the Kent family farm, that is, the mythical 'heartland'. The series of match-frame dissolves that occur towards the end of the title sequence metaphorically bind the characters into a series of family resemblances; the individual portraits culminate in a family portrait of the Kents before the credit sequence ends with an isolated image of Clark standing in the cornfield, the metaphoric point of origin for the show's conflicts. Clearly questions of family and patriarchy are a constant refrain for the series, and, accordingly, the Kents are the only whole family presented in the title sequence.[2]

The Kents' household is not only the sole nuclear entity, it is also the show's centre, and much of the first season privileges the Kent home as a site of restoration, an arena in which dramatic tensions are aired and resolved, and a privileged vantage point for Clark to muse about the perpetuation of the familial. Clark's telescope is mounted in the Kents' barn loft, his 'fortress of solitude', and ever focused on the activity of his neighbour and muse Lana. Moreover, the loft itself is a confessional site, a place where Clark and Lana sublimate their desire in conversation. Yet as dictated by the open-ended dramatic tension of the serial format, the familial realm is never entirely secured. It is a safe haven that also hides a secret; it is the locus of the domestic, the mundane and the quotidian, but also the harbour of the otherworldly and fantastic. This home is not only a shelter for Clark, but also for his space ship, stowed away in the storm cellar. It is this very vessel that destroys part of the Kent home at the end of the second season. Bringing the threat back home, the destruction is triggered by Clark in a series of events that also result in the loss of Martha's unborn child. In later episodes Lana is symbolically thrust into adulthood after she murders a criminal at the Kent homestead. This incident, riddled with moral complexity, inescapably binds her to the Kent inner circle. She too is charged with a secret, even if it is not the narrative's central one. The programme's title sequence does not keep pace with these specific plot points. In fact most of the title sequences for WB programmes are updated only on a seasonal basis, reworking the basic montage by substituting clips from older episodes with clips from newer ones, and updating cast profiles. Nevertheless, there seems to be an intentionality built into this signifying system as the montage that is out of synch with the development of the programme narrative calls the reader into action, invites the viewer to draw upon a knowledge of more recent events and maps this awareness against the thematic premise embedded in the opening sequence. In accord with the notion of the open text, this active reading is an interpretive process that occurs along the text's complex yet clearly delimited pathways.

Seriality and the Intertextual Commodity

Serial television and serial texts in general require active participation on the part of consumers, and the study of seriality has tackled the role of the active consumer in the grip of a variety of culture industries trying to turn activity into profit. In her cross-media study of the serial form, Jennifer Hayward notes:

> For producers, the advantage of serialization is that it essentially creates the demand it then feeds: the desire to find out 'what happens next' can only be satisfied by buying, listening to, or viewing the next installment . . . Methods of maximizing serial profits have been progressively refined as industrial capitalism developed. (1997:3)

The television serial complicates the standard concept of a seamless intertextual commodity or 'supersystem'. The television text at the centre of the system is not necessarily in harmony with the texts that circulate around it. These texts are not necessarily successfully bound by a meta-narrative, and when an apparent binding narrative can be constructed there may remain an ideological tension that threatens to unhinge the system. David Buxton suggests:

> The more a text attempts to remain faithful to its original project, the more it is forced to renounce narrative development, or strain to return to its point of departure in an unconvincing closure: the more it embraces narrative complexity and movement, the more it is forced to contend with its inability completely to cover over the cracks that open up between the assemblage and the narrative. (1990: 15)

While Buxton's analysis focuses on the television series rather than the serial, contemporary serials do invoke several of the principles of series programming. The serial narrative illustrates an organising ideological project and is dependent on the collection of a number of concrete elements in developing central characters and themes. It may at various points shift the relationship between stasis and development. This is illustrated most clearly in episodes that privilege self-contained problematics and character sets over the systematic development of the programme's main characters.

Most contemporary serial programmes are part of an intertextual super-system that includes both product tie-ins and sponsorships, independently-operated fan sites that house slash fiction (fan-scripted stories that extend the narratives of the programme), chat rooms, bulletin boards, as well as personal blogs (online journals). It also includes those non-products that circulate in commercial spaces, such as the official chat rooms, bulletin boards, 'news' updates and games hosted by the network or production company.

Warner Brothers' *Smallville* home page takes the form of a conventional newspaper; titled the *Smallville Ledger*, the tabloid reports stories that mirror each episode's central plot points, yet each story is written from the 'naturally' limited perspective of the reporter. The viewer has privileged knowledge that the fictional reporter does not. For example, a recent 'top story' reports on the disappearance of Lex Luthor's wife, yet reports certain causal details as unknown. The viewer, however, is quite aware of the circumstances surrounding the incident, for these were conveyed in the programme. Thus the fictional news site adopts the posture of serial logic, embracing the fundamental premise of mystery and foregrounding those secrets that form the heart of the programme narrative. The *Smallville Ledger*'s community calendar links readers to the programme's online message board, a community site governed by the terms of use of Warner Brothers Online. The site also includes a link to *The Torch*, the fictional school newspaper of Smallville High, which includes its own story archive, as well as a makeshift directory of the show's main teen characters. The *Smallville* site is littered with banner ads, some of these support the fictional enterprises of the programme, for example a link to LuthorCorp includes a fully developed corporate profile and an interface that is decidedly distinct from the Warner Brothers main pages. Others are links to real-world enterprises such as America Online (a Time Warner company) and American Greetings.

The *Smallville* website reinforces the narrative dynamic of the show and embeds the programme's fundamental plot points in a new architecture that invites interaction. Interactivity is called for both in the design of the community pages and by virtue of the interface. While the television text relays information in a linear fashion, the website requires a piecemeal accumulation of key textual data by moving across hyperlinks. Though the Warner Brothers television main page includes a link to a *Smallville* episode guide, this site too contains a wide range of textual tangents that call for non-linear movement. The Smallville High Yearbook page invites readers to participate in an online survey, while the E-Card page allows readers to send *Smallville*-themed greeting cards. The site also includes links to *Smallville* merchandise, including action figures, books, the first season DVD as well as links to biographies and trivia quizzes for the individual actors. The site also hosts Allison Mack's blog (complete with Kodak logo), which functions both as a personal diary and a space for further product placement. As the site expands outwards, it informs the central narrative of the television programme in a traditional system of intertextual rewards. Faithful viewers are urged to become faithful browsers, and although no key plot points are relegated solely to one domain, those consumers who navigate both spaces become more embroiled in the mythology, as the net structure allows the programme authors to further articulate the backstory. As the backstory is elaborated, it is clear that the multi-media venture begs for multi-faceted consumptive possibilities. To the degree that these can be contained under one rubric, on the surface there seems to be some ideological harmony across these products, if only because they can be embedded in one seamless net architecture. Even as *Smallville* expands beyond these spaces the programme's diegesis is foregrounded; the Verizon Wireless interplay is one that privileges the show's narrative as product, allowing subscribers to participate in polls and quizzes as well as send and save *Smallville* images. The wireless service is framed as yet another conduit for the WB; as long as the common carrier is positioned as content provider, ideological harmony is guaranteed.

In contrast to *Smallville*'s apparently ideologically consistent supersystem Robert Allen has suggested that:

> Rather than offering a simple message, soaps offer amazingly complex fields of semiotic possibilities which a variety of audience members can use in a variety of ways. It is precisely this openness that makes the soap opera historically unique . . . but which also makes the 'message' or 'ideology' of the soap very difficult to specify. It seems less important to argue that the soap is a closed or open text, in [Umberto] Eco's scheme, than to recognize that in soaps we are dealing with extremely significant [and complex] economic, aesthetic and cultural products. (1983: 105–6)

While the study of serial programming has revealed or codified a generic vocabulary broadly categorised as narratively open and structurally episodic, a consideration of the serial programme as a serial commodity will highlight the various tensions that may emerge in such a trans-media environment. For example, how does overcommodification affect an overcoded serial text[3] and how does cross-promotion bind the fictive and fantastic realm of the television text with the lived and commonplace residence of the utilitarian commodity? How do these these relations impact on the serial form and its apparently unspecified ideological project?

The Slayer and the Final Girl

Imbued with the characteristics of the 'final girl', a term Carol Clover attaches to the female figure that outlasts the killer in 1970s slasher films, Buffy Summers seems to be a faithful extension of this character, which Clover links with sexual repression and both masculinity and femininity (Clover 1992: 35–41). Yet such a reading decontextualises the female protagonist from her role in the narrative and from her role as a commodity that circulates both within and outside the television text. It overlooks certain technological and cultural differences between film and television in terms of a textual system of looking and the socio-cultural nature of the viewing experience as well as the generic references to 1990s horror cinema in *Buffy*. Specifically, the serial format secures the return of the final girl, and the ensemble cast dynamic distributes her key attributes across a number of other characters. Thus in *Buffy*, there are other mainstays of those attributes that were formally displayed along the axis of the final girl: Willow is book-smart, Cordelia is look-smart, while Buffy is overly attentive and physically empowered yet also imbued with attributes (albeit in watered-down form) of her hyper-attributed female companions. Equally notable is that the serial format mandates development and regression, a forward and backward trajectory that continuously plays out the female protagonist's empowerment, disempowerment, re-empowerment. This departs considerably from the uni-directional, though openly valenced, trajectory of the final girl in feature film.

Moreover, Buffy's phallic empowerment (stake in hand) seems to be in conflict with a certain commodity fetishism that functions to contain her overall body – the marketing of Buffy Summers/Sarah Michelle Gellar – and to destabilise the potentially progressive system of signification at work in the text itself. In fact, the self-reflexive nature of the overtly wry critiques of fashion and girlishness seems to endorse the commodification of the teen body precisely by acknowledging that viewers are not cultural dupes. In the show's autumn 1999 season premiere, Buffy does battle with Sunday, a female vampire. On their first meeting, and just before the onset of their first fight, Sunday critiques Buffy's misguided fashion-sense, commenting:

> I think you had a lot of misconceptions about college; like that anyone would be caught dead wearing that.

Buffy is further insulted later in the show, after Sunday's gang steals her possessions from her dorm room. From a rooftop hiding place, Buffy spies the group handling her diary and tossing about her favourite stuffed animal, Mr Gordo. Somehow the group overlooked her trunk of weapons, perhaps because these objects did not register as a girl's things. The episode concludes with Buffy slaying Sunday and her flunkies, and victoriously parading her girlish belongings back to her room, toting her decorative parasol in one hand.

This self-conscious attention to femininity, with masculinity framed as its direct inverse, extends outside of the show and can be found in such fare as official fan sites and fanzines. A column in the '*Buffy the Vampire Slayer*' *Official Magazine* (a property of MVP Licensing and Twentieth Century Fox Film Corporation) gives fans a peek into Buffy's bedroom:

> Aside from the arsenal of wooden stakes and holy water hidden under the toys in her nightstand, Buffy's bedroom seems to be a lot like that of any teenage girl's. But a closer look reveals the dual halves of her persona: the Slayer and the highschooler. Bright colors and butterflies give the walls a cheery look and stand in dark contrast to her violent evening pursuits, while the mirror and shelf on her makeup table exhibit a more expected gothic look.[4]

Sexual repression and the dialectic between masculinity and femininity are written on to Buffy's body and exist at the surface of the text. While these elements may have been written into the seventies films which are the focus of Clover's analysis,[5] in the nineties we are not encountered with a subtext that requires a theorist to elaborate and bring to the surface. Rather, in line with John Caldwell's investigation of the terms of televisuality in post-1980 television culture, we must consider industry personnel – costume designers, set designers, producers, directors – as sophisticated readers and producers of visual culture, and we must also consider the general public's interest and immersion in the politics (and I use the term loosely) behind the praxis (Caldwell: vii–viii). Given that particular theoretical constructs no longer exist as subtext in the text of *Buffy*, one must consider whether certain other constructs still do remain masked, even more so as the text, centred on a group whose secret lives act as a metaphor for adolescent rites of passage, literally foregrounds its 'subtext'. Consequently meaning appears obvious.

As US television is a commercial medium perhaps political economy provides the most useful approach for understanding at least one particular kind of work that remains concealed in texts such as *Buffy*. The fact that TV sells, that TV delivers consumers to advertisers is not an original insight. But what remains to be explored is how this generalisation operates in the particular, for there are certainly different systems of delivery operating across the texts of television – perhaps systems linked by generic boundaries. Critical readings of soap operas have been most productive in pursuing this line of enquiry, examining the links between programme narratives and their advertising/commercial brackets/breaks. The symbiotic relationship has been read along narrative lines, with the soap opera playing out crises in an enormously extended dramatic arc of delayed gratification and the commercial providing quite a different type of narrative – one with quick crisis management, posing problem and solution in a concise dramatic arc that provides a form of fulfilment desired yet not found in the soap.

But the aspects I want to explore are those economic relations and determinations that exist outside of televisual flow and are instead found across media and mediating experiences. What connections can be made from TV to print, for instance, and what connections can be made between the contextual/geographic experiences of watching television and shopping, for instance? Indeed, Margaret Morse has linked TV to the freeway and the shopping mall, mapping out these transitive spaces and experiences that are at once no where and every where; and in this particular programme the connections between television and commerce are quite clear, with the links between the space of the living room and the space of the department store precisely mapped out for prospective viewers/shoppers (Morse 1990: 193–221).

In the official fan magazine, Buffy's costume designer, Cynthia Bergstrom remarks: [Buffy is] 'so independent that she needs to keep a sense of herself and her own uniqueness. Therefore, it comes out in the way she dresses' (1999: 53–4). Bergstrom proceeds to list those stores where she does her wardrobe hunting, listing, among others: Bloomingdales, American Rag, Rampage, Macy's, Tommy Hilfiger, Fred Siegel, Traffic, Contempo Casuals and Neiman-Marcus. The show's fashion formula is thus readily reconstituted by its viewers. At the same time, this department-store inventory reveals Buffy's identity and more significantly her gender as explicitly constructed, though for the moment only one of a myriad of paradigms of that constructedness is being revealed, in this case cross-dressing. Her clothing is not just trendy and fashionable but functional for both Buffy/Gellar and for her once-removed non-fictional self, the stunt double. But form and function are an acknowledged part of identity politics in television fiction, and not surprisingly Bergstrom dresses each character according to that character's psychological make-up and general 'philosophy'. Her comments on the character of Drusilla, a core figure in the show's second season are revealing:

> We first saw her in her ivory gown that to me was a timeless image of a woman . . . She started out as a very sort of insane, willowy, soft, sickly, consumptive woman. I was really taking off from the women that you sometimes saw in the Dracula movies from the '60s. I sort of saw her like that, but not quite so, you know, girly. I toned down the dress, and I just gave her an empire waist. Then, as she grew weaker, I put her in bad clothing. (Golden and Holder 1998: 275)

Costume differentiates the show's characters, but as it does so it also codes the characters along a traditional scale of relative femininity and masculinity; their philosophies are given form by their apparel as is their relative position along this gendering scale. In this regard characters can be in flux throughout the series where clothing is typically attached to that character's mental/physical attitude relative to a particular crisis in the narrative arc of the programme. Significantly, the gender binary is still insisted upon as the foregrounded scale of value, perhaps in this case since Buffy, the overt composite of masculine and feminine, is the show's central character against which all other characters act, develop, and are read. Yet Buffy's ability to exist as both masculine and feminine, as a true cross-dresser, is compromised by her circulation as a commodity, made most apparent by yet another commercial enterprise, one that extends beyond the limits of the fictional register of the programme and thus seems more decisive and final.[6] Not surprisingly, this enterprise is one of body and beauty, and dominantly read as the domain of the feminine. More importantly, however, this enterprise undoes the machinations of both explicit gendering through costume and fashion and implicit gendering indicated in reading *Buffy* through Clover's model.

The programme, the character and Gellar herself have been most directly linked to department-store culture via Gellar's role as Maybelline spokesmodel. Maybelline's tagline, 'Maybe she's born with it. Maybe it's Maybelline,' proclaims the virtues of natural/naturalising femininity at the same time that it acknowledges the potential constructedness of the term. More specifically, when deployed in Maybelline's ad, Sarah Michelle Gellar becomes the target of the enquiry, the 'she' of the inquisitive remark. Yet the statement is certainly a rhetorical trope; it is safe to assume that Gellar is sporting Maybelline cosmetics, for her face is the featured space of the ad.

But more significantly, the ad circulates at the same historical moment as the TV programme (and can also be found on television) and depends upon a symbiotic interplay between ad and programme, between Gellar and Summers. This slippage is perhaps pertinent for different reasons than the Murphy Brown/Candice Bergen slippage (only a source of confusion for Dan Quayle, perhaps, but relevant nonetheless as it was deployed to activate a perceived moral crisis). Brown/Bergen is more significant in terms of political capital, while Summers/Gellar is more significant in terms of economic capital; and the current slippage is certainly not a site of confusion for shoppers/viewers, but rather plays off of conventional models for marketing celebrity. But these spheres of character/celebrity of viewer/consumer co-exist and overlap, and at the textual level these systems of signification are intimately bound with one another.

The Maybelline slogan is a tagline that supersedes Gellar – a generic tagline that was attached to a campaign long before Gellar's introduction as (one of many) spokesmodel(s). Yet as she is inserted as one paradigmatic term along a syntagmatic axis, it is only the perpendicular paradigmatic chain of visual terms mapped out against the syntagmatic chain of verbal terms that is interrupted. The syntagm as literary text is seemingly uninterrupted, for (the word) 'she' is constant, while the paradigm Gellar, introduced as one of many potential 'shes' or faces, is in flux. But these two chains do play off of one another, perhaps inviting different reads and different associations with each new face. Here, however, the 'born' and 'it' seem all too closely aligned with Gellar's fictional counterpart – a slayer who indeed was born with it (born into a particular role as slayer, a role both social and gendered, and invested in a particular form of labour capital).

The ad raises questions that the programme seems to answer; the serial programme is asked to perform an aspect of symbolic restitution. 'Is she born with it?' 'Yes, she is.' And this particular answer is made possible through a system of signification that rewards viewing. Yet at the same time the ad invites a reworking of a central anxiety played out in the programme (Buffy's predetermined role in a system of labour capital) in terms of femininity and beauty, divorced of their economic functions. And the ad space seems more real than the programme, regardless of the virtues of the narratives themselves and their respective participatory pleasures. For Maybelline reminds us we are looking at Sarah Michelle Gellar, and not

Buffy (Gellar's name is printed in the ad space) and her role as an icon of feminine beauty is affirmed even if it is apparently the subject of speculation. Buffy's masculinity is effaced.

The status of this figure in the Maybelline ad is certainly more fixed than the same figure as she appears in, for instance, the national print ad campaign for milk and a televised phone ad. The '1–800-Collect' ad pulls Buffy out of the episodic structure of the programme but allows a figure who is both Summers and Gellar, as Gellar speaks from what appears to be one of the show's sets and remains in character for the commercial spot. Similarly, the 'Got Milk?' campaign cloaks Gellar in the slayer character, while identifying the star in its fine print; this particular ad engages in a sarcastic play with the slayer's dual status as masculine subject and female object in both its text and image. Gellar/Summers sports a bustier beneath her partly opened trench coat; the undergarment emphasises her bustline and exposes her status as sex object, while the outergarment partly conceals her body, emphasising instead her status as active investigator; the ad's text reinforces this by merging 'revealing outfits' and the 'undead'.

Promotional 'ads' for the programme also flirt with this ambiguity, merging Gellar with her fictional counterpart, freely intertwining the terms. The 6 March 1998 cover of *Entertainment Weekly* features Gellar with the caption 'Sarah Michelle Gellar kills vampires for a living,' and the 1 October 1999 issue features Gellar (in a black tank top that reads 'Vampires Suck' – the programme's content is literally transformed into a fashion moniker) and the caption 'Sarah Michelle Gellar is the "Slayer".' Maybelline, however, cannot dabble in this ambivalence and simply recasts it as 'is she' or 'isn't she', insisting on a fixity of gender. Thus participation/speculation/ambivalence and its pleasures are maintained while gender is naturalised and the question is recast in terms of natural or constructed beauty. Consequently gender is forced to be stable. The speculative operation seems open-ended but in fact allows for only a particular set of paradigmatic substitutions and in the end provides a quite restrictive form of free-play that is far more prescriptive than the space of the television narrative. The gender riddle proposed in the TV series is solved, and it seems once again that even a speculative ad can position itself as a site of restitution that is ultimately more privileged than the function of symbolic restitution enacted by the programme. The marketing of Buffy Summers/Sarah Michele Gellar destabilises what is a potentially progressive gender play in the programme *Buffy the Vampire Slayer*. The programme would otherwise allow her to embody both terms of the conventional gender binary of masculine and feminine, as the programme narrative indeed plays off of her conflicted status as active and passive, expressed most explicitly in her dual status as typical girl and atypical slayer. The Maybelline print ad, however, proposes and answers the question of this conflict via the fiction of the series. The Maybelline campaign does so in more general terms as it crosses from print to broadcasting via the fiction of *Buffy*.[7] In doing so, Maybelline seems to close off the probable liberatory readings on gender of the (WB's) television text. Working together as commercial vehicles, programme and ad seem to close off the prospects of negotiation proposed in either.

The goal of this extended analysis of the Maybelline campaign is to suggest how the push and pull of normalcy at the heart of the televisual hybrid of horror and melodrama may in part be undone by circulating texts that substitute the perpetual tension of the serial discourse (centred on a propagation of secrets) with a simple and decided push towards a normative state. Ironically, Buffy's personal negotiation of difference is resolved not by retreating to conventional norms, but rather by advancing the call for difference, activating all of the potential slayers and, as a result, becoming one of many.

Symbolic Restitution

The closing off of liberatory possibilities should not be equated with closure *per se*. The commercial logic that drives seriality embraces the lines of commerce that extend beyond the confines of the TV screen. Further, thematically nuanced ideological tensions that may radiate from programme to product most certainly do not interfere with the rate of consumption of either programme or product.

My reading of *Buffy the Vampire Slayer* and *Smallville* can undoubtedly be extended to encompass related generic texts on the Warner Brothers network, including *Angel* (a *Buffy* spinoff), *Roswell* (which began its run on the WB before moving to UPN), *Charmed* and *Tarzan* (an action-adventure fantasy that nonetheless embraces the mythos of the superhero). These generic permutations speak to the success of the network's formula that is one grounded in economic, aesthetic and cultural relevance as well as the network's very recognition of the value of genre hybridisation.

Like Clark Kent, Buffy Summers leads a double life, a negotiation that pushes the serial forward with the promise of eventual disclosure and perhaps successful synthesis. Both characters find themselves living in environments that are at the same time commonplace and fantastic. And both characters habituate the rather common domains of school and home, which are nonetheless settings for significant dramatic development. Like the Kents' farm, the Summers' house is a principal location and a site of familial investment and restitution, as well as a spatial embodiment of generic convergence where the real and the fantastic meet in the most acute fashion. It is here that in the second season episode, 'Becoming (Part 2)', Buffy reveals to her mother that she is the Slayer; and it is here that in the fifth season episode, 'The Body', that Buffy finds her mother dead and despite the supernatural carnage that surrounds Buffy, her mother dies from an aneurysm. And in a fitting act of closure, as the series concludes the house becomes a refuge for Buffy, her friends and the potential slayers.

Developing Seriality

Horror, science fiction and fantasy are by their very nature connected to the semiotic operations of serial texts; riddled with contradictions, the genres play in the liminal terrain between the real and the fictive, making them open metaphoric vessels that have proven quite malleable and responsive to cultural change. Yet seriality itself no longer defines the classic soap opera text; it can also be used to describe the episodic and open-ended engagement with new media content. Though not identical gestures, the patterns of consumption that accompany web browsing may have some utility for mapping out the shifting terrain of serial viewing, especially given the increasing volume of cross-platform television fare. Hypertextuality is not entirely removed from the premises of the serial narrative, for it solicits fragmentation and interruption, and the net effect of decentredness parallels the experience of multiple plot-lines. Indeed, the Warner Brothers network's apparent interest in the adolescent market – a valuable niche demographic – has undoubtedly lead the network to consider online space as a critical address point for its viewership of internet-savvy teens. Serial fiction has been a cross-media affair, extending from magazines to motion pictures, and ultimately television, and it is not surprising that the mass-market institutionalisation of seriality has bridged new media forms. Moreover, serial enterprises have consistently been aligned with consumerism, binding close programme readership with close advertising readership. The web of institutional relations that has developed in the twenty-first century is not seamless. The hermetically sealed ideological venture remains a myth. Yet this is far from being a problem. Solicitation requires an open channel of discourse. Just as Buffy Summers and Clark Kent negotiate their status as fantastic and real, the teen reader is invited to the heroic heights of textual authority but only through a ritualistic engagement with the routine labours of consumption. It is the prospect of resolving the question of difference, in the transitional period of adolescence, which drives the reader onward.

Notes

1. Since the time that I began my study, *Buffy the Vampire Slayer* shifted networks, moving from the WB to UPN, and subsequently ended its initial series run.
2. While Lex and his father are both present in the credits, they are not depicted together; moreover, the Luthor clan is without a matriarch, and they are a combatively dysfunctional unit out of step with the community's rural traditions.
3. An overcoded text has multiple layers of signifying detail that make it open to multiple decoding strategies.
4. *'Buffy the Vampire Slayer' Official Magazine* 2, no. 2 (Spring 1999): 27.
5. Indeed, series creator Joss Whedon has read Clover's book.
6. My insistence on the potential progressiveness of what I am terming Buffy's 'transvestism' (admittedly Buffy is a rather mild incarnation of that positionality, with her bodied gender always readily evident beneath her clothes) is based on Marjorie Garber's reading of the terms of such an identity; in Garber's analysis, the enabling fantasy is the body as blurred gender, removed from the traditional terms of either-ness (either male or female) (Garber 1992: 6).
7. Perhaps not coincidentally, as *Buffy the Vampire Slayer* is a serial programme (the character-driven narrative develops from episode to episode), so too is the Maybelline campaign; Gellar was cast in three distinct spots for the cosmetics manufacturer. Thus the form of symbolic restitution found in the series (the active engagement with the viewer's imaginary across episodes) is mimicked in the dual media ad campaign (though the ads are quite redundant in the literalness of their singular enquiry).

Bibliography

Allen, Robert C. (1983), 'On Reading Soaps: A Semiotic Primer', in E. Ann Kaplan (ed.), *Regarding Television*, Los Angeles: The American Film Institute, pp. 97–108.

Bergstrom, Cyntia (1999), *'Buffy the Vampire Slayer' Official Magazine* 2, no. 2, 53–4.

Buxton, David (1990), *From 'The Avengers' to 'Miami Vice': Form and Ideology in Television Series*, Manchester: Manchester University Press.

Caldwell, John (1995), *Televisuality: Style, Crisis, and Authority in American Television*, New Brunswick: Rutgers University Press.

Clover, Carol J. (1992), *Men, Women and Chainsaws: Gender in the Modern Horror Film*, Princeton: Princeton University Press.

Ellis, John (1982), *Visible Fictions*, London: Routledge & Kegan Paul.

Garber, Marjorie (1992), *Vested Interests: Cross Dressing and Cultural Anxiety*, New York: Routledge.

Golden, Christopher and Holder, Nancy (1998), *'Buffy the Vampire Slayer': The Watchers Guide*, New York: Pocket Books.

Hayward, Jennifer (1997), *Consuming Pleasures: Active Audiences and Serial Fictions from Dickens to Soap Opera*, Lexington: University Press of Kentucky.

Kozloff, Sarah (1987), 'Narrative Theory and Television', in Robert C. Allen (ed.), *Channels of Discourse, Reassembled*, Chapel Hill: University of North Carolina Press, pp. 67–100.

Morse, Margaret (1990), 'An Ontology of Everyday Distraction: The Freeway, the Mall, and Television', in Patricia Mellencamp (ed.), *Logics of Television: Essays in Cultural Criticism*, Bloomington: Indiana University Press, pp. 193–221.

Sobchack, Vivian (1996), 'Bringing It All Back Home: Family Economy and Generic Exchange', in Barry Keith Grant (ed.), *The Dread of Difference*, Austin: University of Texas Press, pp. 143–63.

Waller, Gregory A. (1987), 'Introduction', in Gregory A. Waller (ed.), *American Horrors: Essays on the Modern American Horror Film*, Urbana: University of Illinois Press, pp. 1–13.

Wood, Robin (1986), *Hollywood from Vietnam to Reagan*, New York: Columbia University Press.

Part III: Receptions

Introduction: Receptions

Michael Hammond

As we left off in the last section we drew comparisons between the industry's approach to the structure and seriality of the series/serial with the academic study of texts. Where formal textual analysis can reveal how the
stories are told, the industry in general looks to ways that will ensure the
appropriate response or affect. Both are concerned with how the text will
provide narrative information. In the case of formalist textual analysis the
concern is with how the visual and aural elements provide 'cues' to relay
story information. Although they are talking about film here, David
Bordwell and Kristin Thompson emphasise viewer engagement and it is
just as applicable to the series/serial television programme, 'As the viewer
watches the film, she or he picks up cues, recalls information, anticipates
what will follow, and generally participates in the creation of the film's
form' (Bordwell and Thompson 1997: 90). The series/serial format as we
have seen works to elongate and intensify this kind of engagement through
the use of both short-term narrative enigmas or problems lasting as short
as one scene or one episode to long developing story arcs which are resolved
at the end of the season and, at times, beyond.

The industry too is concerned with how audiences or viewers engage
with or use texts in order to determine how to encourage 'loyals'. 'Deep
backstory' into characters prompts the creation of new storyworlds which
are not completely developed in the programme but exist and unfold
through episode guides, websites, novel series and comic books. These
offer multiple avenues of interest that can be followed up by dedicated
viewers. For instance the evolution of already existing mythical legends
such as that of *Buffy the Vampire Slayer*, or the revelation of new 'real
worlds' such as that of the undertaking industry in the case of a 'quality'
series/serial like *Six Feet Under* work to lend depth and complexity to
characters and enhance their motivation. In each case they provide varying
levels of engagement for viewers that go beyond the single programme or

the series/serial itself . This is now a standard procedure in the media and television industries and is a means, as Matt Hills demonstrates, of 'superintending' the interpretation strategies that audiences might utilise. Building such features around the programme has clear advantages for the writer-producer of a new series/serial in that it builds upon tried and fairly well understood ways that fans have engaged in previous successful programmes. In fact it is arguably true that the industry practice here has been guided at least initially by the way that fan communities, led by the *Star Trek* phenomenon of the early 1970s where fans succeeded in reinstating the programme after it had been cancelled, have demonstrated the numerous ways that programmes can be not only watched but shaped and even rewritten (Jenkins 1992).

However, in both the academy and the industry much of contemporary attention to television has tried, with varying degrees of success, to explain the ways that viewers engage with these programmes. Formalist analyses such as that of Bordwell and Thompson tend to emphasise the activity of the viewer in the progression of the narrative through cause–effect and enigma–resolution structures. Other forms of analysis such as those associated with spectatorship theory in the 1970s and 1980s sought to determine spectator positions constructed by the text. This approach was superseded in the 1980s by reception studies which emphasised smaller specific or local studies that were able to take into account contingent and tangible contextual material ranging from advertising to popular critical journalism and attempt to explain the text's meaning-making strategies rather than to interpret them. This meant a turn to historiographical methods. The attempt here, generally called historical reception studies (Staiger 1992; Klinger 1994) looks at specific films or television programmes as 'events' which anchor the extra-textual features such as reviews, advertising, interviews and other forms of publicly available information about the specific film or programme within the limits of one film or programme, or director. It does this to avoid the unwieldy task of determining potentially infinite 'possible readings' and in order to outline the 'probable interpretations' encouraged by the text in conjunction with its surrounding 'extra-texts'. Elizabeth Clark's chapter on *The West Wing* (Warner Bros/John Wells Productions, Aaron Sorkin 1999–present) broadly takes this type of approach by drawing on the reviews and the public 'talk' generated on the subject of President Bartlet's relationship to actual White House policy, particularly with the shift from the Clinton White House to the Bush administration and the events of 9/11. Here the seriality of the programme creates shifting positions in debates and reviewers' comments as the programme's serial narrative unfolds alongside the real historical events of national and world politics.

Spectatorship theory of the 1970s and 1980s was criticised for emphasising the spectator as a product of the text without consideration of the social and cultural forces that are a part of each individual person's experience, in other words 'real' audiences. Such criticisms prompted in a general way ethnographic approaches which looked for ways to account for the role that social and cultural factors had on viewers' interpretations of films and television programmes, or even, as we have seen, the 'supertext' of the 'flow' of television (Stacey 1994; Ang 1985). This approach utilises interviews with viewers or by asking them to write or record their impressions and responses to particular programmes. Again, as with historical reception studies, the potential range of responses can be infinite and so ethnographic studies require specific means of limiting the range of the study. This has often taken the form of focusing on one specific text (Ang 1985) or a particular social group (Walkerdine 1985) utilising methods of fieldwork such as interviewing or participant observation to bring together a manageable range of research material. This kind of research has been successful in recognising the various means by which viewers engage with and 'use' the text, although is perhaps limited in making any broad claims for what these studies might say about general audience behaviour beyond the focus study (Geraghty 1998; Morley 1980; Seiter 1995).

One way of thinking about the industry/academic approaches is that they are a kind of doppelganger or that they have shared concerns, particularly around the subject of the behaviour and response of audiences to programmes or 'texts'. Script doctoring and textual analysis share such a relationship as they seek to maximise/explain affective mechanisms within the scripts/texts themselves. Also ethnographic approaches share similar objectives with the industry in their use of audience surveys and market analyses as they try to determine audience make-up and response along class, ethnic, age and gender lines. Another means of exploring the way that audiences respond to programmes or texts is to consider what literary theorist Stanley Fish has called 'interpretive communities' (Fish 1980). These are groups who share similar concerns and agreed upon interpretive strategies, such as fans for *Star Trek*. This is not, however, limited to fan cultures and has been a consistent means throughout media history whereby entertainment companies appeal to the critical community for cultural validation of their products and programming. Lynn Spigel has drawn attention to the way that CBS attempted to create a journal of critical weight as a means improving its image among the US public in the early 1960s. This effort resulted in a book *The Eighth Art*, published in 1960 by CBS and edited by critic Robert Lewis Shayon:

Why then did CBS decide to initiate such a project? It seems likely that in 1960 the network had a lot to gain from becoming a patron of the TV arts. At a time when it was under heated attack, CBS attempted to control the climate of criticism by funding the critics – a true testimony to the power of corporate hegemony and its ability to incorporate dissenting views. (Spigel 1998: 68)

Such appeals to the critical communities of 'high culture' is a way that media industries have tried to upgrade their image as a means of deflating negative public opinion and avoiding the disruptive attention of censoring groups. This approach offers a good example of the overlap that exists between the academic community and the media industries. As Spigel points out, this example demonstrates that 'academic television scholarship was – like programming, audiences, advertising, and all other elements of the system – imagined and, in part, generated by the networks. We [the television academic community] are, in that regard, the wish fulfilment of the industry' (Spigel 1998: 67). More broadly the approach of recognising 'interpretive communities' in academic research has its reflection in the industry's reliance on the journalistic critical communities who help guide audiences' interpretations, if only to offer countervailing principles and opinions.

The industry's programming policy- and decision-makers can be seen to be a kind of interpretive community as they make decisions and indeed interpretations which line up with brand images. Janet McCabe outlines the way that Channel Four in Britain and its newly launched digital channel E4 positioned their programming of *ER* within their policy of offering quality programming for an 'independently minded' viewer. Positioning as 'quality' a series/serial which offers fast-paced editing and steadi-cam work with sensational although realistic special effects in depicting the behind-the-scenes activity of an inner-city *American* emergency room seems somewhat anomalous on a channel with a 'quality' remit. However, as McCabe demonstrates, notions of quality shift as companies and programmers work to negotiate their decisions about what constitutes quality within their target audience.

Naturally it is obvious that the industry has specific outcomes for its attention to audiences and research which have to do with determining markets and reducing financial risk. In this regard scriptwriters and 'hyphenate writer-producers' pay attention to the construction of scripts with particular intent and specific audiences in mind. The development of styles, the progression of characters and storylines are all made with at least a vague sense of who their audience might be. Of course this is not new; throughout the history of film and television audiences have consistently been consulted by producers in various ways. Pre-view screenings had become a staple of the production process in Hollywood from at least the 1920s and to this day remain a vital means of test marketing. However, the reception sites and various forms of fan culture such as websites, slash fiction, fanzines, which have been the subject of audience research in Film and Television studies (Jenkins 1992; Stacey 1994), have also been brought into play by scriptwriters and producers. For example, the official website for *Lost* (Touchstone Television/ J. J. Abrams, 2004), a series/serial which puts fourteen survivors of a plane crash on a deserted Pacific Island is only in its ninth episode of the first season at the time of writing (2004) and is at a crucial moment in its existence. It has generated considerable media attention in its opening episodes and the official website builds in the various elements that encourage audience 'talk', which not only includes an episode guide section and backstory on each character but also has a section called 'community' where visitors are encouraged to talk about the show under headings 'general', 'plot' and 'characters' (http://forums.go.com/abc/thread?start=0&threadID=111399). Consider this exchange in the character section prompted by a question concerning the Iraqi character Sayid (played by Narveen Andrews):

Specie8470: I wonder what Sayid's view on the current war in Iraq is. I wonder if he is for or against the war considering he was once part of the Republican Guard.

LBD: This is one of the traps I pray ABC doesn't fall into. You saw how divisive [sic] all the political talk on this board was. If we actually have Sayid give a strong opinion one way or the other we could be heading into trouble. Right now we have a man who has overcome initial suspicion and cultural differences to prove himself a vibrant leader of the community. If they make his story a political statement it will only cheapen the entire show. Unfortunately, looking at the shots already released for episode 9 I'm afraid we are going to wallow in stereotype.

Dargay: I hope the show does not go into politics. I watch tv to escape from the world around me and I am depressed enough with bozo Bush's re-election.

The response to this question was extensive but the significance was that these allow a kind of instant feedback for producers. It also allows the shows to develop and monitor a sense of 'up-to-dateness' using contemporary controversial (and potentially audience-losing) subject matter to see how it plays out in chat rooms. High-energy action/conspiracy series/serials such as *24* (20th Century Fox Television/Joel Surnow and Robert Cochran, 2001–present) and *Alias* (Touchstone Television/J. J. Abrams,

2001–present) both utilise such topical subjects to build in suspense and heighten the sense of paranoia in the shows' diegetic worlds. Having access to audience opinion in this way is one means of developing future story-lines. It is commonplace for scriptwriters and producers and creative personnel associated with series/serials to consult fans. Nancy Holder, who wrote the *Watcher's Guides* for *Buffy the Vampire Slayer*, states: 'I go on the web . . . If I don't know something the fans will' (Hammond 2004: 162).

Series/serials such as *Lost* make use of the serial format in order to build into the programmes various ways to 'enter' the text for audiences. The stated pre-fix to series/serials 'Previously on . . .' was only the most obvious way of giving background to each episode which would allow viewers to both refresh their memory and to 'catch up' on the broader story arcs. This has been extended effectively through industry perception of and responses to the way that viewers and fans have shaped the programmes they watch to their own ends. Of course questions of how much control viewers have over their programmes have been at the heart of academic debates and the industry has followed suit with this concern, with the pursuit of maximising profits and market share. This section on receptions and audiences considers such questions either directly as in Hills' study of the episode guides, or indirectly in the consideration of how various aspects of the industry from producers to programmers rationalise their choices and strategies.

Both the academy and the industry have for the last twenty years been working with an intensifying and shifting sense of audience self-determination through technological change from video home-viewing and recording in the early 1980s to the advent of TiVos in the early years of the twenty-first century. This environment and pace of perpetual change shows no sign of abating. Arguably the series/serial format offers the industry one solution in this rapidly changing 'mediascape' to holding on to audiences as well as being the product of thinking differently about identifying and appealing to different segments of the market. In its turn television studies has been involved in exploring the reception of serial format programmes for a long time, but now, as these studies show, the series/serial is amending and lending depth to knowledge about the way viewers encounter, respond to the programmes and their many varieties of 'additional extras'.

Bibliography

Ang, Ien (1985), *Watching 'Dallas': Television and the Melodramatic Imagination*, London: Routledge.

Bordwell, David and Thompson, Kristin (1997), *Film Art: An Introduction*, 5th edn, Madison: McGraw Hill.

Fish, Stanley (1980), *Is There a Text in this Class?: The Authority of Interpretive Communites*, Cambridge, MA: Harvard University Press.

Geraghty, Christine (1998), 'Audiences and "Ethnography": Questions of Practice', in C. Geraghty and D. Lusted (eds), *The Television Studies Book*, London: Arnold, pp. 141–57.

Hammond, Mary (2004), 'Monsters and Metaphors: *Buffy the Vampire Slayer* and the Old World', in S. Gwenllian Jones and R. E. Pearson (eds), *Cult Television*, Minneapolis: University of Minnesota Press, pp. 147–64.

Jenkins, Henry (1992), *Textual Poachers: Television Fans and Participatory Culture*, New York: Routledge, Chapman & Hall.

Klinger, Barbara (1994), *Melodrama and Meaning: History Culture and the Films of Douglas Sirk*, Bloomington, IN: Indiana University Press.

Morley, David (1980), *The 'Nationwide' Audience*, London: British Film Institute.

Seiter, Ellen (1995), 'Mothers Watching Children Watching Television', in B. Skeggs (ed.), *Feminist Cultural Theory*, Manchester: Manchester University Press, pp. 137–52.

Spigel, Lynn (1998), 'The Making of a TV Literate Elite', in C. Geraghty and D. Lusted (eds), *The Television Studies Book*, London: Arnold, pp. 63–85.

Stacey, Jackie (1994), *Star Gazing: Hollywood Cinema and Female Spectatorship*, London: Routledge.

Staiger, Janet (1992), *Interpreting Films: Studies in the Historical Reception of American Cinema*, Princeton, NJ: Princeton University Press.

Walkerdine, Valerie (1985), 'Video Replay', in V. Burgin, J. Donald and C. Kaplan (eds), *Formations of Fantasy*, London: Routledge, pp. 167–99.

CHAPTER 10

Cult TV, Quality and the Role of the Episode/Programme Guide

Matt Hills

The pleasures of television viewing have often been academically recorded as pleasures of seriality, familiarity, order and repetition, 'Television is very much part of the taken for granted seriality . . . of everyday life. Broadcast schedules reproduce (or define) the structure of the household day' (Silverstone 1994: 20; see also Ellis 2000; Fiske 1987). As well as this 'onto-logical security' of TV's soothing, ritualised seriality and everydayness (Silverstone 1994: 5), the pleasure of narrative knowledge – being devel-oped over time by dedicated audiences – has been posited as a crucial element in appreciating that most serialised of TV forms, the soap opera (Hayward 1997: 153). However, seriality has not just been discussed in relation to TV's 'essential' characteristic of ritualised repetition, or with reference to soaps as a leading television genre: it has also been a compo-nent in much work on cult TV, and it is this strand of work on television and the serial that I will focus on here.

As I have previously argued (Hills 2002, 2004), it is difficult to define cult television as a distinct genre; it is better thought of as a range of texts that typically fall into genres such as fantasy/horror/science fiction/ comedy, and which share qualities such as creating detailed, expansive diegetic worlds (or even universes) as well as displaying 'endlessly deferred narrative' (Hills 2002: 134). Cult TV series like *Angel*, *Babylon 5*, *Blake's 7*, *Buffy the Vampire Slayer*, *Doctor Who*, *Monty Python's Flying Circus*, *The Prisoner*, *Star Trek*, *Twin Peaks* and *The X-Files* hence tend to be marked by sustained enigmas, and by ongoing or unresolved mysteries about their characters, character relationships, or aspects of their invented worlds. Regardless of how cult TV narratives progress – or, in the case of a surrealist sketch show like *Monty Python*, fail to progress – there is a sense in which what we see on screen is only a part of a much wider nar-rative world, always implying further events and developments. It is this detailed hyper-diegesis at the heart of cult TV series that fans of *The*

X-Files capture when they talk about 'myth-arc' stories (stories that focused on the series' ongoing mythology and continuity), or which *Buffy the Vampire Slayer* fans are concerned with when they debate details of 'the Buffyverse'.

One early study of cult TV series *Doctor Who* carried the subtitle *The Unfolding Text* (Tulloch and Alvarado 1983), very much gesturing to the intertwining of seriality and cult status. More recently, Sara Gwenllian Jones has testified to the significance of cult TV's serial nature:

> Paradoxically, the repetitive structures of cult television series and the repetitive viewing practices of fans facilitate the series' lack of closure. The repetition of the already-known releases fans from the thrall of causality . . . The predictability of the cult series decisively relocates the pleasure of viewing, shifting it away from the anticipation of major story events and towards the always-unfolding and unforecloseable *how* of the metatext. (Jones 2002: 83)

Jones is arguing against the TV studies orthodoxy that views seriality as inevitably involving 'pleasures of the familiar' (Harrington and Bielby 1995: 125), suggesting that fans' repeated viewing of their favoured cult TV shows, and the seriality of these shows, actually allows the fan audience to move outside of strictly hermeneutic (narrative/causal) concerns. But Jones also indicates something else important about cult TV; it is appreciated by fans not just at the level of 'the text itself' (that is the televised episodes), but also through a variety of surrounding inter-texts:

> This 'What Is', in cult series, is the vast, elaborate and densely populated fictional world that is constructed episode by episode, extended and embellished by official secondary-level texts (episode guides, novelizations, comics, magazines) and fan-produced tertiary texts (fan fiction, cultural criticism essays, art, scratch videos). Cult television's serial and segmented forms, its familiar formulae, its accumulated multiple storylines, its metatextuality, its ubiquitous intertextuality and intratextuality . . . work together to overwhelm the processual order of cause and effect, enigma and resolution. (Jones 2002: 84; see also Hills 2004: 514–17)

Certain types of fan-produced 'tertiary texts' (for example fan fiction and fanzines) have formed the basis for much academic discussion (beginning with Bacon-Smith 1992 and Jenkins 1992). By contrast, what Jones terms 'secondary texts' (following Fiske 1987) have been rather underexplored in studies of cult TV and its fans. For example, whilst including a whole chapter on fan fiction in *Textual Poachers* (1992), Henry Jenkins notes only of 'program guides' that:

> Guides to series such as *Doctor Who*, *The Avengers*, *The Twilight Zone* and *The Prisoner* are . . . in wide demand. Where such professional program guides are unavailable, fans produce their own . . . When professional program guides appear, they lack both the accuracy and detail of the fan versions; such books typically make mistakes such as misnaming minor characters . . . and distorting narrative actions and their consequences. (Jenkins 1992: 69–70)

Despite its relative academic invisibility, the episode guide has become an increasingly prominent companion to cult TV serials. Unlike the 'continuous serial' such as the soap opera (Dolan 1995), whose constantly ongoing nature renders episode-by-episode guides redundant other than as teasers or as narrative reminders (typically published in newspapers, given the intensely time-sensitive nature of such 'guides'), cult TV's series/serial hybridity often combines soap-operatic elements with limited runs or 'seasons' of episodes concluding with a cliffhanger. It is this series/serial combination which has especially facilitated the rise of the cult TV episode guide.

In this chapter, then, I want to address the fact that work on cult TV has somewhat neglected the role of official and fan-produced episode/programme guides. I will argue that the phenomenon of the episode guide can tell us much about cult TV's seriality, thus challenging Jones' and Jenkins' suggestions that episode guides contribute to an erosion of 'the processual order of cause and effect, enigma and resolution' or that they 'distort . . . narrative'. What these arguments share with the position I want to develop here is the notion that cult TV's narratives and very seriality are *actively worked on and worked over by secondary texts such as the programme guide*. However, in what follows, I will suggest that this textual activity, this 'feedback' into the 'primary text', is not clearly a matter of dispersal or distortion; both Jones and Jenkins seem to view the episode guide as somehow inimical to the seriality of cult TV shows. Against this assumption, I want to propose that official and unofficial episode guides appeal to fans of cult TV as a tool to manage seriality and make its repetitions and differences, its temporal unfoldings, more orderly and immediately present to fans as 'archived' knowledge.

Examining a range of cult shows and their various guides suggests that approaches to seriality cannot restrict themselves to formal analysis of 'the TV series' as an isolated 'text' (as in Thompson 2003), but must also consider the ways in which seriality is produced, managed and activated in secondary materials such as the episode guide. Such guides also construct a corpus of canonical televised episodes, allowing for comparative aesthetic evaluations and the attribution of discourses of 'quality' to cult TV series.

If a show merits an episode-by-episode 'guide' then the implication is that said TV show must display culturally valued criteria of aesthetic development, complexity and coherence. Both official and unofficial programme guides – *contra* Jenkins' authenticity claims – typically adopt a specific stance in relation to 'their' show: one of cultural valorisation and celebration. In the next section I want to focus on the idea that episode guides provide an active 'superintendence of seriality', smoothing out continuity problems and/or interpreting cult TV series' narratives as organic wholes rather than as *ad hoc* or pragmatic/contingent sequences of production decisions. I will then move on to consider issues of 'quality' and the cult TV series' episode guide.

Activating Seriality

In this section I will draw on reading formation theory, considering episode guides not as innocent (or distorting) 'reflections' of cult TV serials, nor as 'background' material which can be unproblematically integrated into academic textual analyses, but rather as secondary texts which seek to actively shape and police readings of cult TV's seriality (see Couldry 2000). Tony Bennett and Janet Woollacott's (1987) book *Bond and Beyond* puts forward a detailed exposition of reading formation theory. This theoretical framework opposes the idea that meaning is inherently 'in' a text, suggesting instead that different readers activate different meanings by reading a text in relation to other texts (termed 'inter-texts'). For example, one group of fans may read *Buffy the Vampire Slayer* in relation to other vampire fictions, therefore placing an emphasis on the vampire characters in their interpretation, whilst a further group of fans may consume 'secondary texts' focusing on Sarah Michelle Gellar's star image, and may thus read the show as a star vehicle for Gellar. Neither set of meanings is simply 'in' the cult TV programme. They are specifically activated by readers drawing on given inter-texts. Similarly, different audiences may respond to *Buffy* (or other cult shows, for example *The X-Files*) as belonging to horror or romance genres, depending on what inter-texts they draw on (see Branston and Stafford 2003: 86–8). The concept of 'reading formations' therefore:

> refers, specifically, to the inter-textual relations which prevail in a particular context, thereby activating a given body of texts by ordering the relations between them in a specific way such that their reading is always-already cued in specific directions that are not given by those 'texts themselves' as entities. (Bennett and Woollacott 1987: 64)

Different reading formations hence differently organise relations between ranges of texts, supporting specific types and forms of interpretation (see Klinger 1991). Bennett and Woollacott's argument does not imply that texts have absolutely no form of their own that can 'be analysed objectively' such as 'a definite order of narrative progression' (Bennett and Woollacott 1987: 65). However, it does support the notion that fans of a cult TV show may read it differently when compared to interested audiences who are nevertheless not a part of socially organised fandom; fans will supplement and inflect their readings through inter-texts such as fanzines, online discussion and extra-textual, industry information and so on. By contrast, interested (but not self-professed 'fan') audiences may use a different range of inter-texts to cue and sustain their interpretations, such as interviews with star actors in 'mainstream' magazines and media sources, or content from TV listings/journalistic/publicity material, but they probably wouldn't read fanzines, for example. As Bennett and Woollacott state:

> a reading formation is . . . the product of definite social and ideological relations of reading, composed . . . of those apparatuses – schools, the press, critical reviews, fanzines – within and between which the socially dominant forms for the superintendence of reading are both constructed and contested. (Bennett and Woollacott 1987: 64–5)

Different reading formations thus govern how a text is to be read. They provide their own 'superintendence of reading' (see Jenkins 1992: 88–9 on how fans are socialised into the 'right way' of reading cult TV as a fan).

It is interesting to note that when Bennett and Woollacott give an example of formal properties that do inhere 'in' texts themselves, it is 'narrative progression' they refer to. This may suggest that although meaning is not 'in' a text – according to this theoretical framework, at least – seriality ('a definite order of narrative progression') nevertheless *does* belong to 'texts themselves'. Indeed, this formalist assumption has underpinned much textual-analytical work on the TV serial such as Hagedorn (1995) and Dolan (1995), as well as Ndalianis (see Chapter 5). Dolan traces an institutional and televisual history in which the 'episodic series' (individual stories per episode, resolved at the conclusion so that a narrative status quo is restored) gives way to the 'sequential series' (overarching plot-lines moving across single-episode stories) as an industry norm in the 1980s, with this movement often being linked to markers of 'quality' and of TV-as-innovative (1995: 33–4; see also Feuer 1995 and also Chapter 2, and Catherine Johnson, Chapter 4 in this book). Hagedorn similarly presents a narrative of the developing TV series/serial hybrid which emphasises the move from strictly episodic formats to shows such as *Star Trek: Deep Space Nine*, where:

its writers often refer to elements of one episode in subsequent ones and, even more significantly, link episodes with characters and events from the original *Star Trek* and *Star Trek: The Next Generation* series, the effect of which is to create a sense of fictional space, history and character development that is far more sophisticated and intricate than that of classic series programming. (Hagedorn 1995: 39)

Dolan (1995), Hagedorn (1995) and Feuer (1995) all discuss cult TV (*Twin Peaks*; *Star Trek: The Next Generation* and *Deep Space 9*; *thirtysomething*) when considering the rise of sequential series and series/serial hybrids, once again indicating the importance of seriality to cult successes. As well as such formalist accounts, it is also seemingly true at a banal level that cult TV narratives (from the 1990s onwards) unfold in a specific sequence, and that episodes are made to be – and are – shown in a specific order (although this is not always the case: Joss Whedon's *Firefly* was transmitted in a different sequence to that intended by the series' producers, then reinstated in an 'authorially intended' narrative sequence for its DVD release).

However, these apparent narrative truths of TV textual form and transmission mask a more complex state of affairs for cult TV's fan audiences. Just as fans read cult TV distinctively, they also respond to and activate cult TV's serial nature in distinctive ways. Reading formation theory can thus throw some useful light on just how cult TV's serial forms are received by fans who actively *collapse, navigate and teleologise* seriality rather than merely responding to cult TV's 'sequential series' as a 'fixed' or essential textual attribute. In what follows, I will explain what is meant by the three different types of activated seriality referred to – that is, collapsed, navigated and teleologised seriality.

What I am terming 'collapsed seriality' refers to fans' tendency to convert temporally 'unfolding texts' into spatially organised or archival/encyclopaedic forms of information (such as an 'A–Z guide' alphabetically listing all diegetic characters, planets, jargon etc.). This encyclopaedic reading formation acts as a specific superintendence of fan interpretation by stressing the importance of knowledge about all aspects of a serial narrative. Janet H. Murray (1997: 83) has suggested that 'digital environments are encyclopaedic', giving the example of fan cultures using the internet:

> as a giant bulletin board on which . . . episodes from different seasons [can be] juxtaposed and compared. For instance, the web site for the intricately plotted space drama *Babylon 5* contains . . . plot summaries that document the many interwoven stories portrayed over multiple seasons. (Murray 1997: 85)

However, Murray's somewhat technologically determinist emphasis on digital media as encyclopaedic neglects the point that cult TV fans display such encyclopaedic readings – comparing and contrasting episodes from widely different seasons and widely different years of transmission – in printed episode guides long pre-dating the advent of online discussion. As such, rather than using cult TV fans to exemplify digital media's 'encyclopaedic' qualities, we might instead think of cult fans as participating in an encyclopaedic reading formation which is similarly played out in online and offline publications. As Murray observes, 'this kind of [encyclopaedic audience] attention' has been characteristic of 'series with cult followings like *Star Trek* or *The X-Files*' (Murray 1997: 85).

Returning to Murray's earlier example of cult TV, *Babylon 5*, Kurt Lancaster (2001) has paid close attention to an official CD-ROM guide to the series. This rare example of a detailed study of a cult TV programme guide notes how the:

> CD-ROM gives encyclopaedic background information about the various religious, political, and social factors comprising the various alien species depicted on the television series that fans may never learn by simply watching it. But this contradicts the opening scene of the CD-ROM, where the designers set up the users' expectations that they are about to embark on a virtual tour of the station [Babylon 5]. (Lancaster 2001: 116)

Although Lancaster criticises this digital guide for its non-immersive interface and design, arguing that it functions more as a 'high-tech book' (2001: 118), his analysis does call attention to the way that such guides collapse seriality and its temporality into spatial metaphors. Rather than encountering an unfolding narrative, fan readers here pick (or click) their way through 'one-liners' or 'captions' (2001: 122) and paragraphs of text. The serialisation of the televised series *Babylon 5* is transformed into an archive of 'factual' material about the diegesis, with the TV text's seriality being rendered almost invisible via its rewriting (and fan rereading) as an archive of (diegetic) data rather than as a narrative progression. Such guides thus treat cult TV's seriality as concluded and finished, superintending and marshalling fans' readings as responses to *Babylon 5* as a static whole rather than as responses to specific, unfolding episodes.

The fact that many cult TV programme guides render serialisation – its narrative lures, delays and cliffhangers – invisible is also alluded to in David Howe and Stephen James Walker's (1998) foreword to Doctor Who: *The Television Companion*. They comment that 'the pages that follow give full details of every one of *Doctor Who*'s wonderful cliffhanger episode endings . . . something . . . that, perhaps surprisingly, has never been done in any previous book about the series' (Howe and Walker 1998: iv). This remark points up how the fan experience of narrative delay and suspense is over-written by the encyclopaedic reading formation which short-circuits and collapses seriality into a more immediately available and co-present store of fan knowledge. This mode of fan reception, stressing the need to accu-mulate facts about one's beloved TV show, doesn't distort or erode cult TV's seriality so much as seek to oppose and erase its temporal obstacles to (fan) knowledge.

A second mode of fan response to cult TV's serialisation – 'navigated seriality' – indicates the way that fans can use episode guides (again, as a source of fan knowledge) to re-organise serial narratives thematically, then viewing re-sequenced episodes on video or DVD so that a specific narra-tive development is strongly activated and emphasised (such as one char-acter's psychological/personal growth), or even so that a story other than that given 'in' the televised texts themselves is activated (i.e. fans may choose to screen selected episodes and leave out later stories where unwanted or unpopular narrative developments occurred). Whereas 'col-lapsed seriality' approaches TV texts as spatially organisable stores of information or data rather as narratives, navigated seriality attempts to cut into and across televised narratives. Seriality is thus not undermined here, but is rather reworked by fans' reading formations: cause and effect remain important, but they are temporarily subordinated to associative theming, with episodes being juxtaposed in order to play up, or even construct, res-onances and parallels across the work of different writers or across differ-ent seasons.

Writing in the edited collection *Seven Seasons of Buffy*, Justine Larbalestier gives an example of such 'unofficial' fan readings and practices:

> I create my own Buffy mini-festivals! . . . All that's required is some judicious episode selection. Start with the obvious, say a series of relationship festi-vals: Spike and Buffy (first 'School Hard' 2–3; next 'Halloween' 2–6, and so on), or Cordelia and Xander ('What's My Line, Part 2', 2–10; 'Ted', 2–11; 'Bad Eggs', 2–12; and 'Innocence', 2–14; etc). Or you could have a Jonathan festival . . . or a Ripper retrospective . . . Then you can graduate to the less obvious: the Anya's-Afraid-of-Bunny-Rabbits festival, the Conveniently-Located-Axe festival, and the Slutty Clothes festival. (Larbalestier 2003: 77)

The fan activity of focusing on specific relationships is also a reading strat-egy that is superintended by the official *Buffy* programme guide, *The Watcher's Guide*. This includes a section entitled 'Bloodlust' detailing Sunnydale's various 'love connections' by quoting dialogue from relevant episodes (Golden and Holder 1998: 164–94). And the notion of linking together themed episodes by character has also been commercially co-opted with the release of official *Buffy* DVDs which pre-organise episodes in this way, for example *The Slayer Collection: Spike*, which features the episodes 'School Hard'/'Lie to Me'/'Lovers' Walk'/'Fool for Love' (other themed DVD collections focus on the characters of Angel, Faith and Willow). These commercial releases correspond only to Larbalestier's most 'obvious' mini-festivals, not approaching her more quirky compilations which display ever-more-detailed and 'authentic' fan knowledge. In a review of these DVDs, Mark Sinker says 'perhaps Hollywood's plunge into a swirl of . . . DVD remixes . . . is . . . an aesthetic battle with the problem of the ending, an issue television – by nature episodic – has always been at war with' (Sinker 2004: 79). Viewed as a form of 'DVD remix', such themed concatenations of episodes that are de- and re-contextualised from their original place in *Buffy*'s televised sequence do appear to stall the final closure of the show's serial narrative. As such, they partly resonate with Sara Gwenllian Jones's argument that cult TV's predictable formats can be opened out, by fan readings and responses, into an 'always-unfolding and unforecloseable . . . metatext' (Jones 2002: 83). At the same time, though, this navigation of seriality, this cutting-across of a sequential series, means that different layers and levels of seriality can be brought into focus. As Mary Hammond has commented:

> In *Buffy* the TV series the repressed that returns is polysemous, multifaceted, *serialized*. There is a new demon, a new development, and a new character in focus almost every week, co-existing alongside a slower-maturing narrative (usually Buffy's . . .) across and between several episodes and/or an entire season . . . This seriality mobilizes a different kind of viewing experience from that available in narrative cinema, positing different types of closure or open-endedness. (Hammond 2004: 150)

Fan reading formations that stress reading for character or reading for repeated details such as 'Anya's-Afraid-of-Bunny-Rabbits' thus partly re-open and re-work a text's seriality by mining it for specific iterations or developments. Such fan responses neglect the overarching narrative progression of cult TV series as a whole in order to more or less creatively (or more or less resistantly) re-contextualise episodes in terms of fan-defined 'series' or 'mini-festivals' (a language which positions the fan as curator or as festival 'programmer'). Such fan reading formations link into the 'secondary texts' of programme guides, using them to navigate a TV series. Once again, a given series is treated as a co-present resource (i.e. as something immediately available on DVD or video), albeit this time, a resource to be narratively rather than informationally plundered. Levels of seriality 'in' the texts of cult TV are not just emphasised here; forms of quirkier 'seriality' that are somewhat (or entirely) incidental to any overarching narrative progression are also activated as meaningful by fans.

A third type of fan response to cult TV's serialised form is 'teleologised seriality'. This refers to the fan practice of analysing serial narratives as if earlier events already presupposed later incidents and were thus inevitably moving towards them. Hence the TV series concerned is assumed to be fully teleological and coherent. A striking example of this occurs in the unofficial and unauthorised guide to British cult TV show *Blake's 7*, *Liberation*. Its writers Alan Stevens and Fiona Moore use their analysis of the series' final episode as a kind of summing up of the whole programme:

> From the very beginning we have been left under no illusion that being a rebel is a safe occupation, with the deaths of characters who were introduced as if they were to be regulars, followed by the deaths of the actual regulars Gan and Cally . . . We have . . . seen an idealistic movement degenerate, over the course of four seasons, into a marginal band of pirates and criminals . . . The whole series has thus been predicated on the idea that revolution is a grim process . . . easily co-opted by greed and venality . . . It is fitting, then, that as the credits roll, there is no Seven anymore, and certainly no Blake. (Stevens and Moore 2003: 196)

This programme guide reads the events of the series' final episode as a 'fitting' restatement and resolution of the series' 'predicating' idea, interpreting narrative developments from different seasons as forming part of a unified whole. Decisions made by various actors not to renew their contracts, or different writers' visions of the programme, are hermeneutically conceived as fitting into an overarching progression. TV seriality and its readings are therefore superintended in a specific sense by this activation of meaning. Analysing reasons given for *Twin Peaks*' eventual failure, Marc Dolan isolates out one type of fan complaint which he argues was based on:

> Anglo-American Romanticism . . . [treating the TV text as] a unified conception on the part of the artist . . . These neo-Romantic viewers, who sometimes suggested that *Twin Peaks* should have been a miniseries or limited-run series, probably also thought of the first season as 'David Lynch's *Twin Peaks*'. (Dolan 1995: 31)

'Teleologised seriality' in fans' receptions of cult TV thus appears to accord with 'well-established, "legitimate" aesthetic doctrines' (Dolan 1995: 31). In Bennett and Woollacott's terms, it draws on apparatuses such as schooling and critical reviews 'within . . . which the socially dominant forms for the superintendence of reading are constructed', and hence works to construct cause and effect across a TV series (*contra* Jones' argument cited above). Although this process may 'distort narrative', as Henry Jenkins has alleged, it is a distortion that operates in line with ideological norms of neo-Romantic 'art' discourses, essentially working to valorise cult TV rather than seeking to falsify its televised narratives.

What these examples of fan-negotiated seriality all demonstrate is that rather than merely being 'in' the text, cult TV's serialisation is variously activated by fan readings. On this account, seriality appears not as simply occurring 'in' TV's 'primary texts'; it is also specifically activated, managed and conceptualised (as neo-Romantic etc.) in so-called 'secondary' texts that 'overflow' from televised material (Brooker 2003; Caldwell 2002, 2003).

The programme or episode guide plays a significant role in these activations of seriality, allowing fans to rework, rewrite and reread televised sequences of episodes by erasing the temporality of unfolding seriality and rendering TV texts as immediately consumable data; by supporting the navigation of seriality and the compilation of 'themed' episodes; and by treating cult 'sequential series' or 'series/serial hybrids' as Romantic, coherent and teleological wholes. As such, the prominence of cult TV episode guides can be considered as part of the superintendence of seriality, indicating its simultaneous fan – and commercial – management, ordering, re-opening and exploitation. In the next section I will go on to discuss another key aspect of how episode guides function to value and contextualise cult TV's serialisation, building on my reference to 'neo-Romantic' discourses: the matter of 'quality'.

Activating Quality

Whether fan-produced or commercial, the episode/programme guide typically reinforces an ideology of 'quality' surrounding its cult TV series. For example, by assuming that episodes and seasons of *Angel*, *Babylon 5*, *Blake's 7*, *Buffy*, *Doctor Who*, *The Prisoner*, *The X-Files* and so on require 'guides' – sources of supplementary information to point out, say, the self-reflexivities and popular cultural references of 'primary texts' – then notions of textual non-ephemerality and detailed audience attention can be materially supported, as can the 'ranking' of episodes according to specific aesthetic and interpretive criteria. Various cultural practices of 'quality' are hence constructed and indicated by such guides (cf. McCabe 2000; Kuppers 2004).

Commercially available cult TV guides also adopt different approaches to the production and management of seriality, ranging from thematic digression (Genge 1998; Tracy 1998) to critical analysis of greater or lesser complexity (Kaveney 2004; Muir 1999). Different *Buffy* episode guides, for instance, call up an array of different inter-texts, ranging from those which predominantly cite filmic inter-texts (Mann 1999), to those which are more broadly pop-cultural in their activation of inter-texts and those which are focused around topics (such as the vampire) and themes (such as romance or 'bloodlust' as in Golden and Holder 1998).

Episode/programme guides therefore represent one cultural site where notions of 'quality' are constructed around cult TV series (see Hills 2004: 516 for a related discussion). As in Dolan's analysis of 'neo-Romantic' readings of cult TV seriality, which stress the role of the author, Henry Jenkins – drawing on the work of Michel Foucault – has analysed the 'author-function' promoted in secondary texts surrounding ur-cult-programme *Star Trek*. Jenkins suggests that:

> [Gene] Roddenberry's contribution to [the reference book] *The Making of Star Trek* and subsequent extra-textual discourses allowed him to articulate a personal vision for the series and to define a canon of core episodes . . . which conform most closely to that philosophy. (Tulloch and Jenkins 1995: 189)

By discussing the 'author-function' either explicitly or implicitly, Jenkins and Dolan mark out how cult TV tends to be valued by its fan readers. However, notions of the author-function assume that texts are demarcated as possessing 'quality' primarily through nominations of their artist-creators. In this argument, the notion of a TV 'text' is omnipresent: all TV is made up of texts, it is just that some are discursively positioned as 'authored' by their executive-producer-creator hyphenates (and hence are 'artful' or 'innovative'; see Pearson, Chapter 1) while others are not (being viewed as industrial/ephemeral or entirely 'generic'). This assumption – that all TV is equally 'textual' – fits with structuralist and poststructuralist forms of thought that have fed into TV studies.

However, what episode/programme guides achieve is not *only* the nomination of cult TV's author figures (though they often do achieve this); such guides also serve what might be called a kind of 'text-function', constructing specific series as instances of textuality that can be divorced from a surrounding flow of generic ideas or forms of inter-textuality. Programme guides thereby inevitably bid for the distinctiveness and value of their show, often marking it out as a textual 'event' in TV history. These processes build on what John Thornton Caldwell has termed 'program individuation', where 'quality' TV of the 1980s onwards has tended to have a signature 'look' achieved through lighting, cinematography and visually 'distinctive stylization' (Caldwell 1995: 89). If TV shows have increasingly sought to mark out their badges of 'identity' in a crowded media/brand marketplace, then cult TV's official programme guides have furthered that economic logic by discursively reinforcing textual 'individuation'. Thus, it is not only the case that cult TV is construed as authored in its programme guides whilst 'devalued' (and non-cult) TV is implicitly construed as lacking authorship. Cult TV series are also *viewed as more identifiable as a discrete (and sacred) set of texts*, as opposed to other shows which remain viewed as part of television's profane flow of messages, not being discursively cut apart from such flow and installed as a bounded unit of study or programme-guidance.

To take an initial example, Jan Delasara's unofficial exploration of *The X-Files*, part literary-critical reading of the TV series and part fan appreciation or guide, places just such an individualising frame around the show. Delasara discusses 'the persona of the text', suggesting that 'any popular television series takes on a personality for its audience . . . [and that] the persona of *The X-Files* is complex and distinctive' (Delasara 2000: 27). This specific creation of a text-function (rather than author-function) to validate *The X-Files* rather nakedly construes it as unique, and therefore as a 'text' that is distinctively detachable from TV's other (non-textualised) output.

In her analysis of 'Quality Science Fiction', focused on the cult show *Babylon 5*, Petra Kuppers considers another unofficial programme guide:

> In Andy Lane's *The Babylon File*, Lane precedes his episode guide with an in-depth look at the B5 universe and storyline through the lens of Jungian psychology . . . Lane doesn't deny that science fiction has a range of pleasures to offer, but claims that 'Although it can be enjoyed on a purely superficial level as a rollicking adventure yarn with some nifty special effects . . . there are deeper levels in which the main elements and characters of the show cast historical and mythical shadows and deeper levels still in which the overall story arc is essentially a massive replication of Jung's theories of the mind'. (in Kuppers 2004: 52)

This programme guide's invocation of 'quality' discourses cannot be readily disarticulated from the range of other cultural sites where *Babylon 5* is constructed as authored, 'literary' and individuated (see Kuppers 2004: 48 and Feuer 1995: 93), but like Delasara's guide to *The X-Files* it also emphasises the textually bounded nature of *Babylon 5*. Even when discussing pop-cultural or high-cultural inter-textual references, these citations or appropriations are not viewed as inimical to the distinctively bounded 'identity' or 'essence' of cult TV series such as *Babylon 5*, *The X-Files*, *Buffy* or *Doctor Who*. Instead, programme guides position these types of inter-textuality as guarantors of textual individuation: *Babylon 5* is distinguished, for Andy Lane, by its 'massive replication of Jung's theories of the mind', just as *The X-Files* and *Buffy* display their 'textual personae' in Delasara's sense via quoting and reworking 1950s horror, or via hip, punning pop-cultural references. This situation, where cult TV programme guides use inter-textual references as markers of textual identity rather than as indicators of unoriginality, flies in the face of Roland Barthes' infamous pronouncement that:

> We now know that a text is not a line of words releasing a single 'theological' meaning (the message of the Author-God) but a multi-dimensional space in which a variety of writings, none of them original, blend and clash. The text is a tissue of quotations drawn from the innumerable centres of culture. (Barthes 1977: 146)

Whereas, for Barthes, this 'tissue of quotations' appears to put an end to the distinctiveness of singular texts, such a literary-theoretical conclusion evidently fails to anticipate the popular 'text-function' of cult TV series and their fan cultures' episode/programme guides. Several studies of cult TV have concluded that a shift in producer–fan relations underpinned moves in the 1990s towards self-consciously target-marketed and target-designed cult television, and these narratives of cult TV's rise also typically stress the textual distinctiveness of such shows:

> Rather than being simply oddities and nuisances, producers came to recognise that fans could be vital to the development of shows . . . While television has traditionally been discussed in terms of habitual viewing and televisual 'flow' (Williams 1974), the trends outlined above suggest that contemporary television has witnessed the emergence of 'must-see TV', shows that are not simply part of a habitual flow of television programming but, either through design or audience response, have become 'essential viewing'. (Jancovich and Lyons 2003: 2; see also McCabe 2000: 148–53)

I have argued here that contemporary TV has not merely 'witnessed' the emergence of cult shows that magically divorce themselves from the (meta)seriality of TV's flow. Rather, this separation is discursively reinforced – if not discursively constructed – through cult TV episode/programme guides that seek to exercise a 'text-function' (as well as various 'author-functions') by nominating cult shows as distinctively bounded and hence as fenced off from other pop-cultural derivations, inter-texts and generic patterns. Although fans' experiences of watching specific cult TV shows may also work to divorce these shows from the surrounding TV 'flow', official and unofficial programme guides nevertheless refine this phenomenology of viewing into a bid for 'quality' status, neo-Romantically demarcating cult TV series as non-ephemeral, complex and unique, without always or necessarily invoking a clear author-function. As Janet McCabe has suggested – via an unfortunate use of fan stereotypes – this situation puts the cult TV fan in an intriguing position with regards to 'quality' TV:

> Niche audiences are nothing new, already associated with 'cult TV'. Much more than a television geek though, the devoted viewer is an active agent in the shaping [of] contemporary TV culture. In a sense, *the nerd has evolved into an arbiter of quality programming*. (McCabe 2000: 152, my italics)

And yet it is not just 'the nerd' who is a newfound arbiter of discourses of quality; McCabe's argument shares an excessive clarity or sharpness of focus with that of Jancovich and Lyons (quoted above), since both pieces appear only to address 'cult television' and 'cult audiences' without considering cult television culture's range of 'secondary texts' or inter-texts. It is secondary texts – especially those that negotiate with, manage and activate cult TV's seriality and its very status as 'a text' – which have been significant in anchoring cult TV to multiple (authored; textually bounded; Romantic-unified) notions of the 'quality' serial (Hills 2002, 2004). Furthermore, it is secondary texts such as episode/programme guides which have also superintended seriality by enacting and licensing fans' reading strategies of collapsed, navigated and teleologised serialisation. If 'quality' and 'meaning' aren't innocently or formally 'in' cult TV's 'texts themselves' – both these terms now routinely being investigated via discursive models in the wake of reading formation and poststructuralist theory – then, as I have proposed here, we might profitably explore cult seriality and its fan reception through a similar lens.

Bibliography

Bacon-Smith, Camille (1992), *Enterprising Women: Television Fandom and the Creation of Popular Myth*, Philadelphia: University of Pennsylvania Press.

Barthes, Roland (1977), *Image-Music-Text*, London: Fontana Press.

Bennett, Tony and Woollacott, Janet (1987), *Bond and Beyond: The Political Career of a Popular Hero*, Basingstoke: Macmillan.

Branston, Gill and Stafford, Roy (2003), *The Media Student's Book*, 3rd edn, London and New York: Routledge.

Brooker, Will (2003), 'Conclusion: Overflow and Audience', in Will Brooker and Deborah Jermyn (eds), *The Audience Studies Reader*, London and New York: Routledge, pp. 322–34.

Caldwell, John Thornton (1995), *Televisuality: Style, Crisis and Authority in American Television*, New Jersey: Rutgers University Press.

—(2002), 'New Media/Old Augmentations: Television, the Internet, and Interactivity', in *Realism and 'Reality' in Film and Media*, Copenhagen: Museum Tusculanum Press, pp. 253–74.

—(2003), 'Second-Shift Media Aesthetics', in Anna Everett and John T. Caldwell (eds), *New Media: Theories and Practices of Digitextuality*, New York and London: Routledge, pp. 127–44.

Couldry, Nick (2000), *Inside Culture: Re-imagining the Method of Cultural Studies*, London: Sage.

Delasara, Jan (2000), *PopLit, PopCult and 'The X-Files': A Critical Exploration*, Jefferson: McFarland.

Dolan, Marc (1995), 'The Peaks and Valleys of Serial Creativity: What Happened to/on *Twin Peaks*', in David Lavery (ed.), *Full of Secrets: Critical Approaches to 'Twin Peaks'*, Detroit: Wayne State University Press, pp. 30–50.

Ellis, John (2000), *Seeing Things: Television in the Age of Uncertainty*, London: I. B. Tauris.

Feuer, Jane (1995), *Seeing through the Eighties*, London: BFI Publishing.

Fiske, John (1987), *Television Culture*, London: Methuen.

Genge, N. E. (1998), *The Buffy Chronicles: The Unofficial Companion to 'Buffy the Vampire Slayer'*, London: Boxtree.

Golden, Christopher and Holder, Nancy (1998), *The Watcher's Guide*, New York and London: Pocket Books.

Hagedorn, Roger (1995), 'Doubtless to be Continued: A Brief History of Serial Narrative', in Robert C. Allen (ed.), *To Be Continued: Soap Operas around the World*, London and New York: Routledge, pp. 27–48.

Hammond, Mary (2004), 'Monsters and Metaphors: *Buffy the Vampire Slayer* and the Old World', in Sara Gwenllian Jones and Roberta E. Pearson (eds), *Cult Television*, Minneapolis: University of Minnesota Press, pp. 47–64.

Harrington, C. Lee and Bielby, Denise (1995), *Soap Fans*, Philadelphia: Temple University Press.

Hayward, Jennifer (1997), *Consuming Pleasures: Active Audiences and Serial Fictions from Dickens to Soap Opera*, Kentucky: University Press of Kentucky.

Hills, Matt (2002), *Fan Cultures*, London and New York: Routledge.

—(2004), 'Defining Cult TV: Texts, Inter-texts and Fan Audiences', in Robert C. Allen and Annette Hill (eds), *The Television Studies Reader*, London and New York: Routledge, pp. 509–23.

Howe, David and Walker, Stephen James (1998), *'Doctor Who': The Television Companion: The Official BBC Guide to Every TV Story*, London: BBC Books.

Jancovich, Mark and Lyons, James (2003), 'Introduction', in Mark Jancovich and James Lyons (eds), *Quality Popular Television: Cult TV, the Industry and Fans*, London: BFI Publishing, pp. 1–8.

Jenkins, Henry (1992), *Textual Poachers*, New York and London: Routledge.

Jones, Sara Gwenllian (2002), 'The Sex Lives of Cult Television Characters', *Screen*, 43(1), 79–90.

Kaveney, Roz (ed.) (2004), *Reading the Vampire Slayer: The New, Updated Unofficial Guide to 'Buffy' and 'Angel'*, London and New York: I. B. Tauris.

Klinger, Barbara (1991), 'Digressions at the Cinema: Commodification and Reception in Mass Culture', in James Naremore and Patrick Brantlinger (eds), *Modernity and Mass Culture*, Bloomington: Indiana University Press, pp. 117–34.

Kuppers, Petra (2004), 'Quality Science Fiction: *Babylon 5*'s Metatextual Universe', in Sara Gwenllian Jones and Roberta E. Pearson (eds), *Cult Television*, Minneapolis: University of Minnesota Press, pp. 45–59.

Lancaster, Kurt (2001), *Interacting with 'Babylon 5': Fan Performances in a Media Universe*, Austin: University of Texas Press.

Larbalestier, Justine (2003), 'A *Buffy* Confession', in Glenn Yeffeth (ed.), *Seven Seasons of 'Buffy': Science Fiction and Fantasy Writers Discuss their Favorite Television Show*, Texas: Banbella Books, pp. 72–84.

Mann, Peter (1999), *A Completely and Utterly Unauthorised Guide to 'Buffy the Vampire Slayer'*, Harpenden: Pocket Essentials.

McCabe, Janet (2000), 'Diagnosing the Alien: Producing Identities, American 'Quality' Drama and British Television Culture in the 1990s', in *Frames and Fictions on Television: The Politics of Identity within Drama*, Exeter: Intellect, pp. 141–54.

Muir, John Kenneth (1999), *A Critical History of 'Doctor Who' on Television*, Jefferson: McFarland.

Murray, Janet H. (1997), *Hamlet on the Holodeck: The Future of Narrative in Cyberspace*, Cambridge, MA: The MIT Press.

Silverstone, Roger (1994), *Television and Everyday Life*, London and New York: Routledge.

Sinker, Mark (2004), 'And Life (or TV) Goes On', *Sight and Sound*, March 2004, 79.

Stevens, Alan and Moore, Fiona (2003), *Liberation: The Unofficial and Unauthorised Guide to 'Blake's 7'*, Tolworth: Telos Publishing.

Thompson, Kristin (2003), *Storytelling in Film and Television*, Massachusetts: Harvard University Press.

Tracy, Kathleen (1998), *The Girl's Got Bite: The Unofficial Guide to Buffy's World*, Los Angeles: Renaissance Books.

Tulloch, John and Alvarado, Manuel (1983), *'Doctor Who': The Unfolding Text*, London: Macmillan.

Tulloch, John and Jenkins, Henry (1995), *Science Fiction Audiences: Watching 'Doctor Who' and 'Star Trek'*, London and New York: Routledge.

CHAPTER 11

Creating 'Quality' Audiences for *ER* on Channel Four

Janet McCabe

British Audiences, American 'Quality' Dramas: introduction

Despite Channel 4's past success with imported American programming, Steve Clarke wondered how viewers would react to its new acquisition, *ER* (NBC, 1994–present), when first transmitted on British terrestrial television in February 1995:

> The problem was that while *ER* (Emergency Room) was obviously the more original of the two [*Chicago Hope* (CBS, 1994–2000) being the other], it was so different that viewers might be put off by its frantic pace. (Clarke 1995: 3)

Even at the beginning of series seven, shown first on Channel 4's new pay-TV entertainment digital channel E4 in January 2001, reviewers still expressed concerns that new viewers would find its frenetic pace and dense plotting an unnerving experience. Matthew Baylis explains:

> Many new viewers feel nauseous after an *ER* encounter . . . *ER* is a confusing experience. An episode can feature up to seven storylines, which compared to the sedate three or four of British soaps, is like exposing GCSE maths students to quantum physics. (Baylis 2001: 17)

Despite reservations, *ER* was dubbed 'must-see TV' from the start (Hildred 1995; Massingbred 1995: 29; Viner 1995: 29). So important is *ER* (along with popular US situation comedy, *Friends* (NBC, 1994–2004)) to Channel 4 that in 1996 the company became embroiled in a vitriolic price war with Channel 5 to keep the British syndication rights for the American shows. Channel 4 reached an agreement with the programme's distributor, Warner Bros, to share the drama series with Sky One, in a deal believed to have cost £60 million (Smith 1996: 20). In 1999 the network paid out a reputed £86.2 million for the exclusive British rights to *ER* and *Friends*,

outbidding BSkyB for first-run privileges as well as the renewal of its terrestrial rights and full access to the archive (Dams 1999: 1). Even in its
seventh season *ER* was 'still popular enough for Channel 4 to have gambled
large amounts of their budget on squeezing Sky out of the running to show
it here' (Morrow 2001: 6). The ex-director of programmes at Channel 4,
John Willis, justifies the high prices paid in terms of the demands placed on
Channel 4 by its audience, 'We have a responsibility to our viewers to get
good acquisitions. C4 has been doing that since week one' (Smith 1996: 20).

This chapter investigates how Channel 4 imagines its audience as it
repositions *ER*, the medical drama series set in an emergency room of
the fictional Cook County General Hospital in Chicago, into the British
television flow. New series of *ER* (along with *The Sopranos* (HBO,
1999–present), *The West Wing* (NBC, 2000–present) and *Six Feet Under*
(HBO, 2001–5)) are flagship shows for the digital channel E4; and, as Paul
Rixon contends, Channel 4 is now 'a second run channel' (Rixon 2003: 55)
for these programmes. The constant repositioning of, and rethinking
about, *ER* within the press, promotional and advertising campaigns and
television schedules has something to tell us about how such American
dramas function in an ever more complex television landscape. I thus aim
to suggest how Channel 4 constructs knowledge about its audience for *ER*
as it defines and strengthens its own corporate identity; how in turn these
series are positioned as 'quality' through imagining viewers based on lifestyle choice and modes of readership; and what in turn this has to say about
how American series operate in British television culture. The point here
is that *ER* emerges as a distinctive quality televisual product within the
abundant and highly competitive television flow precisely because it is *contained* and *represented* by institutional frameworks that say that this is what
it is.

Underpinning this argument is the idea that what defines the *ER* text as
a generic product is self-containment. *ER* possesses a recognisable internal formula: a unique visual style, dense narrative plotting and a combination of episodic and accruing storylines. Even while a viewer can sit down
to watch an episode for the first time, the multiple layers of *ER* encourage
repeated viewing to clarify and consolidate narrative information, and to
appreciate the richness of the inter-personal relationships and dense
medical knowledge. In so doing it invites an intense audience loyalty.

Identifying a Quality Demographic

British broadcasting policy documentation has always had an ideal television viewer in mind when putting forward its beliefs about quality tele-

vision. The 1968 Pilkington Report for example identified a reactive and uncritical television audience in need of platonic protection (Pilkington 1962). The vulnerable Pilkington viewer justified Reithian ideals of public-service broadcasting based on balancing education with entertainment to constitute an informed and enlightened democracy. Quality television in this context is associated with a cultural paternalism, about those high-minded and socially advantaged individuals (for example the educated middle-class elite) able to make appropriate programming decisions on behalf of those who could not (for example the working-class mass). This conservative idea of quality TV saw a shift in drama production, from writer-led original works in the fifties and sixties to hugely prestigious literary adaptations in the early eighties, such as Granada Television's *Brideshead Revisited* (1981) and *The Jewel in the Crown* (1984). Charlotte Brunsdon identifies literary source, the best of British acting, high production values and a nostalgic sense of British heritage as defining these series as 'uncontroversial signifiers of quality' (Brunsdon 1990: 85–6). Broadcasters demonstrate a middle-class paternalist attitude towards their audience as one in need of moral protection and cultural guidance.

Another definition of quality emerged during the seventies. The new type of viewer associated with the emergent notion of quality television was able to make informed choices for him- or herself, both as a discerning consumer and socially responsible citizen. It is an idea embedded into the Peacock Report, which advocated a new 'consumer sovereignty' in 1986:

> Our own conclusion is that British broadcasting should move towards a sophisticated system based on *consumer sovereignty*. That is a system which recognises that viewers and listeners are the best ultimate judges of their own interests, which they can best satisfy if they have the option of purchasing the broadcasting services they require from as many alternative sources of supply as possible. There will always be a need to supplement the direct consumer market by public finance for programmes of a public service kind . . . supported by people in their capacity as *citizens* and *voters* but unlikely to be commercially self-supporting in the view of broadcasting entrepreneurs. (Peacock 1986: paras 592, 593, emphasis added)

John Ellis elaborates further to contend that this emergent idea of quality emphasised, 'a varied service which enhanced the life of the citizens and enabled them to participate more fully in their society. It also stressed the importance of innovation in keeping in touch with the audience to avoid predictable programmes and to continue to engage and surprise their audience' (Ellis 2000: 149). Quality is redefined in relation to a television consumer-cum-citizen as about offering experimentation and variety to the newly empowered audience capable of making responsible choices for themselves.

Apparent from these two definitions of quality, defining British television culture is not so much that viewers dictate the form and content of quality programming but that a discourse about the typical viewer, embedded into broadcasting policy, defines how quality television is understood. Identifying a new robust consumer with discerning cultural tastes and sense of social (rather than class) responsibility justified new types of quality programming, scheduling practice and modes of delivery at the beginning of the eighties. Such a conceptualisation of a liberated television viewer coincided not only with the 1979 conservative general election victory and socio-political re-categorisations of modern Britons as meritocratic citizens (McCabe 2000: 147–8), but also made visible the emergence of a dynamic and highly competitive television landscape. As institutional developments and new forms of delivery changed what audiences watched, remote controls and VCRs altered how they watched television. Deregulation – as outlined in the Broadcasting Bill (1990) and the 1988 White Paper, *Broadcasting in the 90s: Competition, Choice and Quality* – and increased competition from cable, video and satellite companies during the nineties fragmented the British television audience even further.

Increasingly lifestyle choice (or fantasies of self) informs a definition of quality television. John Willis mobilises knowledge about an intelligent and demanding consumer when justifying Channel 4's programming decisions and scheduling patterns:

> Television is changing. Like Adam and Joe [from *The Adam and Joe Show*, C4, 1996–2001], viewers will increasingly make programmes or schedule their viewing themselves so existing notions of ownership and power will change. [. . .] However, young or old, rich or poor, Channel 4 viewers are independently-minded. . . . They will watch Italian soccer and Cezanne, current affairs and Chris Evans. Above all, they don't want easy answers but to make sense of the world themselves. (Willis 1996: 22)

Willis' statement delivers up an egalitarian model of the average Channel 4 viewer as a television citizen able to make discerning choices for him- or herself from a discursive range of options positioned within the television flow. By evoking an emancipated viewer Willis justifies Channel 4's ambition to be '*the* television broadcaster that is most likely to explore new ideas and connect with new ways of thinking' (Channel 4 1998b: 5). These statements further beg the question: what are these new programme ideas and how does Channel 4 imagine they will appeal to the 'independently-minded' viewer?

Audience research continues to tell us that television viewers are becoming ever more demanding about what they watch. Recent scholarship identifies how American networks responded to the problem of attracting and – more importantly – retaining audiences faced with numerous television choices (Feuer 1992; Thompson 1997; Reeves et al. 2002: 42–57). Instead of appealing to a mass audience, television companies increasingly began to think about audiences as a 'differentiated mass possessing identifiable demographic categories' (Feuer 1992: 152). Particular networks such as NBC and CBS started to introduce 'a new type of complex and sophisticated programming aimed directly at an upscale audience' (Thompson 1997: 30). What this emergent institutional philosophy presents us with is another definition of quality related to economic survival, niche marketing and the search for quality demographics. It would be fair to say that quality television drama can be encoded as targeting the group most prized by sponsors and advertising agencies: that is, the 18–40-year-old urban, educated, up-scale viewer. Given the instability and fragmentation of the television marketplace, the need to find a lucrative niche audience provides an incentive for encouraging experimentation and product differentiation.

It is, however, not enough to attract this valued group but to retain them as loyal viewers who tune in week after week. Jimmie Reeves, Mark Rogers and Michael Epstein define this devoted viewer as someone who 'will make arrangements to watch every episode . . . For the devoted viewer, a favourite show is a "special event" that disrupts the flow of television and inspires more intense levels of identification and attention than typical television fare' (Reeves et al. 1996: 26). Such an avid viewer may for example tape and archive episodes. Yet, would it not be more appropriate to think about how and why the devoted viewer is conceived by networks and television production companies in the first place? To this end, television institutions relentlessly construct knowledge about devoted viewers for certain programmes within which a series of statements about lifestyle choice, intellectual tastes, social aspirations and cultural identities are made. This knowledge is further embedded into the formal style and textual address of dramas like *ER* but is also generated and reinforced by inter-textual material like official websites (http://www.ertv.com/) and online discussion groups as well as ancillary merchandise such as books, videos/DVDs, coffee mugs, T-shirts and even scrubs. It is in and through such a discourse that individuals are positioned to see themselves as devoted viewers, to understand their relationship to the rest of the niche audience and the construction of subjectivity in relation to the drama. By means of this institutional discourse, how a particular drama series becomes known is invariably determined by who watches the show, which in turn justifies form and content, modes of reception and the ways in which the drama will be talked about.

With its Finger on the TV Pulse: Channel 4, *ER* and its Imagined Audience

Reliance on American syndicated material has helped Channel 4 build a distinct corporate brand identity for itself. Channel 4 began transmission in November 1982 with a public-service remit designed to appeal to those viewers ignored by pre-existing terrestrial television channels in terms of class, gender and ethnicity. Channel 4 admits that it does not aim to cater for a mass audience. Instead it aspires to foster 'the new and experimental in television' (Channel 4 1998b: 1–2). Soon schedulers tried to attract a more affluent, upscale, media-literate group similar to the 'yuppie, TV-literate baby boomers' (Feuer 1995: 8) targeted by American networks for the quality dramas described above. Far from aping US television production methods, Channel 4 buys in American drama to serve the interests of its own network identity, which encourages diversity, innovation and experimentation, a mandate that professes a commitment to 'fresh and invigorating television that challenges the norm' (Channel 4 1998a: 1). In a new television era of availability, and the proliferation of consumer and lifestyle choice represented by multi-channelled television (Ellis 2000: 61–73), Channel 4 makes sense of *ER* as a quality television drama precisely by imagining a quality demographic that 'expect curiosity, challenge, controversy' (Willis 1996: 22).

ER was initially launched in Britain as bringing prestigious Hollywood talent to the small screen, '*ER* is written by Michael Crichton and produced by Steven Spielberg. I knew I was going to be hooked before the opening titles had finished,' wrote A. A. Gill (1995: 3). Before the pilot first transmitted in 1995, Channel 4 promised a unique televisual experience. Through promotional trailers and newspaper articles, the marketing campaign focused on Spielberg, whose Amblin Television company produced the series, and Crichton's 'man of the moment' (Ogle 1995: 17) status, post-*Jurassic Park* (Spielberg, 1993). Most previews chronicled Crichton's ten-year quest to option his script, based on his experiences as a medical intern at Massachusetts General Hospital, and his first meeting with Spielberg (Ogle 1995: 17; Bond 1995: 47; Clarke 1995: 3). Press coverage tended to pass over *ER's* little known cast to focus instead on what Crichton and Spielberg brought to the writing and visual direction of the show, '[The] sense of relentless chaos is perfectly and accurately delivered – thanks, largely, to adrenaline editing and Crichton's fat-free scripts'

(Hunt 1995: 67). Authoring the drama gave meaning to *ER*'s dramatic urgency, complex characters and numerous plot-lines as cutting-edge television, 'The author, Michael Crichton, calls it the "rock 'em-sock 'em" pace, and says that most television is too slow. "I wanted to crank it up to something resembling reality"' (Purves 1995: 5). Establishing a link with those whose creative reputation had already been established in the highly commercial and competitive world of Hollywood cinema suggests that *ER* is no ordinary medical drama but prestigious *zeitgeist* television.

One does not have to look too far to find the source of the media hype. Press releases from Channel 4 reveal that the company's initial marketing campaign was built around past Crichton/Spielberg associations. Much was made by Channel 4 of Crichton and Spielberg's ability to elevate the tried and tested medical generic formula on television to the level of block-busting cinematic entertainment. Pre-publicity branding deliberately evokes pre-existing media cultures and past cinematic experiences. Offering associations and pleasures not normally allied with medical TV dramas, Channel 4 presented *ER* as a daring and innovative new televisual experience. Through statements made by Channel 4, the production of knowledge about *ER* became an uncritical reproduction of various assumptions and beliefs about those viewers to whom the show was initially meant to appeal. Not only were these viewers imagined as adept at decoding media texts and marks of authorship, similar to an independent art-house spectators, but they were also positioned as desiring a unique and challenging televisual experience. In so doing, Channel 4's advertising campaign elevated *ER* to the status of exclusive designer-label television for *cinéphiles*.

Two episodes stand out as Channel 4, with its reputation for sponsoring innovative, low-budget independent films (FilmFour), activated new associations for the drama. The first was Quentin Tarantino's directorial effort, 'Motherhood' (23: 1). When the episode first aired in 1995 Tarantino had only recently shot to fame as Hollywood's latest creative genius, praised by critics for his trash aesthetics and uncompromising depictions of violence. Many heralded his 1992 debut, *Reservoir Dogs*, as having changed the semiotics of contemporary American cinema; and the 1994 follow-up *Pulp Fiction* (remaining the highest-grossing independent film in American cinema history) consolidated his *auteurist* celebrity status. His reputation as the quintessential nineties American *auteur* guaranteed 'Motherhood' would be the most eagerly awaited episode in season one:

> Tarantino's direction . . . took the programme into a different league. It was the best instalment of *ER* I have ever seen. He brought much needed humour to a series that is horribly earnest about itself. (Pile 1995: 12)

Head Nurse Carol Hathaway's (played by Julianna Margulies) and Dr Susan Lewis' (played by Sherry Stringfield) stroll through the E.R. in dark glasses, the scuffle between two gang girls, one holding a severed ear, or Dr Peter Benton's (played by Eriq LaSalle) graphic handling of the bone saw could be unlocked by those who understood the episode's *auteur* underpinning, 'Last night, the series must have doubled its ratings with all the movie nerds who were watching just to check Tarantino's *auteur* touch in the surgery scenes' (Romney 1995: 11). Mapping Tarantino's maverick reputation for visceral set pieces, graphic violence, ultra-hip dialogue and his geekish fixation for popular culture on to the *ER* text was promoted as elevating the TV generic form with its predictable and low cultural visual aesthetics to the level of innovative film art. Tarantino's foray into the E.R. confirmed the assessment that '*ER* is fast, funny and always surprising' (Hildred 1995: 27). Such knowledge was used by Channel 4 to court a pre-existing fanbase that might not have otherwise tuned into the show. But it also rewarded regular viewers with something special.

Ewan McGregor's guest appearance as the ill-fated Duncan in the season three grocery-store armed-robbery episode ('The Long Way Around', 15: 3) is the other example. McGregor's cameo role inspired similar copy, 'Cinema's Coolest Junkie Visits the Small Screen's Hippest Hospital,' declared *The Observer*'s headline review (Brooks 1997: 10). McGregor, star of British cult films such as *Shallow Grave* (Danny Boyle, 1994) and *Trainspotting* (Danny Boyle, 1996), made the temporary cross-over from film to television because he was a fan, 'I didn't want the part in order to crack into the States. I wanted it because I really like *ER*' (Brooks 1997: 10). This was convenient given the strong identification his image has with Channel 4's FilmFour trendy lifestyle-choice corporate image. Both episodes, plucked from their original narrative contexts, were repeated back to back early in 1999, reasserting the distinctiveness of the tele-cine experience and bolstering Channel 4's reputation as an investor in innovative, independent film production. These episodes were uniquely positioned as small experimental 'movies'. That both celebrities were identified as 'big' *ER* fans, and that their star images were used to lend originality to the *ER* text leads one to conclude that the institutional text produces an identity for *ER* as innovative, generically ground-breaking and stylish precisely by bringing such high-profile admirers into its own discourse. Aligning viewers with other *ER* fans like McGregor and Tarantino is less about the series' popularity than a concept of *ER*, and a viewer identity defined by lifestyle choice, hip attitudes and fantasies of self.

Bringing in famous names to play cameo roles is now an established part of the *ER* formula. Season six finds Alan Alda joining the medical team as distinguished E.R. specialist Dr Gabriel Lawrence, hired by Dr Kerry Weaver (Laura Innes), much to the chagrin of Dr Mark Greene (Anthony Edwards) ('Greene With Envy' 3: 6). His expertise in emergency medicine immediately evokes past associations with his role as Benjamin Franklin 'Hawkeye' Pierce in the hugely successful *M*A*S*H* (20th Century-Fox, 1972–83). Such self-referentiality speaks about the maturation of the television generation growing up watching TV. Television now has a history. Audiences are invited to remember it when decoding contemporary texts and they are also nostalgically positioned to see themselves as part of that cultural history. Although Lawrence departs the E.R. once his Alzheimer's becomes public, our previous knowledge of Alda as Hawkeye is deliberately played upon as Dr Lawrence advises his colleagues on emergency procedures based on his experiences in Vietnam. Jason Jacobs claims that '*M*A*S*H* was . . . the first hospital drama that routinely rejected and ridiculed consensus-based depictions of medical care' (Jacobs 2003: 8), and *ER* certainly inherits its liberal humanism with the site of conflict transposed from the Korean War and a nation torn apart to an inner-city Chicago-based hospital with its troubled urban communities. Dr Greene is, as Jacobs rightly observes, the 'natural successor' (Jacobs 2003: 146) to Hawkeye. Yet it is the knowing-ness created in the text, especially given Greene's distrust of Dr Lawrence and his unconventional methods practised in combat, that shapes this generic inheritance in the minds of the media-literate viewer. That the *ER* text has a memory in terms of its narrative is in no doubt, but that *ER* self-consciously remembers a television (as well as film) history must be acknowledged as an important source of pleasure for audiences invited to take enjoyment in the act of remembering.

ER continues to enjoy a high profile in Channel 4's schedule. So much so that the show is central to its new pay-TV entertainment channel, E4. The launch night in fact kicked off with a double bill of the latest series of *Friends*, followed by brand new *ER*, 'No point in waxing lyrical about how good Thursday nights are,' declared the advertising campaign. 'Have a look at the line up below. It speaks for itself' (Channel 4 2001). Along with other so-called quality American dramas such as *The Sopranos* (HBO, 1999–present), *The West Wing* (NBC, 2000–present) and *Six Feet Under* (HBO, 2001–5), *ER* is shown first on E4, before appearing on Channel 4 (although the delay has narrowed considerably in recent time), and was key to its Big Thursday marketing campaign (although E4 now spreads its TV pleasures across the week). Just as NBC generates anticipation for *ER* through its media campaigns (Martín 2003: 34–5), E4 and Channel 4 create a buzz around the new series with its tantalising trailers and subliminal 'emergency room' messaging. The first-run discourse elevates *ER* from popular mainstream drama to exclusive quality television by evoking a viewer prepared to spend money on digital services to catch the first glimpse of the American import. Compared to the 35 million viewers the show gets in America, Channel 4 only expects 4 million. The figure is even smaller for the pay-TV service (Hiscock and Boshoff 1998). An American prime-time mass audience is translated into a quality niche audience interested in original programming and willing to pay for it. Such profiling justifies Channel 4's substantial investment in the series, and assures the station cultural kudos as an innovative network, 'That means a channel willing to try the new in both form and content' (Willis 1996: 22).

Something any channel must have above all else in the now congested marketplace is a robust and distinct brand identify. E4 builds on Channel 4's unique and long-standing reputation for bringing audiences cutting-edge and risk-taking entertainment, and is described 'as one of the coolest TV Channels' (Deans 2002: 2). Its reputation for 'creating a youthful and funky atmosphere' (Deans 2002: 2) is now well established. Yet as the *ER* formula turns from ground-breaking to normal with viewers used to the house style, *ER* increasingly seems to sit uncomfortably with the E4 brand label. Despite delivering large audiences, *ER* 'does not necessarily sit so well with the intended cutting edge image and draw their audiences from a wider demographic than the channel's supposed 16–34 target audience' (Deans 2002: 2). Yet, its continued ability to attract high ratings gives pause for thought; and might it say something about how *ER* as a new kind of generic product finds ways of holding on to its audience?

Repeat Prescription: Building Audience Loyalty and Modes of Readership

Describing how her writing is shaped by the *ER* actors, Carol Flint, writer and *ER* producer, implies how 'long-running TV series can take on a creative life of their own' (quoted in Jacobs 2003: 34). Extending her thinking leads me to ask if there is something about the internal logic (the visual style, the multi-layered narrative) that hooks in and retains the audience. It seems to me that what enables a dramatic series like *ER* to keep its viewers in this crowded and competitive marketplace is how it deliberately builds an intense televisual experience into its very form. It is meant to be consumed more than once; and as such has something to tell us about the relationship between contemporary television form and viewing practices.

When *ER* first burst on to screens, its fast visual pace was designed to appear original and inventive to viewers:

The sullen atmosphere and herky-jerky camera movement bring the game up-to-speed with present television conventions. But *ER* has established its own eccentric rhythm . . . This subtle work is backed up by smart editing – *ER* cuts away from a scene about two seconds before most shows would, not in any disconcerting way, just enough to alter television's visual pace. (Whitehead 1994: 54)

ER seemed to inject a cinematic energy into the medical drama TV formula. 'With its breathless pace, taut writing, dizzy camera-work and razor-sharp editing, *ER* is a visceral treat akin to seeing a big-budget Hollywood action movie' (Gritten 1995: 1). Shooting on film before transferring to videotape, non-traditional lighting systems (such as fluorescent bulbs) and camera style (for example use of the Steadicam) and fast editing (700–800 cuts as opposed to the standard 300–400 edits for a one-hour drama; Oppenheimer 1995) gave the show its distinct look. Mimi Leder[1], co-executive producer and director (first two seasons, including 'Love's Labor Lost'), describes how the programme-makers took risks, to give *ER* 'a real action feel: an intense, frenetic look, different from other medical programs' (Oppenheimer 1995: 46–7). With 'the viewer's attention . . . not allowed to flag for a moment' (Massingbred 1995: 29), the exhaustive sensory experience was dubbed 'channel-surfing without hitting the button' (Purves 1995: 5). Such an intense visceral experience is designed to grab and hold on to the viewer's attention, 'Pace is necessary because if we slow down for a few seconds the audience can go to one of 100 other channels,' explains *ER*'s executive producer, John Wells (Brooks 1997: 10). Short audience attention spans may justify the need for visual/narrative speed; but the rapid tempo appears designed to impress those watching *ER* for the first time with an energy not seen before on television (Odone 1997: 38). Compulsive viewing becomes reconfigured as an addiction to *ER*'s visceral energy and dramatic tension.

Reliance on Steadicam tracking shots draws the audience into the narrative action in ways that more conventional camerawork and editing fail to do. Viewer proximity is achieved through being allowed to closely tail the staff, as if we were medical students traipsing after the E.R. medics. The Steadicam tracking shot gives us unprecedented access to the action, and places us in the trauma rather than watching it from a distance, 'It's almost as if somebody is going to hand you, the viewer, a scalpel' (Oppenheimer 1995: 50).

Viewers are positioned to expect innovation from *ER*. Across the ten seasons, the series continues to foreground its ability to experiment and reinvent itself (especially if ratings dip). In response to losing ground to other new dramas in the States, *ER* went out live in 1997 ('Ambush' 1: 4).

The episode was filmed as a fly-on-the-wall documentary with a film crew spending the day in the emergency room recording the staff going about their daily duties. 'Live television has a visceral kick: mistakes, spontaneity and unpredictability become a welcome part of the viewing experience' (Gritten 1997: 26). *ER* later achieved another first by becoming the first American network show to be aired in wide-screen format. Such a move responds to current trends in high-definition TV broadcasting as well as changes in what and how audiences are watching television. Eric Taub describes the incentive behind the switch, 'With increasing numbers of viewers watching letterboxed movies on DVD and creating home theatres with large, wide-screen sets, [Jonathan] Kaplan [an *ER* director] felt the time was right for a change' (Taub 2001: 22). It was first introduced in the season seven episode, 'The Visit' (6: 7). Guest-starring Oscar-winning actress Sally Field, as Abby Lockhart's (played by Maura Tierney) bipolar mother, Maggie Wyczenski, her appearance was meant to 'overshadow any technical change' (Taub 2001: 22). Yet, and alongside the last-minute decision by NBC to add 'Presented in Wide-Screen' at the beginning, the episode gave audiences a movie-style experience. More recently, the wide-screen format enabled the show to experiment with form. Contrasting the fortunes of Dr John Carter (Noah Wyle) on the day shift with Dr Greg Pratt (Mekhi Phifer) working the night, the two-hundredth episode, 'When Night Meets Day' (21: 9), uses a split screen to build the dramatic tension with both doctors handling the same trauma but separated by time. Being innovative with form makes *ER* look modern and cutting edge; as Taub notes, 'the new shooting style energised the production' (Taub 2001: 22). Kaplan felt the wide-screen format liberated the audience, allowing them to explore the dramatic space for themselves: 'I want to take the audience where they want to go' (Taub 2001: 22).

The plot-dense formula is another feature of *ER* The series is 'fond of ellipses, revelation is parcelled out, subplots dangle to be picked up in their own sweet time or are tied [together] so imperceptibly [that] they barely seem to have been tied up at all' (Whitehead 1994: 54). It is also known that '*ER* . . . tells stories from [a range of different generic categories] and . . . its research team has interviewed emergency personnel, people with real stories that lend an authenticity to the show' (Feldshuh 1995: 4). Multiple storylines, scenes fractured into mini-scenes and conversational snippets inter-dispersed with incomprehensible medical jargon offer up a narrative space designed to appeal to the broadest television constituency as possible. It also keeps the viewer alert. Wells says, 'People have told me they can't miss a minute, can't go to the bathroom while it's on, because they're afraid they'll miss how one of the stories works out. There's no time to grab your remote and see what's on the other channels' (quoted in Gritten 1995: 1). The point here is not whether or not the story is true but that the drama with its sense of dramatic urgency and information overload positions viewers to feel this way about what they are watching.

Viewers are spoken about as being able to keep pace with the different plot-lines and numerous characters, 'its multi-layered storylines show a respect for the viewer's intelligence not always apparent in British television drama: *ER*'s first dose contains no fewer than 45 medical stories' (Clarke 1995: 3). Yet there remains something about the narrative that demands a second viewing. Back in 1996 the first season run on Wednesday nights was immediately repeated on Saturday evenings and since 2002 new episodes seen on Big Thursday are shown again on Sundays (otherwise known as Second Chance Sunday). There is even the opportunity to review the whole series again on Channel 4 in the usual Wednesday night 9 p.m. slot. Over time, the delay has shortened and now E4 episodes can be viewed only a week later on terrestrial. Repeated watching means the viewer can easily catch up with missed episodes but it also gives them another chance to make sense of the fast narrative pace and blur of medical procedures. Having another look at the drama armed with knowledge means new meanings can be found and fresh connections made. But, as one reviewer notes, 'Not being able to follow what on earth is going on remains one of the peculiar charms of the breakneck American hospital drama, *ER*' (*The Daily Telegraph* 1996: 31). Such a comment also reveals that there is something elusive about these texts which encourages us to avidly consume and keep coming back to decipher meaning. Readership becomes an ongoing accretional rather than complete process.

Movement from its prime-time evening slot to daytime repositions the *ER* text once again. It is often shown daily on Channel 4, either in the mornings or early afternoon (but not during school holidays), either as one episode or two back to back. There is nothing new in recycling previously aired programmes (it allows the show to pick up new audiences) but a series like *ER* appears to anticipate the process in its very form. Viewing the *ER* archive offers different reading pleasures. Retrospective reading becomes in part a nostalgic experience. Pleasure is generated from a pleasure revisited, in which memory and repetition play an important role. It also means that the series takes on an elegiac tone, viewing an episode now ten years old. Jacobs reads Mark Greene as 'a doomed character' (2003: 150–1) for example. Yet such a judgement is only made possible once you know what eventually happens to him. Certainly there is a melancholy surrounding his character from the start. But the despair he expresses in the live episode, 'Ambush', and the vulnerability he feels after being violently assaulted in the male rest-room ('Random Acts', 20: 3) come to have added poignancy once we know how his narrative arc gets played out. Reviewing the text knowing what becomes of Mark and of his death from brain cancer ('The Letter', 20: 8; 'On the Beach', 21: 8) enables us to rethink earlier episodes and reconsider the choices he makes in relation to the series arc rather than an individual episode. More importantly, retrospective reading – acquired knowledge accumulates and becomes deeper, associations not previously apparent are identified and new meanings (some of which cannot have been anticipated in earlier seasons) located – reveals the important role played by the self-reflexive viewer in making meaning. This active reading process creates an intimate bond between audience and the series, turning the regular viewer into a loyal fan tailoring meaning and reordering the narrative for his or her own pleasure. As television increasingly moves over to a consumer-led market (with personal video recorders like TiVo, which select programmes according to user profile), texts like *ER* position the viewer as being able make personal selections (watching repeats, reviewing favourite episodes, fast-forwarding) and owning meaning.

(Re)viewing the show when the visual pace is no longer innovative but familiar finds the drama taking on a more decidedly melodramatic quality. While *ER* is prone to sentimental narratives (with dashing paediatricians fighting to save vulnerable 'crack' babies, or a recently divorced doctor looking on as an elderly man embraces his dying wife for the last time), there is a sentimentality embedded in the reading process related to intimacy and familiarity. There is a sense that over the ten seasons the viewer has invested time in these characters and the series. Watching the show every day also allows for what Laura Stempel Mumford calls 'another kind of intimacy and emotional intensity' (1994/5: 186) based on exposure to daily screenings and the looping of the series. Knowing what is to come does not just provide an inescapable inevitability about particular events, such as when Benton goes on his first date with Carla Reese (Lisa Nicole Carson), or when Greene begins rowing with his wife over his commitment to work, but gives an additional emotional weight provided by the omnipotent viewer.

Conclusion

Dramas like *ER* break generic rules while transforming them. While I have discussed the impact of such dramas on cultural identities elsewhere (McCabe 2000: 141–54), the aim here has been to understand how a television text produces meaning. Positioned as quality 'must-see' TV finds

Channel 4 employing promotional strategies that will make *ER* look special: something that we look forward to and will make special arrangements to see. It flatters the audience to see themselves as a sophisticated, media-literate audience and, even during the day, *ER* is positioned as a cut above the usual soap operas that fill the daytime television schedules.

Yet, there is something inherently robust about the *ER* text which is designed to be constantly consumed. Scheduling reruns is not so much about repeating episodes but about an ongoing televisual experience in which viewers are invited to frequently return and watch the series – time and again. Looking at how the *ER* text positions viewers to make sense of the drama reveals that they are meant to experience and understand it differently each time. Quality television in this context is about a complete cultural viewing experience that imagines proactive consumers owning the text – selecting when they will watch it and engaging in the meaning-making process.

Acknowledgement

With grateful thanks to Kim Akass and Mike Allen for listening to me ramble on about *ER* (again) and sharing their insightful thoughts.

Note

1. Mimi Leder went on to direct the fast-paced action-adventure *The Peacemaker* (1997, starring George Clooney and also featuring Goran Visnjic as a Bazta sergeant) and the special effects-driven disaster movie, *Deep Impact* (1998, which featured Laura Innes and Ron Eldard, who played Ray Shepard, Carol Hathaway's love interest in season two).

Bibliography

Barnard, P. (1995), *The Times*, 2 February, p. 47.
Baylis, M. (2001), 'Back to the Suture', *The Guardian*, 18 January, pp. 16–17.
Bond, M. (1995), *The Times*, 9 February, p. 47.
Brooks, R. (1997), 'Cinema's Coolest Junkie Visits the Small Screen's Hippest Hospital', *The Observer*, 13 April, p. 10.
Brunsdon, C. (1990), 'Problems with Quality', *Screen*, 30(1), Spring, 67–90.
Channel 4 (1998a), *Channel 4: New Developments and Future Ambitions*, London: Channel 4.
Channel 4 (1998b), *Channel 4 Licence*, London: Independent Television Commission.
Channel 4 (2001), *Da Launch Night*, London: Channel 4.

Clarke, S. (1995), 'A Medical Drama to Quicken the Pulse', *The Daily Telegraph:* ('TV and Radio'), 28 January, p. 3.

The Daily Telegraph (1996), 4 January, p. 31.

Dams, T. (1999), 'C4 bags Sky Rights to *Friends* and *ER*', *Broadcast*, 17 December, p. 1.

Deans, J. (2002), 'When Will E4 Get An Audience? Bet Now', *The Guardian* ('Media'), 14 January, pp. 2–3.

Ellis, J. (2000), *Seeing Things: Television in the Age of Uncertainty*, London: I. B. Tauris.

Feldshuh, D. (1995), 'Doctoring the Truth', *The Sunday Times* ('Culture' section), 29 January, p. 4.

Feuer, J. (1992), 'Genre Study and Television', in R. C. Allen (ed.), *Channels of Discourse, Reassembled: Television and Contemporary Criticism*, Chapel Hill: University of North Carolina Press, pp. 138–59.

Feuer, J. (1995), *Seeing through the Eighties: Television and Reaganism*, London: BFI Publishing.

Gill, A. A. (1995), *Sunday Times* ('*Culture*'), 5 February, p. 3.

Gritten, D. (1995), 'Why They Do It Better', *The Daily Telegraph*, July, p. 1.

Gritten, D. (1997), 'The Show That Set a Nation's Pulse Racing', *The Daily Telegraph*, 23 October, p. 26.

Hildred, S. (1995), *The Sun*, 16 February.

Hiscock, J. and Boshoff, A. (1998), 'TV Network Pays £8m a Show for Hospital Drama', *The Daily Telegraph*, 16 January.

Hunt, R. (1995), 'Theatre of Blood', *The Guardian* (Guide), 28 January, p. 67.

The Independent (1997), 'TV Crossover is no Emergency for Film Star Ewan McGregor', 28 March, p. 2.

Jacobs, J. (2003), *Body Trauma TV: The New Hospital Drama*, London: BFI Publishing.

McCabe, J. (2000), 'Diagnosing the Alien: Producing Identities, American "Quality" Drama and British Television Culture in the 1990s', in B. Carson and M. Llewellyn-Jones (eds), *Frames and Fictions on Television: The Politics of Identity within Drama*, Exeter: Intellect Books, pp. 141–54.

Martín, N. San (2003), 'Must See TV: Programming Identity on NBC Thursdays', in M. Jancovich and J. Lyons (eds), *Quality Popular Television*, London: BFI Publishing, pp. 32–47.

Massingbred, H. (1995), 'Healthy Diagnosis for Medical Drama', *The Daily Telegraph*, 16 February, p. 29.

Morrow, F. (2001), 'Series Seven, and No Sign of Heart Failure', *The Independent*, 25 February, p. 6.

Mumford, L. Stempel (1994/5), 'Stripping on the Girl Channel: Lifetime, *thirtysomething* and Television Form', *Camera Obscura*, 33/34, May–January, 166–91.

Odone, C. (1997), 'A Medical Drama in Perfect Health', *The Daily Telegraph*, 15 May, p. 38.

Ogle, Tina (1995), 'Forceps Saga', *Time Out*, 1 February, p. 17.

Oppenheimer, J. (1995), 'Diagnosing ER's Practical Approach', *American Cinematographer*, October, 46–52.

Peacock, A. (1986), *Report of the Committee on Financing the BBC*, Cmnd 9824, London: HMSO.

Pile, S. (1995), *The Daily Telegraph*, 15 July, p. 12.

Pilkington, Sir Henry (1962), *Report of the Committee on Broadcasting*, Cmnd 1753, London: HMSO.

Purves, L. (1995), 'Supercharged, Supercool, Superior', *The Times* ('Vision' section), 28 January, p. 5.

Ramsey, T. (2002), '*ER*', *The Evening Standard*, 27 February, p. 36.

Reeves, J. L., Rogers, M. C., and Epstein, M. (1996), 'Rewriting Popularity: The Cult Files', in D. lavery, A. Hague and M. Cartwright (eds), *'Deny All Knowledge': Reading 'The X-Files'*, London: Faber & Faber, pp. 22–35.

Reeves, J. L., Rogers, M. C., and Epstein, M. (2002), '*The Sopranos* as HBO Brand Equity: The Art of Commerce in the Age of Digital Reproduction', in D. Lavery (ed.), *This Thing of Ours: Investigating 'The Sopranos'*, New York/London: Columbia University Press/Wallflower Press, pp. 42–57.

Rixon, P. (2003), 'The Changing Face of American Television Programmes on British Screens', in M. Jancovich and J. Lyons (eds), *Quality Popular Television*, London: BFI Publishing, pp. 48–61.

Romney, J. (1995), 'ER, Like, Not Totally Gross', *The Guardian* (Section 2), 13 July, p. 13.

Smith, C. (1996), 'Friendly Rivals', *Broadcast*, 20 December, p. 20.

Smith, G. M. (2003), 'The Left Takes Back the Flag: the Steadicam, the Snippet, and the Song in *The West Wing*'s "In Excelsis Deo"', in P. C. Rollins and J. E. Connor (eds), *'The West Wing': The American Presidency as Television Drama*, New York: Syracuse University Press, pp. 125–35.

Taub, E. (2001), 'A Walk on the Wide Side', *Emmy*, 23(1), February, 22–3.

Thompson, R. (1997), *Television's Second Golden Age: From 'Hill Street Blues' to 'ER'*, New York: Syracuse University Press.

Viner, B. (1995), *Mail on Sunday* 'Night and Day', 11 June, p. 95.

Whitehead, C. (1994), 'When Wards Collide', *Voice*, 11 October, pp. 52, 54.

Willis, J. (1996), 'The Attitude Channel', *Broadcast*, 20 December, p. 22.

CHAPTER 12

The Bartlet Administration and Contemporary Populism in NBC's *The West Wing*

J. Elizabeth Clark

One of the only things that has made life worth living for left-leaning liberals in the United States since George W. Bush became president is the small fact that, for one hour on Wednesday evenings, he is not the president. That honour belongs instead to the fictitious Josiah 'Jed' Bartlet – a three-term US Congressman and two-term governor from New Hampshire who holds a Ph.D. in Economics from the London School of Economics and a Nobel Prize in Economics – who presides over the country's fate on NBC's *The West Wing*. This president, whose American roots, he claims, can be traced back to one of the original signers of the Declaration of Independence, combines academics and politics in a formal way, like his real-life predecessor Woodrow Wilson. His administration is part executive branch, part college classroom, part hippie-loving, sixties-era inspired, grassroots political organising.

Through Bartlet and his industrious staff, *The West Wing* presents a tangible, populist depiction of an imaginary government working for the people to uphold the principles of democracy. The vigour, zeal and passion of this fictional administration, in its responses to real-life political, social and cultural events, operates between fact and fiction, essentially 'rewriting' everyday events to an often 'satisfactory' conclusion. The programme offers audiences the opportunity to engage with a different version of American democracy, one in which serious social problems receive the kind of personal attention a populist vision of the United States fervently desires.

For the first four seasons creator Aaron Sorkin led the show's creative team with support from director Thomas Schlamme. They were backed up by executive producer John Wells, who is largely credited with the fast-paced dialogue and tightly shot scenes characteristic of his other top American television show, *ER*. Sorkin and Wells' success relies on an intricate web of television network politics and the emerging creative control given to what Roberta Pearson in this book refers to as 'the hyphenate' writer-producers (see Chapter 1). The immediacy of *The West Wing*'s plots, for example, its ability to mirror domestic and international incidents with a fictionalised response, particularly in the first four seasons, was due to the Sorkin/Wells/Schlamme hyphenate which gave the team control over the shooting schedule and budget. Sorkin had both creative and logistic control, allowing him to write scripts and then move them into production almost immediately.

The Sorkin/Wells/Schlamme team's success lay in its depiction of the interplay between the fictional, liberal White House staff and their president that intentionally played itself out against a background of thinly veiled references to the actual political milieu of US politics. In short, the programme constructed a liberal populist fantasy in the face of an increasingly conservative political and social reality. The programme began in 1999, following the country's impeachment of President Clinton and at the beginning of an unimpressive Democrat campaign for US president. In seasons one and two, *The West Wing* ran against real-life news stories of political intrigue, charges of mediocrity and an uninspired electorate hesitant to commit to either of the candidates endorsed by the two major American political parties. This fantasy political universe was specifically referred to by *New York Magazine* columnist Michael Wolff in the midst of the election:

> Indeed, it probably doesn't matter much who – if anyone – becomes president in January because the real president will be Josiah Bartlet . . . You can, with not too much difficulty, imagine *The West Wing* replacing national politics or offering some preferable parallel world, like a sort of benign Manchurian candidate. And there's nothing much real politicians will be able to do about it. (Wolff 2000: 44)

Leading up to the November 2000 presidential election, 'NBC's publicity department began an ad campaign trumpeting its own version of "a president we can all agree on." The man in question, of course, was Josiah Bartlet . . . At about the same time, cars in southern California reportedly began sporting bumper stickers that read BARTLET FOR PRESIDENT' (Lehmann 2001). Moreover, Martin Sheen, who plays the earnest Jed Bartlet, has said, 'We know we're a fantasy. But at the same time, there are sometimes periods of history where a fantasy is not a bad idea to focus on every now and then' (Sheen 2003).

This widespread devotion to Jed Bartlet significantly altered the vision of the show. In the beginning, Aaron Sorkin believed that the president would be an ancillary character, with the show focusing on the ensemble cast of Bartlet's staff, much like Well's *ER* (1994–present) or Sorkin's *Sports*

Night (1998–2000), where weekly episodes featured storylines following different members of the cast. Martin Sheen recalls, 'Aaron said, "We just want the President to appear once a month." I said that would be great. I did the pilot, and then went off to find another job' (Ballestero 2000: 38). In part, Sorkin had already explored the role of the presidency in the movie *The American President*,[1] a romantic comedy starring Michael Douglas and Annette Bening – with Martin Sheen playing the role of Douglas' chief of staff. *The West Wing* was an opportunity to explore a different facet of White House politics by examining the role of the president's staff who are charged with carrying out the president's ideas, objectives and policies. This early vision for the show is reflected in the pilot, where the president comes in at the very end of act four, with the preceding portions of the episode introducing each of the key members of Bartlet's staff.

The Idealised Presidency: Bartlet as Cultural Icon

The premise of *The West Wing* was that the public would be interested in this critical consideration of the intermediaries in American government – those unelected officials who are responsible for a significant amount of American governing. What Sorkin soon discovered, however, was that the audience was far more interested in an honest and in-depth portrayal of the relationship between an American president and his carefully selected staff. In an article on the representation of the presidency in *The West Wing*, Bartlet 'rat[ed] higher than both Bush and Clinton' in an examination of three key character traits: 'principled', 'engaging' and 'common' (Holbert et al. 2003: 435). The study further found that 'The positive images of the American presidency found on the show translated to more positive images within viewers of the sitting President Bush and former President Clinton' (Holbert et al.: 437). Aaron Sorkin has said that his idea for the show was, in part, to endorse public service, presenting the president and his staff as flawed heroes of the contemporary age:

> Our leaders, government people are portrayed either as dolts or as Machiavellian somehow. The characters in this show are neither. They are flawed, to be sure, because you need characters in drama to have flaws. But they, all of them, have set aside probably more lucrative lives for public service. They are dedicated not just to this president, but also to doing good, rather than doing well. The show is kind of a valentine to public service. (Sorkin 2000)

In its first and second seasons, *The West Wing* received widespread critical acclaim, winning thirteen Emmy Awards in its first season alone, a record for the most awards given to a show in a single season. It has also received additional Emmy Awards in subsequent seasons, a Peabody Award, a Humanitas Prize, five Golden Globe nominations, one Golden Globe Award and three Television Critics Association Awards.

While President Bartlet has run into occasional troubles in his fictitious administration, no American president, real or fictitious, could boast such popularity without extensive policies in addition to charisma. *The West Wing*, week by week, rolls out shows in which President Bartlet and his staff address – and sometimes compromise – real-life policy objectives, all while appealing to a large cross-section of American and international viewers. In essence, beginning with Clinton's impeachment, *The West Wing* began to take over where Clinton policy left off. More importantly, the serial format of *The West* Wing allowed for longer story arcs to develop across episodes where the decisions and actions of earlier episodes are the source of events and crises of later ones. Using this format, Sorkin, Wells and Schlamme created a show in which a liberal political agenda – in seasons one and two – went unchecked by the reality of American politics and instigated a cult status among its left-minded audience.

From the very first episodes, *The West Wing* revealed an administration willing to work for (and sometimes reject) traditionally left-wing political stances such as environmentally sensitive policies (episode 1: 8, 'Enemies'), the death penalty (episode 1: 14, 'Take this Sabbath Day'), reparations for African-American slavery, increasing the role of Latinos in government (episode 1: 18, 'Meetings before Lunch'), AIDS drugs for Africa (episode 2: 4, 'In This White House'), a patient's bill of rights (episode 2: 11, 'The Leadership Breakfast'), international women's rights *and* representations of American veterans (episode 3: 9, 'The Women of Qumar'), the decriminalisation of marijuana *and* the role of the US Surgeon General (episode 2: 15, 'Ellie'), Affirmative Action *and* US naval testing on the island of Vieques (episode 3: 13, 'The Two Bartlets'), abortion rights (episode 4: 18, 'Privateers') and presidential pardons for felons serving long sentences for first-time drug offences (episode 5: 11, 'The Benign Prerogative'). Chris Lehmann, in a widely touted article, 'The Feel-Good Presidency' appearing in *The Atlantic Monthly*, argues that the Bartlet administration's dedication to such issues is significant:

> *The West Wing* sets out, week after week, to restore public faith in the institutions of our government, to shore up the bulwarks of American patriotism, and to supply a vision of executive liberalism – at once principled and pragmatic; mandating both estimable political vision and serious personal sacrifice. (Lehmann 2001)

Aaron Sorkin believes that the in-depth portrayal of such issues is one of the keys to the show's success, commenting 'One of the things I like about this world, or at least the way we're presenting this world, is these issues are terribly complicated – not nearly as black and white as we're led to believe.'[2] In fact, the show is so packed with references to real-life struggles that the show's official website has a weekly 'Hot Topics' page with references to actual policies and issues often addressed by the show so that viewers can get additional information.[3]

Yet, in many ways, the Bartlet administration, by virtue of its fictional representation of the presidency, takes on only the sexier – and most dramatic – issues of American politics, offering positive resolutions to often real-life issues. Further, some critics, like Lehmann, argue that the presentation of issues is one-sided at best:

> Team Bartlet is constantly consumed by the minutiae of high cultural warfare . . . In a second-season episode, 'The Midterms,' there's a high-handed showdown between Bartlet and one Dr Jenna Jacobs – a moralizing radio talk-show host clearly modeled on Dr Laura Schlessinger . . . Bartlet takes her on a rapid-fire declamatory tour of the follies of biblical literalism, a punishing performance whose like has not been seen since the climax of *Inherit the Wind*: 'I'm interested in selling my youngest daughter into slavery, as sanctioned in Exodus 21: 7 . . . what would a good price be?' . . . Why is Bartlet expending such heavy artillery and so much precious time on humiliating a radio talk-show host? And why is he unable to resist a final victory dance over her seated person and prostrated intellect – especially by invoking the majesty of his own presidential eminence over the discredited authority of biblical tradition? ('One last thing,' he shouts. 'While you may be mistaking this for your monthly meeting of the Ignorant Tight-Ass Club, in this building when the President stands, nobody sits.') The answer, of course, is that such displays – which occur nearly every week in Bartlet's White House – cost the Administration precisely nothing politically while ratcheting up its sense of cultural superiority exponentially. (Lehmann 2001)

Lehmann's final sentence indicates the extent to which the boundaries between fiction and reality are blurred in popular discussions of the show. He treats the administration as if it really exists and has a political significance outside the realms of fictional television. This reality–fiction relationship holds pleasures for liberal-minded viewers and offers a voice usually shouted down on right-wing talk radio shows. As Lehmann observes, Bartlet is in the enviable position of addressing a Dr Laura-like character, raising many of the critiques liberals have offered of Schlessinger's show in less public forums. Throughout US television history shows like *Dragnet* (1967–70), *Hill Street Blues* (1981–7), *St Elsewhere* (1982–8), *Law and Order*

(1990–present), *NYPD Blue* (1993–present), *ER* (1994–present), *The Practice* (1997–2004), *Boston Public* (2000–4), and *CSI* (2000–present) have had fictional 'ripped from the headlines' stories that parallel real-life events. But *The West Wing* moves beyond the salacious details of daily news articles, taking headlines of current political and social issues from the streets into the fictitious Oval Office. (Of course, the writers for the show also play with the idea of banality in *The West Wing*. In 'Take Out the Trash Day' (episode 1: 13), Bartlet observes of the slow news, 'Unless a war breaks out, I'll be spending much of my day talking about bananas.')

What has been called a 'liberal bias' by many critics – with some right-wing commentators going as far as dubbing the show 'The Left Wing' – has been apparent from the very first episode. In the series pilot, during which 'POTUS' (The president of the United States) crashes his bicycle, Bartlet enters at the end of the episode, coming in on a contentious meeting between Josh, Toby and members of the religious right; we finally learn that the bicycle accident was due, in part, to anger. Bartlet reveals that he went out riding when he was 'about as angry as I've ever been in my life'. Turning to the group of conservative religious leaders, he asks them: 'From what part of Holy Scripture do you suppose the Lambs of God drew their divine inspiration when they sent my 12-year-old granddaughter a Raggedy Ann doll with a knife stuck through its throat? You'll denounce these people, Al. You'll do it publicly. And until you do, you can all get your fat asses out of my White House.' Thus the pilot episode closes, receiving critical acclaim for a president unwilling to be cowed by religious interest groups.

No Mr Smith: Bartlet's Twenty-first-Century 'Populism'

Jed Bartlet's is a complicated presidency, a complexity that has manifested itself increasingly over five seasons. This 'Yankee President', whose genealogy ties him to the roots of American democracy, is hardly common. A deeply intellectual president, Jed Bartlet eschews the naivety of a Capra-esque populism represented by Jefferson Smith in *Mr Smith Goes to Washington*. Jimmy Stewart's 1939 portrayal of an 'average Joe' within the American political system romanticised the notion of 'populism' in film, suggesting that the 'everyman' (at least as 'everyman' was defined in the 1930s as a white, good-looking, earnest man) could take on – and win – against the political machine. Mr Smith's form of populism was an appeal to the people, a political empowering of the 'common man'. Jed Bartlet, however, is an insider to the political system, a long-time political animal; in other words, Bartlet is not your average populist. Jed Bartlet is neither simplistic nor jingoistic in his relationship to the American democratic system, but he is unquestionably idealistic.

Jed Bartlet is not a man against the machine; Jed Bartlet is the man who unmasks the machine. The populism of *The West Wing* – much like real-life candidate Howard Dean's assault on traditional means of building popular support as he linked his candidacy to the media and web savvy electorate, yoking his early success to grassroots organising through the internet – assumes a media-savvy public. Former President Ronald Reagan, with his background in acting, made an art of the public appearance: the presidency as performance. *The West Wing* inverts that performativity, pulling the viewer behind the scenes as it deconstructs the public face of political office by exposing the private realm of American democracy.

Traditional notions of populist political theory focus on populism's 'appeal to the people, the claim to empower the "common man", the capacity to motivate largely unpolitical individuals to participate, the emphasis on welfare policies, or the professed aim of restoring some dignity to politics' (Arditi 2003). Bartlet's populism comes from a combination of seeking to establish – and sometimes failing – legislation and policies to benefit the largest segment of the American public, his accessibility (particularly to viewers) and his staff. Week to week, Bartlet engages in political struggles with Congress, the Senate and even the Supreme Court as he works for issues such as better health care, protecting women's rights, and ensuring access to public education.

Increasingly throughout the series, however, Bartlet feels removed from those issues that compelled him to seek office. In season five's 'Disaster Relief' (episode 5: 6), he refuses to return from the site of a hurricane because he believes that he can affect more good by offering solace to his wounded citizenry than returning to Washington to confront political battles that repeatedly mean compromising his ideals. In the same episode, Donna introduces Josh to her 'What a Shame Folder', a collection of ideas that the administration has stopped pursuing – the very issues and ideas that pushed them into the political realm. Even Abigail Bartlet feels removed from her ability to do good work; in 'An Khe' (episode 5: 14), she begins volunteering at an impoverished medical clinic (violating her promise to give up practising medicine until after Jed's term of office has ended because of her violation of medical ethics in treating his Multiple sclerosis).

Political scientist Benjamin Arditi offers two critiques of populism which, when taken together, most accurately characterise the Bartlet administration's political enterprise and appeal. Arditi argues, 'Populism appears to be a fellow traveller of contemporary, media-enhanced modes of representation at work' but can also be understood as 'participatory channels hidden behind the morality of democratic procedures'. The Bartlet administration – part traditional populist government, part media-savvy contemporary government – succeeds because of the careful balance between public and private. By season five, Bartlet's failures become less about a lame-duck presidency and more about a warped and ineffective political machine, one against which Bartlet can only make so many gains. Ironically, the populism of Bartlet's administration within the fictional 'parallel universe' of the US political reality, that which makes *The West Wing* so real to viewers, is also that which has affected the show's later success. The more realistically *The West Wing* portrays politics, the further it strays from a successful, idealised left agenda, the more difficult it becomes to engage viewers in the fantasy of democracy.

While critics agree that the show promotes the ideals of democracy, some critics disagree that the show fosters populist notions of the presidency. Critic Patrick Finn argues that the show is not fundamentally populist in nature, appealing instead to a widely educated and intellectual audience:

> Through its interaction with America's founding documents, and through the repackaging of current political issues, this transcendent form of media reaches beyond coaxial cable and into the everyday lives of Americans. It offers a new public space for debate, presided over by a new kind of virtual public intellectual. (Finn 2003: 124)

Despite this, however, the Bartlet administration – by virtue of its visibility and the intimacy of the act of viewing Bartlet's most private moments – becomes transparent, as the viewer understands the relationship between a leader and his policies. Bartlet makes intellectualism, as well as the presidency, accessible. More importantly, *The West Wing* mixes the administration's policies with a detailed look inside the government, pulling the viewer into the rooms of the White House to participate in the conversations behind the discussions in a way that Donnalyn Pompper argues, 'offers audiences a means for democratic engagement that journalism alone cannot' (Pompper 2003: 31). While in the early seasons this initially meant the rush of behind the scenes work to effect change, increasingly, the transparency of government reveals that even Mr Smith would fail more often than he would succeed.

Complications of the Office: Fallibility in Public Service

Where *The West Wing*'s president becomes more likeable, and his failings more forgivable, then, is in the ability for viewers to enter into the White House, to see decisions being made, to understand what motivates the president, to understand the compromises he makes. Even when the policies he desires fail, the viewer understands that failure in the context of the other workings of government. The classic strategy of revealing the personal and emotional terrain that exists in the professional environment, apparent in various forms in shows such as *ER* and *Ally McBeal*, is taken to the 'highest office' in *The West Wing*. The carefully crafted fictional moment allows for an empathetic exchange between viewer and fictitious president and his staff and creates an impression of a president more tangible, than the carefully crafted sound bites and photo opportunities of any real president.

Soon after the pilot, in 'Take This Sabbath Day' (episode 1: 14), Bartlet has to decide whether or not to grant clemency to a Federal prisoner facing the death penalty because of drug-related crimes. Quickly expanding on the pilot and Bartlet's fierce liberalism, President Bartlet's character reveals a multi-faceted and complex idealism. Patrick Finn maintains that Bartlet 'is outside of power because he maintains a split position on key issues such as abortion and the death penalty (he is against both in principle, but upholds their application). Thus he is more an embodiment of the complexity of the issue than an ideologically driven proponent of one political vision' (Finn 2003: 107). While championing traditionally liberal views, Bartlet is not a liberal paper doll cutout. In this episode, a practising Catholic, Bartlet relies on his religion as a moral, ethical touchstone. In a parallel plot-line, Toby attends synagogue, where his rabbi offers an anti-death penalty message.

Despite the seriousness of the episode's theme, the staff stays true to its fast-talking, wry wit. In considering capital punishment, Sam Seaborne says to presidential aide Charlie Young, 'The US is one of five countries on earth that puts to death people who were under the age 18 when they committed their crime.' Charlie responds by attempting to guess the other four countries. 'Nigeria?' he asks. 'Pakistan,' Sam replies. 'Saudi Arabia and Iraq?' Charlie tries again. Sam affirms his answer by saying 'Yeah, so that's a list we definitely want to be on.' Such quick-witted banter is a hallmark of the show, underscoring Sorkin and Well's construction of the populist intentions of the Bartlet presidency. Jed has surrounded himself by a staff who supports his agenda – like the president, his staff are largely against the death penalty. And, more importantly, the staff will support the president's decision – whatever it is – because they trust him to actively apply democratic principles.

At the same time, however, Bartlet is depicted as a complicated, thoughtful and often thought-provoking president. He argues that he cannot grant clemency because that decision would undermine the

American law of capital punishment; Bartlet reasons that the laws of the country cannot be enforced at the whim of the president. Clearly struggling with the decision, Bartlet asks his childhood priest to visit the Oval Office to hear his confession. The episode ends chillingly with Bartlet on his knees in the centre of the Oval Office, a clear visual contradiction between his personal ideology and the national policies he is elected to uphold.

Similarly, in season five's 'HAN' (episode 5: 4) Bartlet welcomes a North Korean pianist, Jai Yung Ahn, on a good-will mission from what staffers call 'the most unstable regime in the world'. In a semi-private moment, the pianist autographs a CD for Bartlet, on which he writes that he wants to defect. As the State Department is in secret negotiations with North Koreans, Bartlet is conflicted over whether he should support the pianist's request. C.J. struggles with the staff's debates over the issue, arguing that Ahn must be offered sanctuary, appealing to the core beliefs of the Bartlet White House: 'If we blithely exploit this young man's ignorance then I don't know who we are anymore.' Later, as Bartlet and Ahn sit at the piano together, Bartlet tells Ahn he cannot support a move to defect, asking Ahn to sacrifice choice to the perceived betterment of his country. As C.J.'s comments reveal, however, Bartlet also makes a sacrifice of personal principles for what he believes to be the higher cause; while C.J. can maintain an ideologically strict stance, Bartlet has to negotiate his personal beliefs within a larger national and international agenda. The way the scenes are shot indicate the strategy of evoking empathy for Bartlet's position. The camera closes in on Bartlett and Ahn as they sit together on the piano. This serves to bring the audience into their intimate conversation and to separate us from the North Korean attendants who would no doubt whisk Ahn away if they knew what the pair was talking about. In the sequence with C.J., the shot reverses, positioning the audience with Bartlet and as she directs her comment, her eyeline is just slightly off a direct address to the camera. Hence, the audience is aligned with Bartlet textually and therefore emotionally. In this struggle, the fictional president displays the emotional and ethical stresses of the office. Such depictions of personal/professional conflict enhance Bartlet's appeal, and *The West Wing*'s success relies on the depictions of fallibility and the weight of public office.

Public Presidencies: Factual Fiction/Fictional Fact or, How *The West Wing* Makes it 'Real'

American politics have always relied on the charisma of a president; the best-known and best-loved American presidents have not necessarily been the most intellectual or the best policy-makers. The best-loved American presidents have not been scandal-free. Years later, the public continues to speculate about the workings of the Kennedy administration's 'Camelot' and the salacious details hidden behind the walls of the White House; the romance between Franklin Deleanor Roosevelt and his wife, Eleanor, is the subject of many biographies; Nancy Reagan consulted astrologers; Clinton's relationship with Monica Lewinsky threatened to bring down his presidency. The American public wants – sometimes desperately – to connect with the highest elected officials on a personal level, but that movement into the personal makes a public official vulnerable; the distinction between public and private is guarded at the highest levels and the 'real' moments shared between an American public and its president are either speculative or superficial. *The West Wing*'s depiction of this public/private divide buys into the iconicism of the American president at the same time it places the responsibility for the Bartlet administration's efficacy on the shoulders of its competent staff.

What is interesting about the Bartlet White House, then, is the focus on both policy and intellectually guided decisions. Furthermore, like all administrations, it has not been without scandal and controversy. Early on in season one, in 'He Shall, From Time to Time' (episode 1: 12), after Bartlet collapses before the State of the Union, we learn that Bartlet has hidden his degenerative multiple sclerosis from the American public. Abbey enables this public omission by treating her husband for the disease privately. In subsequent seasons, this leads to investigations and the eventual censure of President Bartlet by Congress – despite this public reprimand, Jed still wins his campaign for re-election. Reflecting on their lives, in 'Abu El Banat' (episode 5: 9), Abbey says to Jed over a disastrous Christmas dinner during which their daughters are angry with Jed, 'We've never been Currier and Ives.' It is exactly this fallibility that connects Bartlet to the leaders who have come before him.

While Bill Clinton was impeached for lying about his sexual relationship with White House intern Monica Lewinsky and Ronald Reagan endured the Iran Contra Affair, as well as a private struggle with Alzheimer's that is public knowledge, their very intangibility accounts, in part, for the American fascination with their lives and dealings. R. Lance Holbert and others write: 'Although a fictional account, this show provides something to the American public that it cannot get from any other source, a vision of what it is like to be president on a daily basis ' (Holbert et al. 2003: 427). Real-life American politics are widely perceived to rely heavily on the 'representative' part of representative democracy.

Yet, in large part, this piece is often missing from *The West Wing*. The other structures of federal power – the Congress, the Senate, the judiciary – are often only presented when they are at odds with the Bartlet administration. While some episodes, particularly those around Supreme Court nominations, seek to explain the federal process, more often, the Bartlet White House is a 'Lone Ranger' within American politics, working to effect political change alone. The other facets of American government are important to the storyline only when they can be blamed for the Bartlet administration's inability to implement a particular piece of legislation.

Instead, *The West Wing* holds up the presidency as the absolute office – much as the media and the American electorate do – the one that Americans should rely on for political change. American presidents are like American rock stars; this was no more evident than in the years of the Clinton presidency. From the earliest episodes, critics and cultural-studies pundits claimed connections between the show and the Clinton presidency. While Sorkin denies modelling any of *The West Wing* staffers on real-life Clinton staffers, he did make extensive use of former White House staffers like Dee Dee Myers and Patrick Caddell to ensure accuracy in his scripts. Critics like John Podhoretz, however, continue to maintain that characters on *The West Wing* have a Clinton-era corollary: 'Nearly every character in *The West Wing* has a real-life parallel from Clinton's first term, Rob Lowe as George Stephanopoulos, Bradley Whitford as Paula Begala, Allison Janney as Dee Dee Myers, Richard Schiff as Gene Sperling, and Moira Kelly as Mandy Grunwald' (Podhoretz 2003: 222).

Whether or not Sorkin intended the relationship, at times, the distinction between fact and fiction is tenuous at best. 'Take This Sabbath Day' was loosely based on the case of Juan Raul Garza. Although Bartlet does not grant Cruz – the fictional Garza – clemency, President Clinton gave Garza two stays of execution (Garza was later executed in 2001 when Bush refused to give him a stay of execution). When President Bartlet's beloved secretary, Mrs Landingham, dies in a car crash, California Assemblyman Kevin Shelley adjourned a May 2001 California Assembly session in memory of Mrs Landingham and her contributions to her country (Joosten 2004). *Time* magazine's Jay Branegan reported in 2000, 'The life-imitates-art moments have become more commonplace. Last month, while sitting in the Oval Office monitoring a briefing session with Clinton and his Mideast advisers, chief of staff John Podesta jokingly slipped a note to Lockhart that read, 'If this were *West Wing*, C. J. wouldn't be at this meeting' (Branegan 2000: 82). When *The West Wing* featured a plot about campaign finance reform, '*The New York Times* wrote an editorial proclaiming that Washington should imitate *The West Wing*' (Waxman 2000: 94). The cast of *The West Wing* was featured at the August 2000

Democratic National Convention and cast member Martin Sheen actively campaigned for Al Gore and Joseph Lieberman in the 2000 presidential election and Howard Dean in the Democratic primaries of 2004.

Acknowledging the cultural currency carried by *The West Wing*, Bush was featured in a January 2002 documentary special called *The Bush White House: Inside the Real West Wing*, which followed the president and his staff through a day at the White House, essentially challenging the success of the fictional programme. Bush's implied commentary was that Bartlet's, and by extension Clinton's, White Houses are a convenient liberal fantasy. The line between the real and fictitious West Wing politics was furthered blurred with season three's 'Documentary Special', which aired on 24 April 2002. The episode features former White House staffers David Gergen, Dee Dee Myers, Henry Kissinger, Leon Panetta and former presidents Gerald Ford, Jimmy Carter and Bill Clinton, and interspersed scenes from the show with real-life West Wing recollections.

Trading on the mythical stature of the 'The President' and closely paralleling actual political issues and events *The West Wing* provides an opportunity to interrogate the public discussion of 'realism' and the way in which everyday life – in a media-frenzied age – becomes a series of moments constructed for the camera, the microphone, the public display of 'reality'. The average citizen does not believe that he or she has any access to the real workings of democracy. Instead, average American voters compose a disinterested electorate that believes that it is precluded from the decisions of a country, that it is never trusted with the entire rationale for any decision, and that it is often lied to – a supposition widely supported by constant revelations from an ever-active media scrutiny of elected leaders. One needs only to chart the controversy over Michael Moore's *Fahrenheit 9/11* to see that the American public is divided about 'facts' and 'reality'; for some, the lack of evidence surrounding global issues like weapons of mass destruction and the validity of the US attack on Iraq play into an increasingly cynical view of American politics. For others, the leadership of George W. Bush and his promises to defeat terrorism at home and abroad play into the most fundamental notions of patriarchy and safety. Many Americans also believe that the media is often a willing participant in the ignorance of the American electorate, carefully choosing small sound bites released to the public. The recent controversy over the facts leading to the US attack on Iraq demonstrates a public perception that 'reality' is often a carefully constructed media device, one available not only to the creators of a fictional television show about the presidency, but also to the 'real' American presidency seeking to create a willing and pliable electorate.

While *The West Wing*'s success relies on making the presidency real by moving viewers past the 'feel good' presidential decisions, such as telling off the Christian right, and into the compassionate moment of watching Bartlet on his knees, with a rosary, confessing his sins to his childhood priest, its failure stems from the same transparency. What is the difference between watching Bush invade Iraq and Bartlet approve the assassination of a rogue Middle Eastern 'terrorist'?

Although *The West Wing*'s popularity has begun to diminish in seasons three, four and five, the show carries significant cultural currency for certain cultural institutions as well as popular critics. The National Education Association released a statement saying that it '"strongly agrees with President Bartlet's call for more teachers and better funded public schools" . . . The NEA, in a missive that carried no discernible whiff of satire, was reacting to a stemwinder President Bartlet gave on the Oct. 2 episode ['College Kids' (episode 4: 2)] to a (fictional) NEA gathering' (Wear 2002: 23). Similarly, the *Boston Globe* reported that '[as] advocates for a ban on land mines lobbied the Bush administration, they were looking for help from another US president. So they approached NBC's 'The West Wing' hoping to get the land mine issue written into the show.' In an analysis of the land mine activists' action, *Globe* reporter Mark Jurkowitz observed, 'Bartlet . . . may command the nation's bully pulpit for only one hour a week. But in his third year (or season) as president, the words and deeds that emanate from his Oval Office carry genuine political clout, according to activists who work on the issues that fill *West Wing* plots' (Jurkowitz 2002).

What activists have identified as the 'possibilities' inherent in a vocal Bartlet White House is what has also led critics like Myron A. Levine to argue:

> [T]the show is didactic and suffers from serious omissions. While *The West Wing* clearly recognizes how external political concerns – fundraising, constituency pressure, polling, and the media – affect White House strategy and policymaking, the series curiously lacks a similar understanding of the internal politics of the White House staff. In its overly sunny and optimistic portrayal of an idealized president operating in a healthy White House atmosphere, *The West Wing* neglects the more unhealthy aspects of staff competition, factionalism, groupthink, and presidential isolation that also characterize the real West Wing. *The West Wing* is a piece of entertainment. (Levine 2003: 62)

Levine points out that the focus on popular policy has led *The West Wing* to re-imagine the White House as an imaginary paradise both more exciting and less contentious than it actually is. John Podhoretz also focuses on the impossibility of the show stating, 'that's the pornographic appeal of *The West Wing* to liberals. The unholy fantasy of it' (Podhoretz 2003: 226). He continues, arguing that the specific appeal of *The West Wing* is the Clinton-era White House made better for the removal of its most controversial figure, Clinton himself. Podhoretz claims, 'Sorkin has airbrushed Clinton from his own White House as crudely as Stalin airbrushed those he had killed from official Soviet photographs, and in his place has superimposed a paragon of virtue so unsullied by the wear and tear of politics that Parson Weems himself might feel a little abashed' (Podhoretz 2003: 231).

Levine and Podhoretz make a significant point: *The West Wing* can't happen; no president could – or will – open his or her administration to the kind of public scrutiny viewers see each week on *The West Wing*. Only through fiction – and an increasing attempt on the part of its writers to parallel actual political events – does the White House evolve as a truly public sphere, the site of a tangible presidency. For many viewers, faith – if only for one hour a week – restores the ideals of democracy, the promise of a nation and its ideology, and the idea that the president is actually working for the people's good.

Terrorism and the Challenge of Liberalism

In the first four seasons, under the writing direction of Sorkin, *The West Wing* was shot with a quickly written script, one that sometimes mirrored 'real-life' events within days or weeks. This was most evident following the 11 September 2001 attacks on the former World Trade Center and the Pentagon. Sorkin and Wells suspended release of the season premiere and interrupted the chronology of *The West Wing* with an asynchronous episode on terrorism, 'Isaac and Ishmael'.

Issues in the Middle East were a small but recurring theme on *The West Wing* before the terrorist attacks on the United States. In season one's 'What Kind of Day Has It Been' (episode 1: 22) an American pilot crashes in the Iraqi desert and the military has to find him before the Iraqi military. In season two's '17 People' (episode 2: 18) airports are ordered to heighten security after a terrorist is caught with explosives at the border. With the advent of 11 September 2001, *The West Wing* radically changed. Following the elections in November 2000, many critics speculated that the show would have to change drastically to survive in the contemporary political climate. The real White House and the parallel fictional White House were simply too different for *The West Wing* to be anything but a fantasy. Sorkin, however, changed very little about the show. What changed *The West Wing* was the presence of terrorism on American soil by foreign nationals. The struggle to keep *The West Wing* real wasn't a conservative presidency, but the intellectual and ideological struggle to present a tangible, populist government in a time of decreasing civil rights, national panic and fear, and unprecedented public intrusion on privacy in the name of 'national security'.

Sorkin's first stab at the new national climate was the greatly hyped 'Isaac and Ishmael' (episode 3: 1), which aired less than three weeks after the 11 September 2001 attack. Sorkin postponed the season premiere to run this episode, which was written in response to the attack. Instead of the usual opening segment before the credits, the cast appear to introduce the episode; the credits were replaced with information about both the Twin Towers Fund and the Red Cross. The episode features a White House locked down because of a terrorist threat. At the time of the lockdown, a high school tour group is visiting the White House. Josh uses the time to explain American misconceptions about Islam to them. The show essentially turns *The West Wing* into a classroom, complete with the students gathered around a chalkboard in the cafeteria. Josh – with the help of other cast members who walked through the cafeteria at key moments – briefly explains what much of its highly literate audience already knew about the tensions between the Middle East and the United States. The episode also serves as a call to remain committed to the concepts of pluralism and diversity. While Josh is educating his students, Leo is questioning a Middle-Eastern employee named Raquim Ali, an alias for a terrorist. Of course, the interrogation turns out to be a case of mistaken identity, underscoring the message that the Arab-American population of the US is not responsible for 11 September 2001 and that acts of bigotry and hatred are fundamentally opposed to US policy (something which the subsequent registration of Arab immigrant men – in real-life politics – contradicts). Critically, the show was largely dismissed as a Sorkin 'soapbox' episode and a pedantic approach to terrorism, disappointing fans who tuned in to find some way to make sense of a new world order.

In comparison to early episodes featuring Bartlet's angry responses to Christian conservatives – like the Lambs of God and Dr Jenna Jacobs – 'Isaac and Ishmael' does largely the same work; Sorkin presents a fairly standard approach to liberal perspectives on terrorism. The real problem was that while the election of George W. Bush to the presidency represented only a temporary problem – there are always impeachments, censures and future elections – the events of 11 September 2001 challenged liberalism in the United States to its very core. While Sorkin's words rang hollow somehow, they also reflected the uneasiness of the American public.

Seasons three, four and five continued to grapple with terrorism as a prominent subplot. While the Bartlet administration can be character-ised as 'pro-woman', 'pro-working family' and pro-liberal issues, no one theme has dominated the show in the way that terrorism has come to. Interestingly, as the show grappled increasingly with changing life in the United States, the show also began to lose some of its previous popularity; while Nielsen ratings can be tricky to understand, this shift in interest has been blamed on liberal plots too unrealistically written in the current polit-ical climate. This was largely connected to Sorkin's writing of the show. Indeed, a deeper analysis of those same plot-lines, shows an increasingly conservative Bartlet grappling with terrorism and the challenge of main-taining a liberal bias while addressing 'national security'.

In 'The Women of Qumar' (episode 3: 9), C.J. protests the administra-tion's renewal of an airbase in the fictitious country of Qumar, whose Taliban-like government abuses women. In 'Stirred' (episode 3: 18), the staff reacts to the crash of a truck containing uranium fuel rods, trying to determine if it is an act of terror. And in May 2002, in 'Enemies Foreign and Domestic', the administration discovers that Iran has a nuclear bomb facility and C.J. again reacts to the treatment of women in the Middle East by making a public statement about the deaths of Saudi girls. And at the end of the season, in 'The Black Vera Wang' (episode 3: 21) and 'We Killed Yamamoto' (episode 3: 22) President Bartlet makes a decision to have a Middle-Eastern official assassinated on his return home because he was intimately involved in planning a terrorist attack against the US.

Season four followed the repercussions of the terrorist plot and the re-election campaign. Bartlet wins the election, despite concerns about his multiple sclerosis and the scandal that ensued from hiding this information from the American public. Curiously, the terrorist plot – followed up in season four also with 'The Red Mass' (episode 4: 3), when Bartlet approves a strike against a group of domestic terrorists in Idaho – reveals the weakest moment of Bartlet's presidency. Compelled by his advisers to act against his own beliefs – and against international law – Bartlet loses both focus and lustre even as he wins re-election to the nation's highest office.

The terrorist act of 9/11 became a liability for *The West Wing*. Given its transparent structure, the show had no choice but to open the discussions around terrorism to its audience. While Bartlet's tangibility in the terror-ist episodes provides for some of the most compelling and seemingly 'unre-alistic' television, it also reveals the moments when Bartlet functions in the way liberal Americans secretly hope their own 'real' government does not. At the same moment that the Bush administration promises security in the guise of 'threat levels' and a war against Iraq, the fictional president wavers, unsure of how to proceed, unsure of his own beliefs and actions. When he does act, it is to violate the trust of the American public by ordering an assassination. Bartlet's strong leadership around terrorism – something kept largely secret from the 'real' people under his administration – is at odds with what the audience sees. The public is invited into the innermost sanctum of American political life – at a time when the real government is becoming increasingly distant and secretive – to watch the struggles of a very 'real' man in office. In this moment, President Bartlet is humbled by the office and by his position as an American citizen.

This movement towards fallibility is completed when a homegrown terrorist group kidnaps his daughter Zoey.[4] Bartlet, in a moment of supreme imperfection, turns the presidency over to the Speaker of the House, a Republican, so that he can be a father. In a telling moment, Josh confronts one of President Walken's aides in the bathroom. Worried that President Bartlet made the wrong decision to hand over power to his enemies, Josh accuses the aide of campaigning in the midst of a national tragedy. The aide replies, 'You don't get it, do you? The Republicans are in awe of Bartlet. He recused himself in the only way he could. In the way envisioned by the Constitution. The whole notion of the 25th Amendment is that the institution matters more than the man does. Bartlet's decision was even more self-sacrificing because he willingly gave power to his opposition.' The temporary invocation of the 25th Amendment furthers the idea that President Bartlet is, after all, only a human being occupying an office that carries great weight, great solemnity and great power.

As with many significant moments in life, his daughter's kidnapping – and the resulting family chaos that ensues when his wife and daughters connect the kidnapping to the Qumari assassination – allows Bartlet to return to his office more focused and resilient. The function of seriality moves Bartlet through differing stages of a fictional US under attack by terrorists at home and abroad, creating a sustained story arc that complicates Bartlet over time. Consequently, Bartlet becomes both idealistic and compromised. In the end, however, he always returns to his vision for a better country and a better life for his citizenry.

The West Wing's fantasy – engaging its viewers in a blurring of fiction and reality – has evolved and compromised across five years of significant change in US politics, an ultra-conservative administration and the threat of terrorism as an actual administration might do. That evolution, made transparent for the viewer through the intimate access to the White House, suggests that a critically engaged liberal politics is a complicated and continually shifting process. It also underscores that despite the political 'realities' of Bartlet's administration, Jed Bartlet changes in reaction to emerging events while also remaining true to his populist roots. The

Bartlet of season five is still a liberal fantasy compared to George W. Bush, but he is also a liberal fantasy living in a post-9/11 'reality'. The president – at least the fictional one – is more human than demagogue, more tangible than idol, more fallible than omnipotent, particularly when he is providing leadership the people can see. And in these conservative times of 'Homeland Security', despite *The West Wing*'s faults, viewers continue to seek out the safety of a modified fairytale White House.

Notes

1. Rob Reiner (1995), *The American President*, United States: Castle Rock Entertainment and Universal Pictures.
2. Aaron Sorkin, interview by Terence Smith, *Online NewsHour*, 27 September 2000, http://www.pbs.org/newshour/media/west_wing/sorkin.html (January 2004).
3. *The West Wing*, 'Hot Topics' http://www.nbc.com/nbc/The_West_Wing/hot_topics/index.shtml (8 August 2003).
4. Three episodes feature the story arc of Zoey Bartlet's kidnapping: '25', '7A WF 83429' and 'The Dogs of War.'

Bibliography

Arditi, Benjamin (2003), 'Populism, or, Politics At the Edges of Democracy', 53rd Annual Conference of the Political Studies Association (PSA), University of Leicester (15–17 April).
Ballestero, Dana (2000), 'The Sheen Shine', *Hispanic* (July/August), http://www.hispanicmagazine.com/2000/julaug/CoverStory/,
Branegan, Jay (2000), 'You Could Call it the Wonk Wing', *Time*, (15 May), http://www.time.com/time/archive/preview/0, 10987, 1101000515-44567,00.htmland
Finn, Patrick (2003), 'The West Wing's Textual President', in Peter C. Rollins and John E. O'Connor (eds), *'The West Wing': The American Presidency as Television Drama*, New York: Syracuse University Press, pp. 101–24.
Holbert, R. Lance, Owen Pillion, David A. Tschida, Greg G. Armfield, Kelly Kinder, Kristin L. Cherry and Amy R. Daulton (2003), '*The West Wing* as Endorsement of the US Presidency: Expanding the Bounds of Priming in Political Communication', *Journal of Communication*, September, 427–43.
Joosten, Kathryn (2004), Academy of Television Arts and Sciences, http://www.emmys.com/membership/why/joosten.php (10 January).
Jurkowitz, Mark (2002), 'Getting President Bartlet's Ear Hoping To Be Heard, Activists Are Lobbying *The West Wing*', *Boston Globe* (27 March), http://www.boston.com/dailyglobe2/086/living/Getting_President_Bartlet_s_ear.shtml

Lehmann, Chris (2001), 'The Feel-Good Presidency: The Pseudo-Politics of *The West Wing*', *The Atlantic Monthly*, The Atlantic On-Line, http://www.the atlantic.com/issues/2001/03/lehmann-p1.htm (March).

Levine, Myron A. (2003), '*The West Wing* (NBC) and the West Wing (D.C.)', in Peter C. Rollins and John E. O'Connor (eds), *'The West Wing': The American Presidency as Television Drama*, New York: Syracuse University Press, pp. 42–62.

Podhoretz, John (2003), 'The Liberal Imagination', in Peter C. Rollins and John E. O'Connor (eds), *'The West Wing': The American Presidency as Television Drama*, New York: Syracuse University Press, pp. 222–34.

Pompper, Donnalyn (2003), 'White House Narratives That Journalism Cannot Tell', in Peter C. Rollins and John E. O'Connor (eds), *'The West Wing': The American Presidency as Television Drama*, New York: Syracuse University Press, pp. 17–31.

Sheen, Martin (2003), interview by Bob Edwards, *Morning Edition*, National Public Radio, 28 January.

Sorkin, Aaron (2000), interview by Terence Smith, *Online NewsHour*, 27 September, http://www.pbs.org/newshour/media/west_wing/sorkin.html

Waxman, Sharon (2000), 'Inside *The West Wing*'s New World', in Peter C. Rollins and John E. O'Connor (eds), *'The West Wing': The American Presidency as Television Drama*, New York: Syracuse University Press, pp. 203–12.

Wear, Ben (2002), 'Federal File: President Doppelganger', *Education Week*, 16 October, 8.

Wolff, Michael (2000), 'Our Remote Control President', *New York, Magazine*, December, 4 http://newyorkmetro.com/nymetro/news/media/columns/medialife/4148/index.html

Bibliography

Allen, Robert C. (1983), 'On Reading Soaps: A Semiotic Primer', in E. Ann Kaplan (ed.), *Regarding Television*, Los Angeles: The American Film Institute, pp. 97–108.

—(1985), *Speaking of Soap Opera*, Chapel Hill: University of North Carolina Press.

Alvey, Mark (2004), 'Too Many Kids and Old Ladies: Quality Demographics and 1960s US Television', *Screen* 45(1), Spring, pp. 40–62.

Ang, Ien (1985), *Watching 'Dallas': Television and the Melodramatic Imagination*, London: Routledge.

Bacon-Smith, Camille (1992), *Enterprising Women: Television Fandom and the Creation of Popular Myth*, Philadelphia: University of Pennsylvania Press.

Barthes, Roland (1977), *Image-Music-Text*, London: Fontana Press.

Bennett, Tony and Woollacott, Janet (1987), *Bond and Beyond: The Political Career of a Popular Hero*, Basingstoke: Macmillan.

Bernstein, Matthew and Studlar, Gaylyn (1997), *Visions of the East: Orientalism in Film*, New Brunswick: Rutgers University Press.

Booker, M. Keith (2002), *Strange TV: Innovative Television Series from 'The Twilight Zone' to 'The X-Files'*, Westport, CT and London: Greenwood Press.

Bordwell, David, Staiger, Janet and Thompson, Kristin (1985), *The Classical Hollywood Cinema: Film Style and Mode of Production to 1960*, London: Routledge.

Bordwell, David and Thompson, Kristin (1993), *Film Art: An Introduction*, New York: McGraw-Hill.

Branston, Gill and Stafford, Roy (2003), *The Media Student's Book*, 3rd edn, London and New York: Routledge.

Brooker, Will (2003), 'Conclusion: Overflow and Audience', in Will Brooker and Deborah Jermyn (eds), *The Audience Studies Reader*, London and New York: Routledge, pp. 322–34.

Brunsdon, C. (1990), 'Problems with Quality', *Screen*, 30(1), Spring, 67–90.

—(1998), 'What is the "Television" in Television Studies', in C. Geraghty and D. Lusted (eds), *The Television Studies Book*, London: Arnold, pp. 95–113.

—(2000), *The Feminist, the Housewife, and the Soap Opera*, Oxford: Oxford University Press.

Buci-Glucksman, Christine (1986), *La Folie du voir: de l'esthétique baroque*, Paris: Éditions Galilée.

—(1994), *Baroque Reason: Aesthetics of Modernity*, London: Sage Publications.

Buxton, David (1990), *From* The Avengers *to* Miami Vice: *Form and Ideology in Television Series*, Manchester: Manchester University Press.

Calabrese, Omar (1992), *Neo-Baroque: A Sign of the Times*, New Jersey: Princeton University Press. (Originally published as *L'Eta Neobarocca*, Editori Laterna 1987.)

Caldwell, John (1995), *Televisuality: Style, Crisis, and Authority in American Television*, New Brunswick: Rutgers University Press.

—(2002), 'New Media/Old Augmentations: Television, the Internet, and Interactivity', in *Realism and 'Reality' in Film and Media*, Copenhagen: Museum Tusculanum Press, pp. 253–74.

—(2003), 'Second-Shift Media Aesthetics', in Anna Everett and John T. Caldwell (eds), *New Media: Theories and Practices of Digitextuality*, New York and London: Routledge, pp. 127–44.

Caughie, John (1991), 'Before the Golden Age: Early Television Drama', in John Corner (ed.), *Popular Television in Britain Studies in Cultural History*, London: BFI, pp. 22–40.

Cantor, Muriel G. (1971), *The Hollywood TV Producer: His Work and His Audience*, New York: Basic Books.

Cardwell, Sarah (2003), 'The Rise of the Television Mockumentary: From Familiar Genres to New Forms', *Anglo Files*, no. 129, September, 30–41.

Cassata, Mary (1985), 'The Soap Opera', in Brian G. Rose (ed.), *TV Genres: A Handbook and Reference Guide*, Westport, CT: Greenwood Press, pp. 131–43.

Channel 4 (1998a), *Channel 4: New Developments and Future Ambitions*, London: Channel 4.

—(1998b), *Channel 4 Licence*, London: Independent Television Commission.

Clover, Carol J. (1992), *Men, Women and Chainsaws: Gender in the Modern Horror Film*, Princeton: Princeton University Press.

Chion, Michel (1995), *David Lynch*, London: BFI.

Coe, Steve (1995), 'Networks Take a Walk on the Weird Side', *Broadcasting and Cable*, 125(43), 56–7.

Cooke, Lez (2003), *British Television Drama: A History*, Oxford: Oxford University Press.

Corner, John (1999), *Critical Ideas in Television Studies*, Oxford: Oxford University Press.

Couldry, Nick (2000), *Inside Culture: Re-imagining the Method of Cultural Studies*, London: Sage.

Creeber, Glen (ed.), *The Television Genre Book*, London: BFI.

Delasara, Jan (2000), *PopLit, PopCult and 'The X-Files': A Critical Exploration*, Jefferson: McFarland.

Deleuze, Gilles [1988] (1993), *The Fold: Leibniz and the Baroque*, trans. Tom Conley, Minneapolis: University of Minneapolis Press.

Dolan, Marc (1995), 'The Peaks and Valleys of Serial Creativity: What Happened to/on *Twin Peaks*', in David Lavery (ed.), *Full of Secrets: Critical Approaches to 'Twin Peaks'*, Detroit: Wayne State University Press, pp. 30–50.

Dow, Bonnie (1996), *Prime-Time Feminism: Television, Media Culture, and the Women's Movement Since 1970*, Chapel Hill: University of North Carolina Press.

Ellis, John (2000), *Seeing Things: Television in the Age of Uncertainty*, London: I. B. Tauris.

—(1982), *Visible Fictions*, London: Routledge & Kegan Paul.

Fellezs, Kevin (2002), 'Wiseguy Opera: Music for *Sopranos*', in Lavery (ed.), *This Thing of Ours: Investigating 'The Sopranos'*, London: Wallflower Press, pp. 162–75.

Feuer, Jane (1984), 'The MTM Style', in Jane Feuer, Paul Kerr and Tise Vahimagi (eds), *MTM: 'Quality Television'*, London: BFI, pp. 31–60.

—(1992), 'Genre Study and Television', in R. C. Allen (ed.), *Channels of Discourse, Reassembled: Television and Contemporary Criticism*, Chapel Hill: University of North Carolina Press, pp. 138–59.

—(1995), *Seeing through the Eighties: Television and Reaganism*, London: BFI Publishing.

Feuer, Jane, Kerr, Paul and Vahimagi, Tise (eds) (1984), *MTV: 'Quality Television'*, London: BFI.

Fish, Stanley (1980), *Is There a Text in this Class?: The Authority of Interpretive Communites*, Cambridge, MA: Harvard University Press.

Fiske, John (1987), *Television Culture*, London: Methuen.

Furedi, Frank (2003), *Therapy Culture: Cultivating Vulnerability in an Uncertain Age*, London: Routledge.

Genge, N. E. (1998), *The Buffy Chronicles: The Unofficial Companion to 'Buffy the Vampire Slayer'*, London: Boxtree.

Geraghty, Christine (1990), *Women and Soap Opera: A Study of Prime Time Soaps*, Cambridge: Polity Press.

—(1998), 'Audiences and "Ethnography": Questions of Practice', in C. Geraghty and D. Lusted (eds), *The Television Studies Book*, London: Arnold, pp. 141–57.

—(2003), 'Aesthetics and Quality in Popular Television Drama', in *International Journal of Cultural Studies*, London: Sage Publications.

Gitlin, Todd (1994), *Inside Prime Time*, rev. edn, London: Routledge.

Golden, Christopher and Holder, Nancy (1998), *'Buffy the Vampire Slayer': The Watcher's Guide*, New York: Pocket Books.

Gripstrud, Jostein (1995), *The 'Dynasty' Years: Hollywood Television and Critical Media Studies*, London and New York: Routledge.

Hagedorn, Roger (1988), 'Technology and Economic Exploitation: The Serial as a Form of Narrative Presentation', *Wide Angle* 10(4), 4–12.

—(1995), 'Doubtless to be Continued: A Brief History of Serial Narrative', in

Robert C. Allen (ed.), *To Be Continued: Soap Operas around the World*, London and New York: Routledge, pp. 27–48.

Hammond, Mary (2004), 'Monsters and Metaphors: *Buffy the Vampire Slayer* and the Old World', in S. Gwenllian Jones and R. E. Pearson (eds), *Cult Television*, Minneapolis: University of Minnesota Press, pp. 147–64.

Harrington, C. Lee and Bielby, Denise (1995), *Soap Fans*, Philadelphia: Temple University Press.

Hayward, Jennifer (1997), *Consuming Pleasures: Active Audiences and Serial Fictions from Dickens to Soap Opera*, Lexington: University Press of Kentucky.

Hills, Matt (1999), 'From *The Radio Times* to *Cult Times*: Market Segmentation in TV Consumption', paper presented at the 'Consuming Markets, Consuming Meanings' Conference, University of Plymouth, September 1999.

—(2002), *Fan Cultures*, London and New York: Routledge.

—(2004), 'Defining Cult TV: Texts, Inter-texts and Fan Audiences', in Robert C. Allen and Annette Hill (eds), *The Television Studies Reader*, London and New York: Routledge, pp. 509–23.

Hilmes, Michele (2002), *Only Connect: A Cultural History of Broadcasting in the United States*, Belmont, CA: Wadsworth.

Hilmes, Michele (ed.) (2003), *The Television History Book*, London: BFI.

Hochschild, Arlie Russell (1983), *The Managed Heart: Commercialization of Human Feeling*, Berkeley: University of California Press.

Holben, Jay (2000), '*The X-Files*: Cinematographer: Bill Roe', *American Cinematographer*, 81(3), 88–91.

Holbert R. Lance, Owen Pillion, David A. Tschida, Greg G. Armfield, Kelly Kinder, Kristin L. Cherry and Amy R. Daulton (2003), '*The West Wing* as Endorsement of the US Presidency: Expanding the Bounds of Priming in Political Communication', *Journal of Communication*, September, 427–43.

Howe, David and Walker, Stephen James (1998), '*Doctor Who*': The Television Companion: The Official BBC Guide to Every TV Story*, London: BBC Books.

Howe, Neil and Strauss, William (1993), *13th Gen: Abort, Retry, Ignore, Fail?*, New York: Random House.

Hughes, David (2001), *The Complete Lynch*, London: Virgin Books.

Jacobs, J. (2003), *Body Trauma TV: The New Hospital Drama*, London: BFI Publishing.

Jancovich, Mark and Lyons, James (eds) (2003), *Quality Popular Television: Cult TV, the Industry and Fans*, London: BFI.

Jenkins, Henry (1992), *Textual Poachers: Television Fans and Participatory Culture*, New York: Routledge, Chapman & Hall.

—(2004), 'Affective Economics 101', in *Flow: A Critical Forum on Television and Media Culture*, http://idg.communication.utexas.edu/flow/?jot=view&id=411.

Jenkins, Steve (1984), '*Hill Street Blues*', in Jane Feuer, Paul Kerr and Tise Vahimagi (eds), *MTM: 'Quality Television'*, London: BFI, pp. 183–99.

Jones, Sara Gwenllian (2002), 'The Sex Lives of Cult Television Characters', *Screen* 43(1), 79–90.

Jurkowitz, Mark (2002), 'Getting President Bartlet's Ear Hoping To Be Heard, Activists Are Lobbying *The West Wing*', *Boston Globe* (27 March), http:// www.boston.com/dailyglobe2/086/living/Getting_President_Bartlet_s_eart. shtm

Kaveney, Roz (ed.) (2004), *Reading the Vampire Slayer: The New, Updated Unofficial Guide to 'Buffy' and 'Angel'*, London and New York: I. B. Tauris.

Kellner, Douglas (1999), '*The X-Files* and the Aesthetics and Politics of Postmodern Pop', *The Journal of Aesthetics and Art Criticism*, 57(2), 161–75.

Kerr, Paul (1984), 'Drama at MTM: *Lou Grant* and *Hill Street Blues*', in Jane Feuer, Paul Kerr and Tise Vahimagi (eds), *MTM: 'Quality Television'*, London: BFI, pp. 132–65.

Kipnis, Laura (1996), *Bound and Gagged: Pornography and the Politics of Fantasy in America*, New York: Grove.

Klinger, Barbara (1991), 'Digressions at the Cinema: Commodification and Reception in Mass Culture', in James Naremore and Patrick Brantlinger (eds), *Modernity and Mass Culture*, Bloomington, IN: Indiana University Press, pp. 117–34.

—(1994), *Melodrama and Meaning: History, Culture and the Films of Douglas Sirk*, Bloomington, IN: Indiana University Press.

Kozloff, Sarah (1987), 'Narrative Theory and Television', in Robert C. Allen (ed.), *Channels of Discourse, Reassembled*, Chapel Hill: University of North Carolina Press, pp. 67–100.

Kramer, Peter (1996), 'The Lure of the Big Picture: Film, Television and Hollywood', in John Hill and Martin McLoone (eds), *Big Picture, Small Screen: The Relations Between Film and Television*, Luton: University of Luton Press, pp. 9–46.

Kuppers, Petra (2004), 'Quality Science Fiction: *Babylon 5*'s Metatextual Universe', in Sara Gwenllian Jones and Roberta E. Pearson (eds), *Cult Television*, Minneapolis: University of Minnesota Press, pp. 45–59.

Lancaster, Kurt (2001), *Interacting with 'Babylon 5': Fan Performances in a Media Universe*, Austin: University of Texas Press.

Larbalestier, Justine (2003), 'A *Buffy* Confession', in Glenn Yeffeth (ed.), *Seven Seasons of 'Buffy': Science Fiction and Fantasy Writers Discuss their Favorite Television Show*, Texas: Banbella Books, pp. 72–84.

Lavery, David (ed.) (1995), *Full of Secrets: Critical Approaches to 'Twin Peaks'*, Detroit, MI: Wayne State University Press.

—(ed.) (2002), *This Thing of Ours: Investigating 'The Sopranos'*, London: Wallflower Press.

Lehmann, Chris (2001), 'The Feel-Good Presidency: The Pseudo-Politics of *The West Wing*', *The Atlantic Monthly*, The Atlantic On-Line, http://www.the atlantic.com/issues/2001/03/lehmann-p1.htm (March).

Levine, Myron A. (2003), '*The West Wing* (NBC) and the West Wing (D.C.)', in

Peter C. Rollins and John E. O'Connor (eds), *'The West Wing': The American Presidency as Television Drama*, New York: Syracuse University Press, pp. 42–62.

Lotz, Amanda D. (2001), 'Postfeminist Television Criticism: Rehabilitating Critical Terms and Identifying Postfeminist Attributes', *Feminist Media Studies*, 1.1, 105–21.

Lowry, Brian (1995), *The Truth is Out There: The Official Guide to 'The X-Files'*, London: HarperCollins.

Lury, Celia (1993), *Cultural Rights: Technology, Legality and Personality*, London: Routledge.

Lury, Karen (2001), *British Youth Television: Cynicism and Enchantment*, Oxford: Oxford University Press.

McCabe, Janet (2000), 'Diagnosing the Alien: Producing Identities, American 'Quality' Drama and British Television Culture in the 1990s', in Bruce Carson and Margaret Llewellyn-Jones (eds), *Frames and Fictions on Television: The Politics of Identity within Drama*, Exeter: Intellect, pp. 141–54.

McLean, Adrienne L. (1998), 'Media Effects: Marshall McLuhan, Television Culture, and *The X-Files*', *Film Quarterly*, 51(4), 2–11.

McLoone, Martin (1996) 'Boxed in?: The Aesthetics of Film and Television', in John Hill and Martin McLoone (eds), *Big Picture, Small Screen: The Relations Between Film and Television*, Luton: University of Luton Press, pp. 76–106.

Mann, Peter (1999), *A Completely and Utterly Unauthorised Guide to 'Buffy the Vampire Slayer'*, Harpenden: Pocket Essentials.

Marc, David and Thompson, Robert J. (1992), *Prime Time, Prime Movers*, Boston: Little, Brown and Company.

Marchetti, Gina (1993), *Romance and the Yellow Peril: Race, Sex, and Discursive Hollywood Strategies in Hollywood Fiction*, Berkeley: University of California Press.

Marshall, Caroline (1998), *Pocket Advertising: The Essentials of Advertising from A–Z*, London: Economist Books.

Martín, N. San (2003), 'Must See TV: Programming Identity on NBC Thursdays', in M. Jancovich and J. Lyons (eds), *Quality Popular Television*, London: BFI Publishing, pp. 32–47.

Martinez, José (1995), 'An Interview with Chris Carter and Howard Gordon', *Creative Screenwriting*, 2(3), 20–3.

Morgenstern, Steve (ed.) (1979), *Inside the TV Business*, New York: Sterling Publishing.

Morley, David (1980), *The 'Nationwide' Audience*, London: British Film Institute.

Morse, Margaret (1990), 'An Ontology of Everyday Distraction: The Freeway, the Mall, and Television', in Patricia Mellencamp (ed.), *Logics of Television: Essays in Cultural Criticism*, Bloomington: Indiana University Press, pp. 193–221.

Moseley, Rachel (2001), 'The Teen Series', in Glen Creeber (ed.), *The Television Genre Book*, London: BFI Publishing, pp. 41–3.

Muir, John Kenneth (1999), *A Critical History of 'Doctor Who' on Television*, Jefferson: McFarland.

Mumford, L. Stempel (1994–1995),'Stripping on the Girl Channel: Lifetime, *thirtysomething* and Television Form', *Camera Obscura*, 33/34, May–January, 166–91.

Murray, Janet H. (1997), *Hamlet on the Holodeck: The Future of Narrative in Cyberspace*, Cambridge, MA: The MIT Press.

Ndalianis, Angela (2004), *Neo-Baroque Aesthetics and Contemporary Entertainment*, Cambridge, MA: The MIT Press.

Newcomb, Horace (1987), 'Toward a Television Aesthetic', in Horace Newcomb (ed.), *Television: The Critical View*, 4th edn, New York: Oxford University Press, pp. 613–27.

Nochimson, Martha P. (1997), *The Passion of David Lynch: Wild at Heart in Hollywood*, Austin, TX: University of Texas Press

—(2003), 'Tony's Options: *The Sopranos* and the Televisuality of the Gangster Genre', *Senses of Cinema*, http://www.sensesofcinema.com/contents/03/29/sopranos_televisuality.html

Nolan, James (1998), *The Therapeutic State*, New York: New York University Press.

Patton, Tracey Owens (2001), 'Ally McBeal and her Homies: The Reification of White Stereotypes of the Other', *Journal of Black Studies*, 32(2), November, 229–72.

Peacock, A. (1986), *Report of the Committee on Financing the BBC*, Cmnd 9824, London: HMSO.

Podhoretz, John (2003), 'The Liberal Imagination', in Peter C. Rollins and John E. O'Connor (eds), *'The West Wing': The American Presidency as Television Drama*, New York: Syracuse University Press, pp. 222–34.

Pompper, Donnalyn (2003), 'White House Narratives That Journalism Cannot Tell', in Peter C. Rollins and John E. O'Connor (eds), *'The West Wing': The American Presidency as Television Drama*, New York: Syracuse University Press, pp. 17–31.

Press, Andrea (1991), *Women Watching Television: Gender, Class, and Generation in the American Television Experience*, Philadelphia: University of Pennsylvania Press.

Probst, Chris (1995), 'Darkness Descends on *The X-Files*', *American Cinematographer*, 76(6), 28–32.

Reeves, Jimmie L., Rogers, Mark C., and Epstein, Michael (1996), 'Rewriting Popularity: The Cult Files', in David Lavery, Angela Hague and Marla Cartwright (eds), *'Deny All Knowledge': Reading 'The X-Files'*, Syracuse, NY: Syracuse University Press, pp. 22–35.

—, Rogers, M. C., and Epstein, M. (2003), '*The Sopranos* as HBO Brand Equity: The Art of Commerce in the Age of Digital Reproduction', in D. Lavery (ed.), *This Thing of Ours: Investigating 'The Sopranos'*, New York/London: Columbia University Press/Wallflower Press, pp. 42–57.

Rixon, P. (2003), 'The Changing Face of American Television Programmes on British Screens', in M. Jancovich and J. Lyons (eds), *Quality Popular Television*, London: BFI Publishing, pp. 48–61.

Rodley, Chris (ed.) (1997), *Lynch on Lynch*, London: Faber & Faber.

Schroeder, Fred E. H. (1976), 'Video Aesthetics and Serial Art', in Horace Newcomb (ed.), *Television: The Critical View*, 1st edn, New York: Oxford University Press, pp. 260–72.

Sconce, Jeffrey (2002), 'Irony, Nihilism and the New American "Smart" Film', *Screen* 43(4), Winter, 349–69.

Seiter, Ellen (1995), 'Mothers Watching Children Watching Television', in B. Skeggs (ed.), *Feminist Cultural Theory*, Manchester: Manchester University Press, pp. 137–52.

Sheen, Erica and Davison, Annette (eds) (2004), *The Cinema of David Lynch: American Dreams, Nightmare Visions*, London and New York: Wallflower Press.

Silverstone, Roger (1994), *Television and Everyday Life*, London and New York: Routledge.

Sinker, Mark (2004), 'And Life (or TV) Goes On', in *Sight and Sound*, March 2004, 79.

Smith, C. (1996), 'Friendly Rivals', *Broadcast*, 20 December, 20.

Smith, G. M. (2003), 'The Left Takes Back the Flag: the Steadicam, the Snippet, and the Song in *The West Wing*'s "In Excelsis Deo"', in P. C. Rollins and J. E. Connor (eds), *'The West Wing': The American Presidency as Television Drama*, New York: Syracuse University Press, pp. 125–35.

Sobchack, Vivian (1996), 'Bringing It All Back Home: Family Economy and Generic Exchange', in Barry Keith Grant (ed.), *The Dread of Difference*, Austin: University of Texas Press, pp. 143–63.

Sorkin, Aaron (2000), interview by Terence Smith, *Online NewsHour* (27 September) http://www.pbs.org/newshour/media/west_wing/sorkin.html

Spigel, Lynn (1998), 'The Making of a TV Literate Elite', in C. Geraghty and D. Lusted (eds), *The Television Studies Book*, London: Arnold, pp. 63–85.

Stacey, Jackie (1994), *Star Gazing: Hollywood Cinema and Female Spectatorship*, London: Routledge.

Staiger, Janet (1992), *Interpreting Films: Studies in the Historical Reception of American Cinema*, Princeton, NJ: Princeton University Press.

Stevens, Alan and Moore, Fiona (2003), *Liberation: The Unofficial and Unauthorised Guide to 'Blake's 7'*, Tolworth: Telos Publishing.

Taub, E. (2001), 'A Walk on the Wide Side', *Emmy*, 23(1), February, 22–3.

Thompson, Kristin (2003), *Storytelling in Film and Television*, Cambridge, MA: Harvard University Press.

Thompson, Robert J. (1996), *Television's Second Golden Age: From 'Hill Street Blues' to 'ER'*, New York: Syracuse University Press.

Tracy, Kathleen (1998), *The Girl's Got Bite: The Unofficial Guide to Buffy's World*, Los Angeles: Renaissance Books.

Tulloch, John and Alvarado, Manuel (1983), *'Doctor Who': The Unfolding Text*, London: Macmillan.

Tulloch, John and Jenkins, Henry (1995), *Science Fiction Audiences: Watching Doctor Who and Star Trek*, London and New York: Routledge.

Van Hise, James (1997), *The Unauthorized History of Trek*, London: Voyager.

Walkerdine, Valerie (1985), 'Video Replay', in V. Burgin, J. Donald and C. Kaplan (eds), *Formations of Fantasy*, London: Routledge, pp. 167–99.

Waxman, Sharon (2000), 'Inside *The West Wing*'s New World', in Peter C. Rollins and John E. O'Connor (eds), *'The West Wing': The American Presidency as Television Drama*, New York: Syracuse University Press, pp. 203–12.

Wear, Ben (2002), 'Federal File: President Doppelganger', *Education Week*, 16 October, 8.

Williams, Betsy (1994), ' "North to the Future": *Northern Exposure* and Quality Television', in Horace Newcomb (ed.), *Television: The Critical View*, 5th edn, New York: Oxford, pp. 141–54.

Williams, Raymond (1974, reprint 1992), *Television, Technology and Cultural Form*, Middletown, CT: Wesleyan University Press.

Willis, J. (1996), 'The Attitude Channel', *Broadcast*, 20 December, 22.

Wood, Robin (1986), *Hollywood from Vietnam to Reagan*, New York: Columbia University Press.

Woods, Paul A. (2000), *Weirdsville USA: The Obsessive Universe of David Lynch*, London: Plexus.

Wyatt, Justin (1994), *High Concept: Movies and Marketing in Hollywood*, Austin: University of Texas Press.

Žižek, Slavoj (2000), *The Art of the Ridiculous Sublime: On David Lynch's 'Lost Highway'*, Seattle: University of Washington Press.

Filmography

The Adventures of Brisco County, Jr (Jeffrey Boam/Carlton Cuse, Boam/Cuse Production, Warner Bros. Television, US, 1993–4)

Alias (Touchstone Television/ J. J. Abrams, US, 2001–present)

Ally McBeal (David E. Kelley, David E. Kelley Productions, 20th Century Fox Television, US, 1997–2002)

Angel (Joss Whedon/David Greenwalt, Mutant Enemy Inc., 20th Century Fox Television, US, 1999–2004)

The Avengers (Sydney Newman and Leonard White, ABC Weekend Television, UK, 1961–9)

Babylon 5 (J. Michael Straczynski, Babylonian Productions, US, 1993–9)

Blake's 7 (Terry Nation, British Broadcasting Corporation, UK, 1978–81)

Buffy the Vampire Slayer (Joss Whedon, Mutant Enemy Inc., 20th Century Fox Television, US, 1996–2003)

Chicago Hope (David E. Kelley, David E. Kelley Productions, 20th Century Fox Television, US, 1994–2000)

Cold Feet (Declan Lowney/Mike Bullen, Granada Television, UK, 1997–2003)

Crossing Jordan (Tim Kring, Tailwind Productions, NBC Studios, US, 2001–present)

CSI: Crime Scene Investigation (Anthony Zuiker, Jerry Bruckheimer Televison, CBS Productions US, 2000–present)

CSI: Miami (Anthony Zuiker/Ann Donohue/Carol Mendolsohn, Jerry Bruckheimer Televison, CBS Productions US, 2002–present)

ER (Michael Crichton, John Wells Prodcutions, Amblin Entertainment, US, 1994–present)

Friends (David Crane/Marta Kaufman, Brioght, Kaufman, Crane Productions, Warner Bros Television, US, 1994–2003)

Hill Street Blues (Steven Bochco/Michael Kozoll, MTM Enterprises, National Broadcasting Company, US, 1981–7)

Homicide: Life on the Streets (Paul Attanasio, Baltimore Pictures, NBC Studios, US, 1993–9)

LA Law (Steven Bochco, Terry Louise Fisher, 20th Century Fox Television, US, 1986–94)

Law and Order (Dick Wolf, Wolf Films, Universal Network Television, US, 1990–present)

Law and Order: Criminal Intent (Alex Chapple/Christopher Swartout/René Balcer/Elizabeth Benjamin, Wolf Films, Universal Network Television, US, 2001–present)

Law and Order: SVU (Dick Wolf, Wolf Films, Universal Network Television, US, 1999–present)

Lost (Touchstone Television/ J. J. Abrams, US, 2004–present)

M*A*S*H (Alan Alda/Hy Averback, 20th Century Fox Television, US, 1972–83)

Miami Vice (Anthony Yerkovich, Michael Man Productions, Universal TV, US, 1984–9)

Millennium (Chris Carter, Ten Thirteen Productions, 20th Century Fox Television, US, 1996–9)

Monk (Andy Breckman, Touchstone Television, NBC Universal Telvision, US, 2002)

My So-Called Life (Winnie Holzman, Bedford Falls Productions, ABC Productions US, 1994–5)

Northern Exposure (Joshua Brand/John Falsey, Universal TV, US, 1990–5)

NYPD Blue (Steven Bochco/David Milch, Steven Bochco Productions, 20th Century Fox Television, US, 1993–2005)

Picket Fences (David E. Kelley, David E. Kelley Productions, 20th Century Fox Television, US, 1992–6)

The Practice (David E. Kelley, David E. Kelley Productions, 20th Century Fox Television, US, 1997–2004)

The Prisoner (George Markstein/Patrick McGoohan, Everyman Films, Incorporated Television Company, UK, 1967–8)

Queer as Folk (Sarah Harding/Charles McDougal, Red Production Ltd, UK, 1999–2000)

Six Feet Under (Alan Ball, Greenblatt/Janolarri Studios, Home Box Office, US, 2001–5)

The Six Million Dollar Man (Edward M. Abroms/Reza Bediyi, Silverton Productions, Universal TV, US, 1974–8)

Smallville (Alfred Gough, Miles Miller, Tollin/Robbins Productions and Warner Bros Television, US, 2001–present)

The Sopranos (David Chase, Brad Grey Television, Home Box Office, US, 1999–present)

Stargate SG-1 (Mario Azzopardi/Dennis Berry, Stargate SG1 Productions, MGM Worldwide Television Productions, US, 1997–present)

Star Trek (Gene Roddenberry, Desilu Productions '66–'6, Paramount Television '68–'69, US, 1966–9)

Star Trek: Deep Space Nine (Rick Berman/Michael Pillar, Paramount Television, US, 1993–9)

Star Trek: Next Generation (Gene Roddenberry, Paramount Television, US, 1987–94)

Star Trek: Voyager (Rick Berman/Michael Pillar/Jeri Taylor, Paramount Television, US, 1995–2001)

Teachers (Tim Loane, Tiger Aspect Productions, UK, 2001–present)

thirtysomething (Marshall Herskowitz/Edward Zwick, Bedford Falls Productions, MGM Television, US, 1987–91)

This Life (Joel Ahearne/Sally Aprahamian, BBC/World Productions, UK, 1996–7)

24 (20th Century Fox Television/Joel Surnow and Robert Cochran, US, 2001–present)

Twin Peaks (David Lynch/Mark Frost, Lynch Frost Productions, Spelling Entertainment, US, 1990–1)

A Very Peculiar Practice (David Tucker, British Broadcasting Company, UK, 1986–8)

The West Wing (Aaron Sorkin, John Wells Productions, Warner Bros Television, US, 1999–present)

The X-Files (Chris Carter US, Ten Thirteen Productions, 20th Century Fox Television, US, 1993–2002)

Index